# Sidney M. Jourard:
## Selected Writings

*Edited by:*

*Michael Lowman, Ph.D.*
*Antoinette Jourard*
*Marty Jourard*

*i*

*Sidney M. Jourard:*
*Selected Writings*

ISBN 0-917982-49-5

PRINTED IN THE UNITED STATES OF AMERICA

Cover: Design by Antoinette Jourard, Jeffrey Jourard
Cover Art: Detail from a painting by the late Florida artist
Hollis Holbrook, 1979

*First Edition, November 1994*

# Acknowledgements

This book is a labor of love for all those who have been involved.

In part, we feel that we have repaid Sidney for the many gifts he has given us. It was a gift to re-read virtually all of his writing, including his travel journals, and in so doing, we have all learned from him once again, anew.

This work has been accomplished with the loving collaboration of Antoinette Jourard and her son, Marty. They have greatly aided us in focusing on the purpose for and the organization of our selected writings.

Other acknowledgements go to our dear friend, Ruth Pritchard, President of Capitol Enquiry, Inc. in Sacramento. Without her love, encouragement, editorial expertise, helpful staff and production facilities, this book would not have happened.

We were given invaluable encouragement, feedback and support from several of our colleagues, including Eleanor Criswell-Hanna, Anne Richards, Peggy Carey, Patty Weston, and Ben Ohs.

Also, an acknowledgement must go to the psychology students at Sacramento City College for undertaking the awesome challenge of reading Sidney's work and then writing a critique relating it to their own lives.

Finally, it is the Jourard family who deserve an acknowledgement, for it has been their love and dedication that made it possible for these selections from Sidney's work to be published. ✦

# Contents

|  | Page |
|---|---|
| **Acknowledgements**. | iii |
| **Dedications** | |
| Sid Jourard—The Compassionate Colleague | |
| *by Ted Landsman* | vii |
| Sid Jourard—the Teacher: One Student's Perspective | |
| *by Martin Amerikaner* | ix |
| **Foreword** *by Antoinette Jourard* | xiii |
| **Introduction** *by Michael Lowman* | xv |

## *I* Cognitive Maps For Human Growth

| | | |
|---|---|---|
| **I-1** | Growing Experience and the Experience of Growth | 3 |
| **I-2** | Fascination and Learning-for-Oneself | 25 |
| **I-3** | An Odyssey Within | 53 |
| **I-4** | Healthy Personality and Self-Disclosure | 63 |
| **I-5** | Reality, Perception and Healthy Personality | 75 |

## *II* Roots of Holistic Psychology: Humanistic/Cognitive/In-Spiriting

| | | |
|---|---|---|
| **II-1** | On Being Persuaded Who You Are | 91 |
| **II-2** | The Laugh That Heals, A Case Study | 99 |
| **II-3** | Growing Personality, Not "Adjustment," Is the Goal in Counseling and Psychotherapy | 125 |
| **II-4** | Somatic Disclosure and Perception of the Soma | 135 |
| **II-5** | The Mystic Dimension of Self | 149 |
| **II-6** | Prophets As Psychotherapists, and Psychotherapists As Prophets | 157 |

# III Psychotherapist as Growth Coach: Teacher, Self-Discloser and Transcender of Facticity

**III-1** The Psychotherapist as Psychedelic Man ............. 169
**III-2** On Becoming a Psychotherapist ........................... 183
**III-3** The Transcending Therapist ................................. 189
**III-4** Psychology: Control Or Liberation? ...................... 197
**III-5** Changing Personal Worlds: A Humanistic
Perspective .......................................................... 209

# IV The Disaster Areas

**IV-1** Marriage is for Life ................................................ 237
**IV-2** Failure of Dialogue .............................................. 255
**IV-3** Some Lethal Aspects of the Male Role .................. 269
**IV-4** The Body Taboo .................................................. 281
**IV-5** The Human Challenge of Automation .................... 289
**IV-6** The Invitation to Die ............................................ 303
**IV-7** Privacy: The Psychological Need .......................... 315
**IV-8** The Fear that Cheats Us of Love .......................... 323
**IV-9** Some Notes on the Experience of Commitment .... 337

# V Appendices

**V-1** Bibliography from *Disclosing Man to Himself* ......... 345
**V-2** Bibliography from *The Transparent Self* ................. 351
**V-3** Sidney M. Jourard Bibliography ............................. 359

# Dedications

## Sid Jourard—The Compassionate Colleague*

*by Ted Landsman*

Sidney Jourard was a man of our times who could not wait for time to change the channels of his profession but who took its future into his own hands and helped make a science of white rats into a science of tender, loving, angry, ecstatic, joyful, tearful, saddened, and frightened, in other words, human, entirely human beings.

Sidney Jourard was a joyous, irrepressible, mischievous, mystic of a man who was a powerful mover of hearts and of thoughts, of ideas and of truths. The body image first excited him, then the idea of a self that was open, that did not seek to hide itself from its friend, its lover, its partner, the transparent self. Then authenticity became his spoken and written vigorous ambition to therapist and to client. It became a watchword of the third force in psychology—a relentless guerilla type intellectual and sentimental movement that reached beyond behaviorism, that loved and left psychoanalysis, and that sang paeans to a new trinity, existentialism, phenomenology, and humanism, all of which were enriched by this surprisingly, severely self-disciplined but always forceful and forever free spirit.

And out of that crazy, delightful cacophony of theory and philosophy of science and mysticism, the voice of Sidney Jourard was heard, a voice of courage and of caution, a voice

* As edited by Michael Lowman. From Humanistic Psychology: New Frontiers, Nevill, Gardner Press, 1977.

of excitement and of balance, declaiming, founding, structuring, not a movement but a science. He disciplined himself to complete research projects on touching, self-concept, self-disclosure, and high level functioning. Was his work finished? He died in a tragic accident. Long before he had begun conceptualizations he wanted to research of enspiriting, of transcendent behavior, of the healthy personality, and in his last week of life, he reinvented renewed purpose for his life with a project to develop a humanistic political party and another one to create a complex grid of studies centering about the various relationships of authenticity between experimenter and subject.

His intense personal and professional friends are a strange mishmash of writers, artists and scientists. Along with these flowed an odd brotherhood of soothsayers, yogis, philosophers, psychologists, I among them. The hand of Sidney Jourard labored to fashion a coherent but still human science.

His heart was where human history had wept, and his mind was in its transformation to joy. His soul was with man's yearning for God and for the heights of *menschlichket*, of personhood. He wrote, he spoke, he shared, he encouraged, he enspirited the papers and the shared searches for the full human meanings in thought and feeling and science. This new science, this old science redefined, these grand words, those grander hopes and dreams and visions—they also are some evidence that one time, even in our days, Sidney Jourard walked proudly and joyously on the face of this earth. ✦

# Sid Jourard—the Teacher:
# One Student's Perspective*

*by Martin Amerikaner*

In *Healthy Personality*, Sid's most recent book, there is a section entitled, "On recognizing a consciousness larger than one's own" (1974). His description of having an enlarged awareness is an apt summary of what being a teacher meant to him. One person wishing to learn, and another, larger person to act as a guide. Through that complex process of exploration, modeling, and laughter he understood so well, teaching and learning would occur. To those of us who spent time with him, Sid was a teacher.

It had little to do with the time of day or where he was. Unlike so many others, Sid did not need those confirming symbols of the teaching role—the lectern and the office—although he was an excellent lecturer and always took the time to listen to students who came to his office. More than this, though, Sid loved his ideas, and wanted to play with them all the time, whether at school, or at parties, or at lunch, or at the beach. However, this was not the dreaded "talking shop" which fills the emptiness at so many social occasions. No, this was a playful passion, an everpresent component of his grown and growing self. He never tired or grew bored with this aspect of his work—as he refilled everybody's glass once again, he would often say, "One can never have too much wine."

Sid's favorite metaphor for growth was that of the journey—that taking off on a voyage to explore and to discover. For Sid, though, a successful trip included the return home. Go out, come back; go out, come back. This model always struck his large class of undergraduates, since, quite literally,

* *From* Humanistic Psychology: New Frontiers. *Nevill, Gardner Press, 1977.*

they were on a voyage of discovery up in Gainesville, but whether from Miami or Moore Haven, they would soon have to deal with returning home. However, this metaphor is also useful in describing why Sidney was such an excellent teacher. The return is a time for incorporating the newly discovered with the older, more stable structure; the time for processing those pictures you took on your trip. It is this time of reintegration that defines real growth, and prepares a larger person for the next adventure. Sidney was always out exploring, but continuously integrating too, and thus the home base from which he dove was getting larger and larger. It was this ever-expanding, revitalized center that made him such a vast and readily accessible resource. When he taught an inter-disciplinary seminar on man and metaphor, or co-taught a course on behaviorism and humanistic psychology, it wasn't a stab in the dark. He would seek out faculty and students and bring together their varied experience. Together they would explore some new combinations of ideas, integrate what was fruitful, and push on.

Integration and expansion—my thoughts keep returning to these words when I think of Sid's teaching. Self-disclosure. The constant process of revealing one's self, while not getting caught up in openness as an end in itself. Letting himself be known while simultaneously becoming new again.

We would be driving across campus to class, discussing the upcoming lecture, when his head would turn, eyes light up, and, "Isn't she lovely," would emerge. Then back to the topic, never missing a beat. He'd be typing a letter to someone when I might come jumping into the office with some ridiculous idea or a new, profound insight. He would listen carefully, with that amused light in his eye, and somehow find something of value in what I was saying. Then he'd rip it apart, because of X, or Y, or Z, and finally convince me to keep at it, because after all, it was a good idea in the first place. I would drift out, vaguely excited, trying to piece together what had just transpired, while the typewriter was already clacking away once again. One did not easily upset the rhythm in Sid's day.

It was always important to build from something. His view of teaching psychotherapy was the apprentice system; the student would work with an experienced guide, making use of him as a model when necessary, and learning from him all he could; from this the student's personal "style" would emerge. Develop a resource base, then strike out on your own. Similarly, in research the idea was to build rather than poke out blindly. Though some did not consider Sid a researcher, he surely understood the process of science, the cumulative nature of a growing body of knowledge. If I would propose some outrageous, but to me, perfectly reasonable study, the criticism would not be of the idea or question itself. More often, he would comment that I wasn't building on what I already knew; I wasn't using information or methods that had previously proven valuable. By no means was this thinking conservative—rather, he tried to convey that in research, as in all modes of development, real advancement is based on, yet goes beyond, what has already been accomplished.

Sid was a teacher who expected one to do things well, or, as he would say, "Do it magnificently." Undergraduates were constantly amazed that their expected "gut" course in humanistic psychology—that soft stuff—would flip from an easy A to a challenge for Bs and Cs. Students who handed in gibberish-laden term papers which they thought sounded nice and "humanistic" would take them home with toughminded comments all over them. It wasn't easy to bullshit old Sid. Yet, those who put care into their work received thoughtful and encouraging criticism. He, not his assistant, read and wrote comments on every paper, and this was in a class of at least 100 students each quarter.

Do it well. Sid was a handball player, and I play tennis. We were always kidding each other about who was better at the other's game, but never getting on the court to find out. Finally, one day we went to the handball court. The first game went about as expected—I was quicker than he, but he knew more about the game. During the contest, he kept complimenting me on my speed and my occasional good shot. He won that game, about 21-14. I then got lucky and real hot, and shut him out, 11-0 in the second game. Still, lots of compliments and lots of enjoyment. Naturally, during the next few days, I made an occasional snide comment about aging athletes and the like, which he merely laughed off. A week later, we went out for another quick game. Still full of kind words, and delighting at my agility, he ran me off the court, about 21-6. Do it well. Enjoy it fully, but do it well. We never did get around to playing tennis.

It's difficult to summarize the teacher-student relationship with Sid. Always very much alive—the true energy source of an often draining psychology building. Encouraging, sensitive, and supportive. During my first quarter at Florida, I went through a very private period of discouragement and depression. He recognized this without any comment from me, and on a particularly gloomy Friday afternoon, I discovered a little note on my desk. He mentioned how much work I had been doing, and that it was going well. But more importantly, it was a confirming statement that I was an important person to him, coming at a time when I was hurting. It was the only note I received from Sid, but as usual, his timing was superb and it helped me turn some things around and truly reinvent my perspective.

Most of all, Sid as a teacher was his own fully human person. As he wrote of himself in *The Transparent Self*, "I don't have a special 'researcher self,' a 'therapist self,' a 'teacher self,' and a 'personal self.' These are names for places to do my thing" (1971, p. 169). This, I guess, was Sid's major statement to me: that human growth was a constant process of beginning new projects while integrating the old, developing new ways of being, while weaving conflicting social roles into one, larger being. He was always active, always challenging, and that laughter—he always had that laughter in his eyes. ✦

### References

Jourard, S. M. Healthy personality: An approach from the viewpoint of humanistic psychology. *New York: Macmillan, 1974.*

Jourard, S. M. The transparent self: Self-disclosure and well-being *(Rev. Ed.). New York: Van Nostrand, 1971.*

# *Foreword*

At some point in 1975 not long after Sidney's death a small group of his friends and colleagues, Robert Isaacson, Fred Richards, Henry Moore, Bob Baringer and myself met at my home with the purpose of organizing Sidney's work into various topics. The idea was to put out a book or books of selections of his work in each area. The amount of material was vast and presented itself in various forms. There were many finished pieces of work in folders, in journals, books and periodicals as well as unfinished works on hand-written notes and scraps of paper (napkins, matchbook covers, note pads, file folders, etc.). A few of the topic headings we had were Change, Education, Professionalism, Comments on Therapy, Religion and even Self-Disclosure, as well as others. Plowing through the vast amount of work was overwhelming and this was coupled by the state of grief everyone was in. We put articles in folders and had many discussions on how to approach this project. We wanted so very much for it to happen but it just couldn't and it didn't. We met only once. We never actually cancelled it but we never met again for this purpose.

In 1975 I approached the Journal of Marriage and Family Counseling to see if they would be interested in publishing a paper Sid had given at a joint meeting of The American Association of Marriage and Family Counseling and The National Council on Family Relations held on October 26 in St. Louis, Missouri, just five weeks before his death. They were quite happy to do so and did. Sid had left his notes on the paper he delivered on the plane when he was returning home and had no other copy. He had mentioned to me that he wanted to have it published but he only had a cassette tape of his talk. He called it "Marriage Is For Life" ("life" meaning "enlivening," not a period of time). The paper was published verbatim from the tape. The response to this journal article was overwhelming. Both the Journal and myself had an enormous number of requests for reprints or permissions to include in publications or to give to students or clients. It was certainly a good move and one that Sidney wanted.

The only other posthumous publication was Sidney's book, *Healthy Personality*, that Ted Landsman lovingly revised. He did a most meticulous job.

But over the years I had a deeply personal need to assemble a book that concisely showed some of the scope and overview of Sidney's work, but it just didn't happen. Then about two years ago in one of my many conversations with my friend Michael Lowman, he mentioned that he was teaching a course on Sidney's work. He had gleaned what he called the "gems" from Sidney's articles and writings that he gave to his students to read and discuss. He felt that with some additions these writings would make a good and much-needed book. He sent me the list of these articles and chapters and after several more phone conversations we met at my home and went through more of Sid's writings, adding and deleting articles. We got these into readable form with the able help of my son Marty, who delved into the project with great enthusiasm. But the bulk of the credit goes to Michael, who selected these "gems" from his extensive knowledge of Sidney's work and organized them into very apt chapter headings. He worked tirelessly and consistently on every aspect of the production. I am most grateful for these efforts and so very pleased to see this book finally become a reality. I feel Sidney would have been happy with it too.

Antoinette (Toni) Jourard
Marina Del Rey, California
August 1994

# *Introduction*

Sidney Jourard's presence was so bright, his beingness so magnificent, that even 20 years after his death, he is still vivid and alive. A part of me feels like it must have been only yesterday or last week that I saw him last. I expect his influence to be with me always.

I have been a psychology teacher at Sacramento City College in Sacramento, California. One of my classes, Human Behavior, involved a cognitive/experiential blending of information about the ingredients of the human growth process. Individuals kept journals and responded to concepts from a personal/spiritual perspective as well as a cognitive point of view.

In past years, I have asked students in these classes to read and write reviews of the Jourard materials and to interrelate his ideas to their own lives. Reading these reaction papers and interacting with current students about Sidney's work convinced me that the contents of these selected writings have a timeless quality—he said and wrote ideas that have never been said better before or since.

My students' feedback has also shown that Sidney's work has a particularly current importance to individuals striving to form values and ways of being larger than those portrayed by the "Me Generation" of the Reagan years. Particularly insofar as cognitive maps or guideposts are concerned, Sidney's work is of the utmost importance for the children of the '90s—the so-called Generation X.

The most current way of describing Sidney's ongoing role in my life is captured in Robert Bly's image of the "Male Mother."

In 1970, Sidney accepted me as a doctoral student in what was then a brand new creation, the Union Graduate School (now known as the Union Institute). I moved to Gainesville, Florida, in the summer of 1970, having completed a master's in counseling from the University of Illinois and three years of doctoral study at Northwestern University's Garrett Theological Seminary in Evanston, Illinois. I found a job counseling and teaching psychology at Santa Fe Community College in Gainesville, which was a wonderful experience in itself. As well, I was one of Sidney's teaching assistants for his huge, ever-popular Psychology 300—Healthy Personality. I found myself office mates at the Community College with Sidney's wife, Antoinette, and soon began to socialize with both of them at their Gainesville home, and, on weekends, at their beach house. I also attended Sidney's graduate seminars at the University of Florida. And, together, we led an overnight marathon encounter group.

I have published my own account of this very extraordinary experience in *The Phoenix: Babblings of a Man Going Sane*. I have also written another book, *Bear of Inverness Ridge: A Tribute to Sidney M. Jourard.** I have become an exemplar of the "experimental existentialist" and have offered my own experience as an example of the viability of Sidney's work to a "lived" life.

In choosing and organizing these selected writings, it has been my intent to "contemporize" and demonstrate how timely and helpful Sidney's work is today. It is my goal that his seminal influence continues to live on. And that his best writings continue to be available. Had he lived, I am certain he would have continued to contribute and lead psychological thinking for his generation, as Maslow and Rogers did for theirs. I will speak to each section of the *Selected Writings* in turn, and briefly introduce Sidney's work into the context of current language.

The first section, **Cognitive Maps for Human Growth**, includes specifics on what a cycle of human growth actually

* Both of these books are available from Bear Valley Press, 1917 20th Street, Sacramento, California, 95814.

looks like: the steps necessary to get "unstuck," to let go of one's usual "mind," confront one's possibilities, choose one's focus, and get on with one's life with a larger project that includes more of one's "beingness"—*a more authentic life lived from the inside out rather than from the outside in*. Sidney also makes it explicit that this is a *process*—to be repeated over and over again in one's life when necessary, in order to stay alive. Stanley Keleman later formulated a similar "loop of growth" which he calls "little dyings" in *Your Body Speaks its Mind*.

Sidney offers specific maps and suggestions on how to detach from old, habitual ways of seeing and being, so that new points of view can be formulated.

The cognitive map of the growth process, including the most difficult step, which is *the return*, depends on individuals connecting with their *fascination* and being encouraged to follow this growth force. More recently, Joseph Campbell has advised his students to "follow your bliss." I have also included "An Odyssey Within," which offers a full account of Sidney's first LSD experience as well as images of the Odysseus myth, one of the central driving forces in Sidney's work and his life. In that myth are all the ingredients for human growth: the departure, adventure, fulfillment, return. Once again, the return, bringing one's new truth or enlarged perspective back to one's community, is the action that completes the cycle of growth.

As a part of the "map" pointing the way to ingredients necessary for growth, Sidney discovered the necessity of having at least one other person in one's world with whom one can be open and self-disclosing. "Healthy Personality and Self-Disclosure" marks the one singular prerequisite for this movement forward into growth and health in a sustained way: the ability to disclose oneself fully to *at least one other person*. The article is a look at the historical evolution of what surely will be seen as Sidney's central, lasting contribution: his research about the effects of self-disclosure on the health of both the therapist and the client (student).

In the chapter "Reality, Perception and Healthy Personality," Sidney incorporates the heart of present-day Cognitive Psychotherapy and offers some very specific suggestions on how to look at and change chronic concepts of ourself and our world which may be impeding our growth.

"On Being Persuaded Who You Are" is the first article in the second section of the book, which I have entitled **Roots of Holistic Psychology: Humanistic/Cognitive/In-Spiriting**. This is an absolute gem: Sidney at his very best. In it he dares to address the "macro" political/social context within which growth occurs, and asks the entrancing question: "Where did you ever get the idea that you had to be like...?"

For the last several years, I have studied the work of the Cognitive Therapists: Beck, Meichenbaum, and so on. In doing so, I have realized that Sidney's work pre-dates and underpins this current expression of psychotherapeutic technique.

Sidney realized that the very first, most crucial, simple, but oftentimes overlooked step in doing psychotherapy is to form a relationship of trust with the client. This is now referred to as the "therapeutic alliance," that *both* the client and the therapist feel united in working together to seek a positive outcome for the client. The presence of this mutual feeling is highly predictive of a successful outcome.

The second step, once genuine trust has been formed, is to call into question the client's self-defeating belief structures which maintain the unwanted or self-destructive behavior. The therapist might also suggest other ways of thinking and acting that might be more productive and generate happiness in the client's life. In addition, the client may be given techniques to remember and implement the new ways of thinking about his or her situation.

I have included a delightful, never-before-published case study—"The Laugh That Heals," to demonstrate how Sidney actually interacted with a client.

In the sense that Sidney was interested in words and their precise use, he was a forerunner of the current cognitive approaches. He was forever challenging his students, clients, and friends to examine their ideas about what was possible, "normal," or assumed as these chronic thoughts form the limits to our human possibilities—how far we are willing to reach.

Another excellent article in the second section which elaborates on this point of view from a humanistic perspective is "Growing Personality, Not 'Adjustment', Is the Goal in Counseling and Psychotherapy." One of the lines from this article has fascinated me throughout my entire career: "A healthy personality lives in and with his body, he is an 'embodied self.' He is not afraid or ashamed to touch his own body or the bodies of other people with whom he is on intimate terms. He is able freely to move his body, which has a look of grace, coordination, and relaxation. 'He dances through life' to state this idea in its most extreme but essentially accurate form." The necessity of changing, or enlivening the physical body as an integral part of the growth process is still not recognized by the vast multitudes of "talk therapists" who have great difficulty in implementing lasting change, since the vehicle for *making change*, the physical body, is never attended to.

Sidney elaborates on this theme of including the full knowledge of the organism in our decision-making process in a heretofore unpublished article entitled "Somatic Disclosure and Perception of the Soma." In this writing Sidney outlines one of his favorite metaphors for the relatively healthy person: the canary in a coal mine.

"Before modern detection devices were invented, miners would take a canary into the mine. If the air was not fit for breathing, the canary would cease singing, and would die before the atmosphere became totally lethal for humans. A number of lines of observation suggests that a person responds bodily to other persons, to landscapes and scenes, such that if he can perceive variations in the state of his bodily being he can detect when the situation enhances his life, and when it diminishes his sense of zest and vitality. R. D. Laing speaks of the 'fantasy' mode of experiencing the world which, typically, is not available to the reflective consciousness but which can be tuned in on if one seeks to. Thus, a person may say, after a transaction with somebody, 'I feel full, or empty, or drained, or sucked dry, or shafted, stabbed in the back, strangled, etc., etc.' These statements are metaphoric and analogical, but they express something real that was going on.... Rather than view fantasy as the unconscious of which Freud spoke, I prefer to view the fantasy mode of experiencing as a special kind of perception—using one's body as a canary....In fact, I propose that we use the term, *somatic perception* to subsume what Freud called the 'unconscious,' Laing calls 'fantasy,' Werner called 'physiognomic' perception, and Scher calls, 'vivacious perception'....Socialization that results in unembodiment annihilates our capacity for 'seeing,' or testing the world with our bodies."

In order to "see through" and therefore begin to erase the power of outdated concepts, roles, rules, and so on, the body must be re-enlivened and validated as a worthwhile source for *knowing* and *acting*. It is a revolutionary act to have one's own perspective. Then, rather than having the knowing and action move only from a fixed law, role or idea (the head), it can *also* come from one's own owned deeper aliveness and realness: the pulsing of the guts, breathing flowing in and out, the beating of one's own heart. The voices spoken by the whole organism are equally important to hear as the head's thinking. We do not wish to negate the intelligence of the brain, but rather to place it in a context of a whole, responsive, functioning being.

Joseph Campbell, in his rightly acclaimed Bill Moyers/Joseph Campbell PBS Series unfortunately implies that the spiritual pathway begins with the opening of the heart and the capacity of one so opened to have compassion and love for another. He further identifies the lower parts of our bodies as our "animal natures" which must be transcended if we are to become fully human.

This, perhaps unintended, pejorative notion of the "animal" as something to be conquered or overcome, as opposed to the "animal" as a positive foundation to be built on, is unfortunate. It may tempt the uninformed seeker to try to go directly to opening the heart and "higher," "more fully human" centers above, without first establishing an open, powerful, and flexible foundation below.

It is clear that one of the most important spiritual practices in our daily lives lies in addressing our bodies; *giving in* to becoming "grounded," trustfully allowing the earth to *support us.* Paradoxically, only when one is more fully grounded in one's own body, can we be more free toward a participation in the *experience* of spirituality.

Two articles which serve as bridges between **Roots of Holistic Psychology** and **Psychotherapist as Growth Coach** are "The Mystic Dimension of Self" and "Prophets As Psychotherapists, and Psychotherapists As Prophets."

In "The Mystic Dimension of Self," yet another previously unpublished "gem," Sidney observes: "The only proper posture for a man is to be off-balance, if not always, then at least periodically. Poets have always lived or experienced the world from this vantage point, assuming that the prosaic view of things-for-use posture is the balanced view." This image, of *allowing ourselves* to be off-balance on occasion is both a metaphoric and literal truth. It is also a central paradox to the process of human growth which must be accepted by the seeker.

In order to let down, find one's own center, inner balance, and ground *to move from*, one must affirm and actually physically practice stances of falling forward into *the unknown.* This posture also involves *faith* and a trust that a new balance point will be found.

The last article in this section, "Prophets As Psychotherapists, and Psychotherapists As Prophets," documents Sidney's re-discovery (or discovery) of Judaism, and also introduces us to some of his most potent metaphors and ideas regarding psychotherapy and the life of the psychotherapist. These images include: Psychotherapist as *Exemplar*, Psychotherapist as "successful" Outsider, Psychotherapist as Double-Agent, and Psychotherapist as Transcender of Facticity.

It is when we examine Sidney's writings of psychotherapy and the role of the psychotherapist in our society, that we see the full brilliance of his thinking and the profound implications of his work for diligent, present-day professional helpers.

Tom Hanna was one of Sidney's dearest friends, and, while I was in graduate school at the University of Florida, was also chair of the Philosophy Department there. Along with Sidney, Tom also served on my doctoral committee. In an article called "The Invitation to Life: Sidney Jourard" Tom states that "for Sidney, it was not a question whether we, in truth, *had* the function of choice, but whether we, in truth, *chose*."

The issue of the possibility of choice remains one of the most hotly debated subjects in the area of psychotherapy and psychology in general. One's feelings, theories and training on this issue greatly affect how a therapist or a teacher addresses a client or a student.

Most systems of personality development, save Humanism, Holism, and Existentialism, view persons as *determined*, as molded and formed by the forces of their history, their environment or by the idiosyncrasies of their biology and genetic "givens."

These deterministic systems also encourage mental health professionals and educators to take charge and set the learning agenda (the diagnosis) for the client or student. This is done by the professional because it is wrongly assumed that the client or student does not have the resources to complete such an agenda. Proceeding on an agenda other than the client's (or student's) is a course bound for failure. The goal of education and psychotherapy is to equip students with skills to identify and follow their own learning priorities *throughout life*, not only when a teacher is present.

"The Psychotherapist as Psychedelic Man," is a light in a world of darkness in exciting the imagination about the true potential of the teacher or therapist. "On Becoming a Psychotherapist" is a delightful, candid snapshot of Sidney's inner life as he writes about his own early development as a therapist, healer, and teacher. He says, "I felt lonely most of my life, now as well as then....I was fascinated with human differences...and wonderment over my chronic feeling of being different, an outsider"—the person who could leave his or her culture and his usual mind on occasion, and then *return*, re-connect, to further contribute to and enrich his or her own locale.

So much of psychotherapy and personality theory is focused on "looking back" to find the answer, and this, alone, has *never* proved to be very effective in helping people live more happy, productive lives. In the extreme, Freud's approach, Psychoanalysis, actually may influence persons to become *less functional* at sustaining a forward movement and, therefore, may be more *debilitating* than helpful. There is a paradox present here as is the case with so many issues regarding human growth. One must be able to look back with the goal of moving forward not forgotten. While it is necessary to understand what happened in one's past, the *primary focus* must be on moving forward, or as Sidney would have phrased it: "Getting on with one's life."

"The Transcending Therapist" continues to probe at the authenticity, or "realness" that heals in the therapeutic encounter. Sidney's work on psychotherapy continues to be *revolutionary and unsurpassed* because it gives permission and encouragement for the therapist, at appropriate moments, to be willing and able to disclose *their real selves* before their clients. This is done to both *model realness* and also to communicate to the client that working together for a positive outcome for the client is a *joint venture*, not something a therapist "does to" a client.

This notion is still radical because it directly challenges the most sacred of Freudian cows: *The Transference.* The general idea of the transference is that in order for a client to get better, he or she must first project their unmet longings, past affronts and humiliations, fears, rages, and so on, *onto the therapist.* Then these past events, inappropriately attached to the therapist's "blank screen" persona, can be analyzed. Through this analysis, presumably, the inappropriate "projecting" will cease and the client will be better able to function in the here and now, healed of old, outdated responses.

But this course has *never* really proven itself to work very well, if at all. Most research on psychoanalysis suggests that persons in such treatments improve at about the same rate as those in control groups who receive no treatment and experience only the passage of time. As I mentioned before, some studies suggest that persons in psychoanalytically oriented treatments actually may become overspecialized at *looking backward*, and may actually become less proficient at getting on with their lives; of finding ways of being happy and productive in their *present lives.*

It is obvious that mere human beings, and not the gods, invent psychotherapies and the theories that bolster them. Not oddly, therapists also produce theories and therapies that protect *their own limitations.* Sidney observes that "Freud might have helped his patients more swiftly if he were not so shy, so reluctant to share his experience with his patients." Unfortunately, Freud's shyness and inability to disclose himself, has been concretized into *present* dogma and unquestioned therapeutic technique.

In "Psychology: Control or Liberation?" Sidney states that "I had begun as far back as 1952 to break my professional anonymity, by sharing with a client any experience of mine with problems comparable to those he was exploring with me. I found that such authentic sharing—within bounds of relevance and common sense—encouraged my patients to explore and reveal their experience more fully and freely than was hitherto the case for me. It was as if I had bungled into a new kind of technique, but one which entailed some risk, indeed, some inclusion of my patient into the world of us, rather than seeing him as one of Them."

Before I move on to make some introductory comments about **The Disaster Areas** segment of this book, I need to explain one phrase used in the title, **Psychotherapist as Growth Coach: Teacher, Self-Discloser and Transcender of Facticity**.

My secretary has repeatedly pointed out to me that there is no such word as "facticity" so I must assume it is a word that Sidney invented himself. In the context of psychotherapy and the psychotherapist's own growth, transcender of facticity means the *ability to choose*, to *overcome* socialization, culture, even biology.

The last article in this section on psychotherapy, "Changing Personal Worlds: A Humanistic Perspective," suggests that any therapist is most effective helping "persons whose suffering grew out of anti-growth forces comparable to those which he himself had tamed." He goes on to "imagine a brochure which listed the names of all the therapists, not by their theoretical orientation but by the kinds of dilemmas, backgrounds, and crises that they had faced and transcended." In essence this is what the Recovery and 12-Step Programs have discovered: the simple truth that no one understands like someone who herself has overcome the obstacle in question—whether it be drinking too much, overspending, sex addiction or whatever. This point of view is also extremely important in that any realistic assessment of therapists' lives demonstrates clearly that there are no perfect, finished, self-actualized persons, only persons in *process of becoming*. It is the journey itself that is crucial, not arriving (or pretending to have arrived) at the *ultimate destination*."

**The Disaster Areas** is a title Sidney was playing with around the time of his death for a new book which, of course, never came to pass. We have decided to use it to organize some of the topics Sidney wrote on with great insight that relate to issues contemporary and timeless: marriage, failure of dialogue, the male role, the body taboo, the challenges posed by the new technologies, suicide, privacy, and so on.

My particular favorites among these writings are "Some Lethal Aspects of the Male Role," and the "The Human Challenge of Automation." As I have said, the "disaster areas" that Sidney identified are still the burning issues of our time.

In "Marriage Is for Life," Sidney introduces several important truths about marriage and human growth. He says, "I take it as true that there is no way to go through life without some pain, suffering, loneliness, and fear. We can help one another minimize the shadow side of life; none can avoid it completely." As a culture we have become pain phobic—the media and Hollywood have brainwashed us into expecting life to come prepackaged, neat, and nicely wrapped. And at the first sign of discomfort, we may leave our project, our companion, our geography.

Yet another of **The Disaster Areas** is "The Invitation to Die." If you've wondered what "existential phenomenology" is, read this gem and you will know. Also, it looks at suicide from an intriguing and thought-provoking perspective: that attempts to kill oneself are the result of a failure of imagination (or of courage) and in part, may be misguided efforts to "grow oneself" or to transcend a *sickening situation*. Sidney states, "I think we need to liberalize and pluralize our social structure, so that people can be taught a theory of personal growth that encourages them to let *an* incarnation die, without killing their embodied selves so that they can invent new ones, and find places and company to live them, until they die of being worn out."

As I have said before, in a marvelous, entertaining and enlightening way, Sidney was a *successful outsider*. He lived fully *in* the culture of his time, but was not totally *of* the culture around him. Even more remarkable was that Sidney had access to the *child spirit* from inside himself and he *loved to play*. Specifically, he loved to play with words and ideas. He remains unexcelled in his power and ability to communicate from this place within himself and connect outward through his writings: gifts that will remain with us, always. Sidney brought himself, totally, to his writings, and the reader of this book will have an experience "of Sidney."

Michael Lowman, Ph.D.
Sacramento, California
August 1994

## Editors' Note

At the time Sidney wrote the articles in this book—the '60s and '70s—it was appropriate to use the words "his" and "man" to refer to all human beings. In his writings it is evident that he championed the rights of women and other minorities. If he were writing today he would not have written in a gender-biased mode. Rather than edit his writings to reflect the present acceptable language, they have been left in the original form, with the understanding that these words were not intended to refer solely to males.✦

# *I* *Cognitive Maps for Human Growth*

# *I-1* Growing Experience and the Experience of Growth*

*Growth has always fascinated man, but he has studied it only from its "outside." None of the scientific accounts of growth and development are informed by the experience of the one growing. Instead, we have accounts of physical and behavioral development, as these appear to the scientist's eyes, or as they leave traces on his recording apparatus, to show up as "growth curves" in a scientific treatise. The other side of growth needs to be shown, if for no other reason than to round out the story. The present chapter offers an essay toward a "phenomenology of personal growth."*

Everything looks different when I visit the neighborhood where I grew up. The stores and houses look smaller, decayed, less imposing than I remember them to have been. My old school chums are balder, fatter; some look defeated and resigned, and others are smug, more self-satisfied than they were when I knew them years ago. Their change appears to me as a kind of fall, a failure to realize many of the dreams which I knew animated them in their younger days. My own change (which I become acutely conscious of at times like these) feels to me like growth. I feel that I have grown, while they have just grown older.

What is growth? What is my growth? How does it appear from the outside, from the point of view of another? Do I experience my growing? Or do I only see a difference, say, between old and more recent pictures of myself and conclude that I have changed. Indeed, I have heard tape recordings of my speech

*The bibliographic numerical notations in this chapter refer to the complete bibliography from Disclosing Man to Himself, which can be found in Chapter V-1.*

and seen moving pictures of myself taken several years ago; and seeing how I looked and sounded makes me almost nauseous. I don't recognize myself as the source of those impressions. I experience myself from the outside, and can't recapture the "feel" of the person I was. Yet at times I have undergone some engrossing experience and, in a flash, realize that I am changed. I experience myself and the world in new dimensions, as if a veil has been suddenly lifted.

What is the essence of this change? Is it growth? What brings it about? Can I help it along, or hinder its occurrence? Can another person bring it on? Prevent it? In this chapter, I am going to speak of growth from an "inside" point of view, of the growth of experience and the changed experience that is growth. There are many accounts available about growth as it appears on the outside, as recorded by instruments or by scientific observers, but few about growing awareness. Since I *am* my awareness, an account of growing, changing awareness must at the same time be an account of my growth.

Growth is the disintegration of one way of experiencing the world, followed by a reorganization of this experience, a reorganization that includes the new disclosure of the world. The disorganization, or even shattering of one way to experience the world, is brought on by new disclosures from the changing being of the world—disclosures that were always being transmitted, but which were usually ignored.

**Being is Change**

Change is in the world. The being of the world is always changing. My body is in the world, and it changes from instant to instant. Things and other people are in the world; and they metamorphose, swiftly or ever so slowly. I may not be aware of the change that *is* the world. The world-for-me may not appear to change; but rather it may seem congealed, constant, fixed. I may also experience my own being as unchanging.

In fact, people *strive to construct* a stable world, a world they can control and get their bearings in. A view of the world exclusively as constant is an achievement—a *praxis*, not a "given." A naïve view of the world sees it as *both* a "buzzing, blooming confusion" and as stable and "structured." We simply cannot navigate in a world that changes swiftly. And so we "freeze" it by pledging not to notice change until it has reached some critical degree, until it has gone so far it can no longer be ignored. Then, we might acknowledge it. If everything changed during the night, and you awakened to a new experience of yourself and the world, you might be terrified. But if suddenly, the world froze, so that as everything now is, it would remain for eternity, you would be horrified. It would be hell—a hell of perfect predictability and boredom.

The disclosure of change is going on all the time. Change is *experienced*, however, only at moments. The awareness of change is frequently the experience of *surprise*: the "unexpected" has just been presented to us.* The world, or my own bodily being, is not as I had believed it to be. My expectations about being, my concepts and beliefs about the world, have just been disconfirmed. The awareness that things are different is not growth, though it is a necessary condition of growth. A growth *cycle* calls for (a) an acknowledgment that the world has changed, (b) a shattering of the present experienced "world-structure," and (c) a restructuring, retotalization, of the world-structure which encompasses the new disclosure of changed reality.

The retotalization of experience which consummates a growth cycle happens when a person sets goals and projects

---

* Psychologists will note the relation of the present phenomenological theory of growth to Festinger's (1957) considerations of "cognitive dissonance." "Balance" theories, as well, as in Heider (1958) or Secord and Backman (1965), also bear upon this question. Shaw's (1966) concept of "upended expectations" is a cognate term, and Kelly's (1955) dialectic of "construing" and reconstruing of experience is likewise related. Murphy's (1947) and Werner's (1948) formulations of the stages in perception, from the global and undifferentiated, through the differentiated, to the integrated or unified stage, is a relevant theoretical formulation of growth, taken over from biological views of physical growth. Finally, the dialectic as formulated by Hegel and Marx, and reformulated by Sartre in phenomenological terms (1960, 1963), and expounded by Laing and Cooper (1964), provides a framework within which the present chapter may be viewed.

for himself, when he envisions a possibility and sets about trying to bring it to fruition. In fact, the growth cycle is often tripped off by a *failure* in goal-seeking. As one sets about trying to make or do something, he finds that his initial concepts and beliefs about what and how things *are*, are false. They do no ground accurate predictions about the world and oneself.[48,94] Faced with failure, he must then suspend his present beliefs and let the world disclose itself to him as it *now* is. If he does this, he can revise his concepts and get on with his project.

A growth cycle can also be triggered when goals and projects turn stale; when money can no longer buy anything that the person wants; when the fame that was once the person's glory has turned to ashes; and when the love of that woman, long-pursued, is now experienced as cloying, suffocating possessiveness. The lack of fulfillment when long-enjoyed goals are achieved signifies, however indirectly, that *our personal being* has changed, unnoticed by us. Our *concept of ourselves*, as the person who would be fulfilled by this pleasure or be made happier by that "success," *has gotten out of touch with the reality of our being*. We are in for some surprises. The boredom signifies the imminence of growth. The time is ripe for the experience of new goals, and new unfoldings of our being. It is time to let the world and ourselves disclose their being to our experience. We may undergo this new experience (if we let it happen) in delight, or in the terrifying realization that we are going out of our minds.

The world is full of Being, of many beings—some human, some animal, some inanimate. Being has many forms. Every being in the world can be likened to a kind of broadcasting station, transmitting signals of its being to other beings in the world. This transmission is ceaseless. As people and things and animals exist, they change; and they broadcast the fact of this change into the world. You and I are both beings, but beings of a special kind. We have (or are) awareness. We are embodied consciousnesses. We experience the transmissions that originate in our bodies; and through our bodies, we experience some of the transmissions of being that originate elsewhere.

As human beings, we originate transmissions of our being, and we receive transmissions from other beings. My being discloses itself to me—I experience my own being—and it is disclosed to you through my appearance and behavior. *My* experience of *my* being is different from *your* experience of *my* being. And my experience of the being you disclose to me differs from your experience of your own being.

## Our Concepts "Freeze" the World and Blind Us

Man is a *concept-maker*. He forms *concepts* of the being of the world, and of his own self-being. A concept is an abstraction from what *is*. From a phenomenological and existential perspective, *a concept is a commitment to stop noticing the changing disclosures (disclosures of change) incessantly being transmitted by the beings in the world.*\* When I identify something as a cow, I rubricize it. I let it disclose enough of its being for me to classify it into the category *cow*. Then, I stop receiving, though the cow hasn't stopped sending. It is a cow. It is this very cow, Bossie. Bossie is that cow which presents itself to me as black and white, of the kind "Holstein," with a big chip flaked off her left front hoof. I "know" Bossie. I can anticipate what she will do, on the basis of her past disclosures to me and my awareness of these disclosures. I can get milk from Bossie. She will kick me if I approach her from the right side. And so on. But Bossie is continually changing, and these changes are continually revealed to the world. So long as I think of Bossie as I always have, I ignore these disclosures. I address Bossie as if she has not changed. Indeed, for the purposes I pursue in my transactions with Bossie, these changes may not make any difference, until enough change has occurred that my predictions about Bossie are not borne out, and my purposes are thwarted. I start milking Bossie, and no milk comes. I say, "Something's wrong. Bossie is different. She has changed. She is not the Bossie I knew." Of course she isn't. She never was. No sooner did I form a *concept* of Bossie (stop

\* *Gendlin's* [24, 25] *formulations have strongly influenced the present exposition. His analysis of personality change is of the most far-reaching theoretical and practical significance, in my opinion.*

perceiving her disclosures) than it was out of date. When I say, "Bossie has change," all I am doing is belatedly acknowledging a change that has been inexorable and continuous. For my purposes (getting milk out of her), she did not change. When my purposes were thwarted, I was forced to expand my awareness of Bossie, to suspend my concept of her being, and to let her being address me. My concept of Bossie (which terminated my perception of the multiple disclosures of her changing being) enabled me to fulfill my milking project. When the project was stymied, my concept became perceptibly incongruent, out of date with the actuality of Bossie's being. In fact, if I propose some new projects that involve Bossie, I may find that my concept of her being requires revision. I may wish to enter her in a race. I believe she is a fast runner and can win me a prize. I test her—I put her in a situation where she can disclose her running ability. I find her slow. My concept of Bossie's being must now include the assertion that "she is slow."

## Growing, Suspended Concepts, and the World's Disclosure-to-Me

Enough of cows, and enough of Bossie. I am going to contend that when my concepts—of myself, of you, of cars, of cows, of trees, and of refrigerators—are shattered, and I again face the world with a questioning attitude; when I face the being in question and *let it disclose itself to me* (it always was disclosing, but I paid it no attention after I conceptualized it); and when I re-form my concept on the basis of this newly received disclosure—then, *I have grown.* I will suspend my concepts when my projects in life (which depend on accurate concepts of reality for their fulfillment) are thwarted, when my predictions about how things will act or react prove wrong. Then, if I adopt the attitude of "let the world disclose itself to me," I will receive this disclosure and change my concepts; and I will have grown.

My concepts of being can change under more pleasant circumstances than failure. In those rare moments when I have gratified all of my urgent needs—I have done my work, I feel good and fulfilled, and I want nothing out of the world just now—then the world will disclose all kinds of new faces to me. I am letting the world "be itself, for itself." I may then notice all kinds of things about my friends, trees, the sky, animals, whatever is there; things that call upon me to enlarge my previous concepts of those same beings. Thus, success and gratification can be psychedelic (consciousness-expanding). They can open up my world for me and let me experience it in new dimensions.

You may notice that I appear different from the last time you saw me. My behavior and my verbal disclosures will show a change to you. You will say of me, "He has changed, he has grown." You will have to modify your concept of me at that time. *If you do, then you will have grown.* Your action toward me will reflect your changed concept of me, your changed experience of me. And I shall then say to you, "You have changed; you have grown." You will feel confirmed in your being. You will feel understood; you will feel that the disclosure of your changed being—in words and actions—has been received and acknowledged by me.

I have a certain concept of my being, of myself. This is my *self-concept*. It is my belief about my own being. My being discloses itself to me in the form of my intentional experience of myself. I experience the feel of my body's existence. I experience my own action from the inside. I form a concept of myself—what I am like, how I react, what I am capable of and what I cannot do—on the basis of this self-experience. You may also tell me what and who you think I am, on the basis of your experience of the outside of my being; and I take your belief into account. We may agree that I am thus and such a kind of person—a man, a psychologist, kind, strong, able to play a fair game of handball, unable to sing in key, etc. Once I have formed this concept of who and what I am, I proceed to behave in the world as if that is all and everything I am or can be. My behavior, my self-disclosure, endlessly confirms my self-concept. It is as if I have taken a pledge to present this and only this as my being.[26]

In fact, my being, like all Being, *is change*. This change discloses itself to me through my experience and to others through my behavior. But if you and I have formed a concept of my being, neither of us pays attention to the ceaseless transmission of my changing being. It is transmitted, but no receiver is tuned in to acknowledge the change. Things can get more complicated. I may notice the changes, and change my concept of myself accordingly. You may not notice the changes. You treat me as if I were the same person. I do not recognize myself as the one you believe I am. I feel you are talking to somebody else, not me.

Or, you may notice the changes before I do, and change your concept of me accordingly. Again, I may not recognize the "me" that you seem to be addressing. Your concept of me is disjunctive from my self-concept.

Or, I may display and disclose the newly experienced facets of my being to you. You may say, "I don't recognize you. You are not yourself today. I don't like the person you seem to be. I'll come see you when you have gotten back into your 'right mind.'" If you thus disconfirm my newly experienced and tentatively disclosed being, and if I am unsure of myself, I may try to suppress and repress my newly emerged being and seek to appear to you and to me as the person I *was*. If I do this chronically, and successfully, I enter an untenable situation; and I may become mad.[54]

### Growing and the Modes of Experiencing

There is also another way in which I might grow through a relationship with you. I may have a fixed concept of you and hence behave toward you in an habitual, stereotyped way. My action toward you is predictable. I always become aggressive in your presence. I experience you as a source of harm to me; and I attack first, to protect myself. My concept of you is that you are menacing, that you harbor ill will toward me. *When I experience you, I may not be undergoing a perceptual experience, but rather an imaginative experience of your being.* I tune out your disclosed being, and replace it by an imaginative experience.[88] Or a fantasy[54] experience. Imagination veils perception. In fact, much of our experience of the people in our lives, even when they are face-to-face with us, is *not* perceptual, but *imaginative*, or fantastical.*

The perceptual mode of experiencing entails the readiness to receive inputs of disclosure from the other, such that one's awareness of the other is a changing awareness. But the imaginative and fantasy modes of experiencing "tune out" fresh disclosures. My image of you remains fixed, unchanged by your disclosures, because I do not pay them any attention. Now, if you can break through my imaginative experience, or my fantasy image, of you; if you can catch my attention, by a shout, a blow, a scream of pain or joy—I may, as it were, "wake up" from my daydream-like experience of your being and undergo a fresh perceptual experience of you. You will surprise me. If you do this, if you get me "un-hung" from fixation on these modes of experiencing you—the imaginative and the fantasy modes—so that I can now perceive you, I shall have grown. My consciousness of you will have expanded. My awareness will have grown; and where I had previously been aware of you only as an image or a concept (though I wasn't *reflectively* aware that this was an image), now I can experience you perceptually, If my consciousness expands so that I can experience you or the world in many more modes than I could hitherto—imaginatively, perceptually, recollectively, in the mode of fantasy—then I have grown. I *am* my awareness; and if my awareness expands, *I* have grown.

My world of awareness may not only be fixed in one *mode* of experiencing, e.g., the abstracting, conceptual mode or the imaginative mode; my world may also be confined to some one or two sensory "channels" of awareness. For example, I may limit my clear awareness only to visual and auditory im-

* *Laing's (1961) analysis of fantasy as a mode of experience is a contribution to phenomenology of high importance. He shows what Freud's "unconscious" is like as it is embodied in our conscious experience of the world.*

pressions and exclude the worlds of smelling, tasting, or the feel of my own body. If you can turn me on to my feelings, to smells, to tastes; if you can wake up my imagination; if you can get me to experience the feel of my body—you will have expanded my awareness and helped me to grow. You could caress me (cf. Sartre,[86] pp. 389-391) out of my "mind" and into my experience of my body.

## Growth Through Suspension of Self-Concept and Self-Consciousness

If I, from time to time, suspend my concept of myself and "tune in" on my being, if I meditate or reflect on my experience, then I must re-form my self-concept. I shall believe myself to be different. I shall act differently. I *am* different. Moments of meditation are the times (rare in our culture) when we try to let the changing flux of our being disclose itself to us.[51, 63] If we learn how to do it or let it happen, meditation can give us the *experience* of transition in our being and can yield transitional experiences.[94] In meditation, too, we let the world disclose more of its changing being to us; and we may find ourselves experiencing more of the variety in the world.

But meditation is not the only occasion when our self-concepts are put into question and temporarily suspended. Whenever we are unself-conscious, whenever our attention is fully focused upon some task or some project, our being changes; and our changing experience of our changed being goes on spontaneously. We let our personal being *happen*. We do not try to monitor and control it so that it conforms to a concept, yours or mine, of my being. Fascinated engagement at *anything* can let change happen and be experienced such that the next time I reflect upon myself, I find my experience of myself different from how I remember it the last time I reflected. And my concept of myself will have to change to encompass the new experiencing I have undergone. Challenge, fascination, total involvement in some task or project such that self-consciousness and self-conceptualizing is *not* the mode of experience, will permit the changed self-being to be experienced.

## Growth Through Dialogue

If I engage in conversation with you, in dialogue; and if you disclose your experience of yourself and of me to me in truth; and if I receive your continuing disclosure; and if I disclose my experience of myself and of your disclosures to you in truth—*then I must be letting change happen* and be disclosed to us both. If I reflect upon my experience of the dialogue, I must notice that I am different from the way I was when we began the dialogue. But if I have (as it were) pledged myself to appear before you and to myself as *this* kind of man and no other, then my intentional disclosures to you will be very selective. Perhaps I will lie to you, to preserve your present concept of me, or at least *my* concept of *your* concept of me. Indeed, if my pledge of sameness is made to myself, then every time my *actually* changed being discloses itself to me, I will become threatened and repress it. I will pretend to myself I did not have the experience of hatred, or of anxiety, or of lust. And I will believe my own pretense to myself. Then, I shall not grow. My concept of myself will become increasingly estranged from the ongoing change of my being. If my self-concept is too discrepant from actuality, the disclosure to me of my changed being will become more insistent. I will then have to pretend and repress much harder. If the change is too great, the experience of change will no longer be repressible. It will declare itself in my experience and perhaps in my behavior; I may become terrified and feel I have "gone out of my mind." Actually, I have, if by "mind" we mean "self-concept." If still I insist on trying to appear to you as the same person I was, I may develop neurotic symptoms. Or if I am terrified enough, I may become psychotic.

## Growth and Your Experience of Me

You can help me grow, or you can obstruct my growth. If you have a *fixed* idea of who I am and what my traits are, and what my possibilities of change are, then anything that comes out of me beyond your concept, you will disconfirm. In fact, you may be terrified of any surprises, any changes in my behavior, because these changes may threaten your concept of me; my changes may, if disclosed to you, shatter your concept of me and challenge you to grow. You may be afraid to. In your fear, you may do everything in your power to get me to unchange and to reappear to you as the person you once knew.

But if you suspend any preconceptions you may have of me and my being, and invite me simply to be and to disclose this being to you, you create an ambiance, an area of "low pressure" where I can let my being happen and be disclosed, to you and to me simultaneously—to me from the inside, and to you who receive the outside layer of my being.

If your concept of my being is one that encompasses more possibilities in my behavior than I have myself acknowledged; if your concept of my being is more inclusive and indeed more accurate than my concept of my being, and if you let me know how you think of me; if you let me know from moment to moment how you experience me; if you say, "Now I like you. Now I think you are being ingratiating. Now I think you can succeed at this if you try"; if you tell me *truly* how you experience me, I can compare this with my experience of myself, and with my own self-concept. You may thus insert the thin edge of doubt into the crust of my self-concept, helping to bring about its collapse, so that I might re-form it. In fact, this is what a loving friend, or a good psychotherapist, does.

There is another way you can help me grow and that is through challenging me and encouraging me to attempt new projects. We actually construe and conceptualize the world and ourselves in the light of the projects we live for. It is our commitment to these which structures our worlds. The beings in the world, including our own being, reveal different faces of themselves to us, depending upon the projects we are pursuing at the moment. The trees in the forest reveal their timber footage to the lumber merchant, the bugs in their trunks to the insect-collector, and their colors to the painter. My muscular strength or weakness reveals itself to me as I try to chop the forest down, and I form a concept of my muscular strength. I may never come to question or doubt this estimate I made. My self-concept gets frozen if my projects are frozen, and if I become too adept and skilled at fulfilling them.

Suppose, when I find my existence dull and boring, I decide to try some new project—to write a book, climb a mountain, change jobs. I tell you of this, at first, faint resolve. I am afraid to try, because, as I presently think of myself, I don't believe I have the capacity to succeed. If you encourage me to try and encourage me and support me when the going gets rough, so that I stick with the project with more and more single-mindedness, I discover in myself transcendent powers I never experienced before and never imagined I had. I do not and cannot transcend my *possibilities*; I don't know what these are and won't know until I stop living. I only transcend my *concept* of what my possibilities might be. You can help me transcend my self-concept by challenging and supporting me in new projects that I undertake.

Even the decision to *attempt* something new results in a new experience of myself and the world, *before* I actually get going. If I decide to start a new book, I begin to experience friends as interferences in this project; movies and television, formerly very inviting, become dull and boring. The whole world and my experience of myself change with the change in projects. If you help me give up old projects that are no longer satisfying, delightful, or fulfilling and encourage me to dare new ones, you are helping me to grow.

## Contemplation, Meditation and Growth

You can help yourself grow if you will engage in aimless contemplation and meditation. To contemplate the world before you, in its visual, auditory, olfactory, and tactual dimensions means simply to let the world present itself to you. You are not searching for anything when you contemplate. Rather, you are letting the world disclose itself to you as it is *in itself*.

You can do this only when you suspend your work, your striving, your goals and projects. When you suspend your projects in this way, you open the "doors of perception," and let birds, trees, other people, in fact everything disclose itself to you. All these beings always were, but you didn't notice so long as you were involved in some task or mission. Such contemplation yields a different experience of the world, which must change your concepts of the world, and it thus fosters growth. Maslow (pp. 109-118)[62] has described such contemplation as "B-cognition," and has pointed out that it has dangers as well as delights. The dangers, of course, are that one might simply revel in the sheer beauty of evil rather than do something about it. But it cannot be gainsaid that contemplation of the world in this aimless way enriches experience.

Instead of gazing upon the world and letting it disclose itself to you through your eyes, ears, nose, and hands, you can meditate upon your own experience of your bodily being. Perhaps close your eyes, or seek a tranquil setting with no sudden distractions. Let your experience happen without direction. Engage in free reverie. You may find yourself now recalling something of the past, now vividly imagining—in playful ways—all kinds of possibilities. You may find yourself experiencing anger for somebody, love for somebody else, you may find you have aches and pains you hadn't noticed before. Some of your self-experiencing may be frightening. It may help you to meditate if, instead of closing your eyes, you gaze with or without fixed focus at a mandala, or a flower. If you gaze long enough, your experiencing may turn on fully and freely. Instead of being frozen into some one mode of experiencing—say, perceiving, or imagining, or remembering—which may be customary for you, you may find that you become "unglued" and then integrated. You experience perceptions fused with memories fused with imagination fused with conceptualizing fused with fantasy fused with emotion. This richness may truly shatter your self-concept, so that when you "pull yourself together," you are truly a different person from the person you thought you were.

As I said before, your being and mine are always in process of change, in consequence of the way we live, the passage of time, and sheer past experience. But living as we do mostly at a conceptual level and for definite projects —dealing, not with concrete things, but with *concepts* of things and people and of ourselves—we reflect quietly upon our awareness of ourselves, we suspend the concepts, and we let our being disclose itself to us. And thus we grow.

## Growing Out of Our Minds

Growing entails going out of our minds and into our raw experience. Our experience is always of the disclosure of the world and of our own embodied being. When we function smoothly, habitually, and effectively in the world, our concepts are confirmed; and we do not receive new disclosure. When we meet impasses and failure in the pursuit of our projects, then our habits, concepts (a habit can be seen as the "outside" of a concept), and expectations are challenged, or upended.[94] Failure of our projects gives us a whiff of the stink of chaos, and this can be terrifying. Our concepts get cracks in them when we fail. Through these cracks, the encapsulated experience "contained" by the concept might leak or explode; or through the crack there may occur an implosion of more being. When there are no concepts, there is nothing—no-thing we can grapple with, get leverage on, in order to get on with the projects of living. There is the threat of pure chaos and situationlessness. If we experience the pure nothingness, we become panicked, and seek quickly to shore up the collapsing world, to daub clay into the cracks in our concepts. If we do this, we don't grow. If we let the concepts explode or implode and do not re-form them veridically, we appear mad, and are mad. If we re-form them, to incorporate new experience, we grow.

Once again, we must consider projects, this time in relation to *integration*, a vital and crucial phase of growth. When our projects are obstructed, because our concepts are out of phase with being, the concepts must explode, or become fractionated, differentiated into parts. We experience chaos. Our commitment to the old projects, or recommitment to new projects, serves as the field of force which organizes the fractionated experience of being into meaningful wholes, concepts, gestalten. Growth is our experience of our concepts and percepts being detotalized and then retotalized into newly meaningful unities.

I know I am ready to grow when I experience surprise—a dissonance between my beliefs and concepts and expectations of the world and my perception of the world.[16] I am also ready to grow when I experience boredom, despair, depression, anxiety, or guilt. These emotions inform me that my goals and projects have lost meaning for me; that my being has gotten too big, too out of phase with my concepts of my being. I have a choice at these moments, if indeed I can experience them. I may have become so unaccustomed to and maladept at reflection and meditation that I simply don't notice these all-is-not-well signals. And I continue to pursue my projects and to believe my beliefs as if experience were confirming them.

But if I do acknowledge the signals, my choice is either to meditate, suspend my concept and preconception of self, and let my changed being disclose itself to me, even when it hurts (it frequently does); or to decide to affirm the project of being the same (an impossible project, but one that many people try to live). If I decide to try to be the same, then I will repress my experience of change, of all-is-not-well signals. I have resolved, really, to stop perceiving myself.

The invitation to suspend preconceptions and concepts, to let being disclose itself, is actually an invitation to go out of one's mind. To be out of one's mind can be terrifying; because when projects are suspended, and experiencing is just happening, myself and the world are experienced as infinite possibility: anything might be possible. Since nothing *definite* is possible, purposeful action is *im*possible. Yet, if a person can endure this voyage within his own experience—his Odyssey within—he can emerge from it with a new concept of his being and with new projects; the new concept of being will include more of his being in it. But this new integration will last only so long, and then the entire process must be repeated again. A sentient life is an endless series of getting out of one's mind and concepts, only to reenter and to depart again.

## Surprise and Growing

The experience of surprise is a sign of one's readiness to grow. Amazement and wonder signify that one's concepts of self and of the world and of other people are "loose," ready to be re-formed. The "know-it-all," the "cool" one, has pledged himself never to be surprised. Everything that the world discloses is no more than an unfolding of what he has expected and predicted, or so he tries to convey to others. But when a man can be dumbfounded and surprised at what comes out of him or at what his friend or spouse is capable of doing and disclosing, he is a growing person.

In fact, if I intentionally adopt the "set" that all of my concepts are tentative and provisional, I invite others, myself, and the world to reveal surprisingly new facets of their being to me, so that even my daily life can be an unfolding of newness, where simply perceiving the world or the self is a source of endless variety and surprise.

If I am with you, and I have willfully adopted the set that I do not know and cannot ever fully know all your possibilities, my very presence embodies an invitation to you to surprise me, to show off, to transcend your (and my) previous concepts of your being. I can tell when I am in the presence of a person with a closed mind. I feel constrained to shut off most of my possibilities. But in the presence of a wonder-er, I feel an absence of prejudgment, a permissive acceptance; and my terror and self-consciousness about revealing surprises is diminished.

In short, if you and I retain our capacity for surprise, we aid and confirm one another's growth.

## Psychedelic Drugs and Personal Growth

There are many ways to "turn experiencing on," whether we are speaking of perceptual awareness in any of the sense modalities; imagination; remembering; or fantasy. I've mentioned the opportunities for this to happen in dialogue, in failure at projects, in boredom, and in fascination. The psychedelic drugs have this power to turn a person on, probably by (somehow) disengaging him from any and all attachments and projects in the "outer" world. This drug-induced liberation from attachments destructures the world of experience and permits all kinds of experiential changes to happen. The world gets unglued and destructured from its usual forms. I shall describe one such experience now, in illustration of some of the points I made earlier.*

### *Psychedelic Drugs: "Not for Everybody"*

The various consciousness-expanding drugs are the subject of keen interest to laymen and to scientists at the present time.[7,58] College students, artists and writers perk up when they hear of personal narratives of a psychedelic trip. Psychiatrists, psychologists, and pharmacologists conduct experiments with LSD-25, mescaline, psylocybin, morning-glory seeds, marijuana, peyote buttons, and anything else that reportedly turns one on. Some psychiatrists include psychedelic drugs as part of their psychotherapeutic armamentarium, using it and sometimes abusing it as a cure-all. I would like to consider here some implications of psychedelic drugs for personal growth and for personal disintegration.

I have said above that a person's consciousness expands whenever he lets more of the possible disclosure of the world reach his perceptual "field," and when he allows his capacities for remembering, imagining, fantasy, thinking, and bodily-experiencing to be activated and admitted to consciousness. Many events and factors can produce such a turn-on of conscious-

*The description of this experience is included in its entirety in a following chapter, "An Odyssey Within." It has been deleted here to avoid repetition.*

ness, as sages and mystics have long known. Thus, the disciplines undertaken by the yogis, the exercises and rituals of the Sufis and of the Jewish mystics, the meditations of the Zen master, all are means that have been adopted in the past to lift consciousness out of its usual rubrics and limits. The Indians who ingest peyote and those who attain ecstatic levels of consciousness through wine or other alcoholic beverages attest the fact that man has always sought to transcend his usual consciousness, and that he has had recourse to pharmacological means. Drug users, both of the opiates and of the non-narcotic varieties, such as hemp, give reports of the alteration of their experience that the drugs induce.[102] The more power psychedelic drugs now available simply reveal technological progress in a quest for new experience that is ages old.

The question I would like to address here is, "What are the values and what are the risks that are entailed in attempting to abet growth through the use of drugs?"

The general answer I would offer is that everything depends upon who is doing the drug-taking, what he is taking the drug for, what is his taking the drug for, what is his preparation for the experience, and with whom is he involved when he takes the drug. I believe that taking such drugs as LSD or hashish for "kicks" is no more or less harmful than taking a ride on a roller coaster or getting drunk. Taken too often, as an escape from a reality that might be changed with a bit of courage or ingenuity, the drugs can be harmful. I have seen patients who sought help because, after 1, 20 or 50 LSD trips, taken without guidance, they found they were so un-hung from usual values and goals that they couldn't find anything worth doing in this world except contemplate the "suchness" of the world. Such "nonattachment" is seemly for a wise old man preparing for his forthcoming death, but appears premature and unearned in young men—especially when there is much to be done in this world and much to be enjoyed. But I have also seen people in their twenties, or forties, who have enlarged their perspectives and liberated long-dormant capacities of feeling, striving, enjoying, and doing, after an experience produced by a drug. The drugs simply yield an enrichment of, and liberation from, one's usual intentional experience. So does a visit to another country, or a dialogue with a teacher or a psychotherapist. Whether or not this experience is worked through and integrated with the total being of the person seems to depend upon whether the person is prepared to grow. And it also depends upon whether or not the person is involved in a *continuing* relationship with some other person who can function as a teacher or guru, or as a spiritual adviser.

In short, I do not see the psychedelic drugs as an unmitigated blessing or menace. I think it a mistake to assign exclusive regulation of their use to physicians. There is no guarantee that physicians are any wiser in the prescription of these consciousness-releasing agents then, say, a minister would be. In fact, if more ministers were educated men of the world and capable of midwifing a man's growth, I could see sense in having marijuana or LSD available in churches, which could then serve as retreats where a person could go to seek healing and growth. But prayer, meditation, and church ritual can also be psychedelic experiences, as can an inspiring sermon, or a dialogue with a clergyman. Since the drugs yield a powerful experience, and since the young and the ignorant are to be guided and protected by the old and the wise, regulation and "dosing" of experience should be in older, wiser hands. But whose hands? Who are the wise ones, the teachers?

The authenticated reports of serious breakdown and deterioration, and of chromosome damage following the ingestion of LSD or mescaline must be taken into account. Instances with which I am personally acquainted have led me to the tentative conclusion that the people so afflicted were brittle, defensive people, incapable of facing *any* intense experience of change. Hence they were ill-advised to take drugs, just as they might have been ill-advised, say, to live in another culture. They were not prepared: they were not involved in a guiding relationship with a therapist or teacher, or the therapists with whom they were involved were not qualified to help the person through the period when ego-disintegration was taking place. ✦

[1968]

# *I-2*  *Fascination and Learning-for-Oneself**

*In the fall of 1965, I attended an "Invitational Conference on Independent Learning" at Milwaukee, Wisconsin. The conference was organized to discuss scientific findings that bear upon the process of learning by and for oneself. It was hoped that such a conference might throw light on the growing problem faced by educators: more and more students are entering the university, with fewer and fewer teachers to guide them.*

*My assignment was to address the problem of independent learning from the standpoint of Personality Theory. I found that I couldn't say much from that viewpoint, except perhaps to report some of the research that had been done on "autonomy." Then, I became fascinated with the question itself, "What is independent learning? Why is it a problem?" And the chapter that follows was the result.*

## Learning for Others and Learning for Myself

The announcement for this conference states: "Recent insights from the behavioral sciences have expanded our conceptions of human potential through a re-casting of the image of man—from a passive, reactive recipient to an active, seeking, autonomous, and reflective being. What are the implications of this impelling new image for our concern with man the learner? Educators are giving increased attention to implementing in practice the recognition that the learner has both the

*The bibliographic numerical notations in this chapter refer to the complete bibliography from Disclosing Man to Himself, which can be found in Chapter V-1.

capacity and the need to assume responsibility for his continuing learning."

How did man come to be conceived of as "a passive, reactive recipient?" By whom was he so conceived, and why? Who recast the image? The peculiar thing about man is that he is no-thing. No "image" can ever do full justice to his being. His being is a question to him. He lives his answers. He can be (as) a "passive, reactive recipient"; and he can also be an "active, seeking, autonomous and reflective being." Each way is a project, a choice, a decision. Another peculiarity of man is that he can let others answer the question of his being for him. If he appears to others and experiences himself as a "passive, reactive recipient," it is because he let himself be persuaded to be that way by and *for* that person. A man may live and show only his passive, reactive possibilities to his teacher, or to a researcher. In solitude or with some trusted other, he may experience and show his active, creative, or other unforeseen possibilities.*

Social intercourse resembles a contest between "definers" of my being. If I experience myself as passive and reactive rather than as active, seeking, autonomous and reflective; and if everyone sees me in this light, we may presume that such consensus is the outcome of a superb job of propaganda, brainwashing, or persuasion. I have yielded to others' definition of me, and thus I define and experience myself. I have a being-for-others, but not a being-for-myself.

If "authorities" are now beginning to say, "You know, we have been wrong, man does seem to have capacity to act, choose, and seek, autonomously," it is because some authori-

---

* This chapter is written from the point of view of "existential phenomenology." Readers interested in this branch of inquiry might consult Luijpen (1963) as an excellent introduction to the writings of Sartre (1956), Heidegger (1962), Merleau-Ponty (1962), and Husserl (1931), among others. For the relationship of existentialism and phenomenology to psychiatry and psychology, see Laing (1960, 1961, 1963), Van Kaam (1966), and May (1958).
This chapter also appears in Gleason, G. T., The theory and nature of independent learning, Scranton: International Textbook Co., 1967.

ties suspended their preconceptions about man, and let some men disclose their experience of themselves to the authorities, who then *listened*.

Others' images of me are, at least in part, a reflection of what I have been invited or permitted to disclose of my experiencing to the Other who is forming an image. We might well wonder why it has taken men so long to disclose their active and creative potentials to the image-makers. And why have the image-makers been for so long blind and deaf to these possibilities that were always there? I suspect the "passive, reactive" image lasted so long because it served a useful purpose to somebody, and hence was imposed on man, who then showed it to the image-makers. Indeed, passive, reactive men are predictable, manipulable, and controllable the very way they should be if they are to serve the interests of someone who can profit from the predicting, manipulating, and controlling.

Independent learning has now become a problem. I believe it is a *pedagogogenic* problem. We produced it, as physicians sometimes unintentionally produce iatrogenic illness. That independent learning is problematic is most peculiar, because man always and only learns by himself. The real question here is *what* does he learn and *for whom*? Learning is not a task; it is a way to be in the world. Man learns as he pursues goals and projects *that have meaning for him*. He is always learning something. Perhaps the key to the problem of independent learning lies in the phrase, "...the learner has the need and the capacity to assume responsibility for his own *continuing* learning." It may well be that those who train young people in the ways of their group (a most necessary task) have overshot the mark; they have trained youngsters to believe that they cannot, dare not, learn anything without a trainer close at hand. The only safe and good learning is learning-for-the-trainer. And the youngsters, being human, independently learned something meaningful to them; namely, that it is dangerous or futile to become *interested* in something, to learn for oneself. It is only safe to learn for the teacher's or for society's approval. One set of image-molders, the teachers, have been commissioned by social leaders to shape youngsters to the acquiescent mode. They implement this commission by invalidating a child's experience of spontaneous curiosity and fascination with aspects of the world. They insist he learn only when and what he is taught. He must learn for others. The teachers and parents have robbed children of their autonomy—their capacity to experience amazement, wonder, and fascination—by invalidating it whenever it appears. Then, they look at their product and find it wanting; they produced a Golem, a humanoid, a "dependent learner." Now we are asked to breathe life into it.

We are caught on the horns of a dilemma. Children must be shown the ways of their group they must be taught and trained. *But they must also be able to transcend this training* and learn for themselves, if they are to experience their lives as meaningful, and if the society in which they live is to grow and change. The question is, how is it possible to reconcile the contradiction between teaching children for society and letting them learn for themselves, such that children can serve their society without loss of freedom and capacity to go *beyond* what they have been taught? This is the same problem, writ large, that every serious teacher—of piano, of art, of psychotherapy, or even of teaching—faces: how can one teach a pupil in the fundamental techniques of this art without producing a mere technician? In any of these arts, we wish the learner to commit himself, to be willing to struggle for objectives *beyond* mastery of exercises and technique (learning experienced as "for-the-teacher") and even beyond current goals. We hope he will seek to make actual *his own image* (not his teacher's image) of beautiful music, pictures, healthy personalities, or independent learners. If the teacher has been effective, he will have shown his pupil that techniques are no more than a beginner's set of tools, to be used up to the point that an impasse is reached. Then, the true artist, the involved therapist, the committed teacher (committed to *his own image* of ultimate goals, not means), gropes and leaps into the unknown, "exercising that courage that is not devoid of fear and trembling," to invent or discover new means to further his project of actualizing the image. If the old versions of ultimate goals have lost meaning, the pupil will envision new embodiments of them.

## The Guru and the Commissar*

Every man must come to terms with what now is. He must learn to speak, move, and even experience the world in the given ways, those deemed right and sane where he lives. It is not easy. It takes a long time. The temptation to stray is strong. "Commissars" stand close, to insure each person conforms to his prescribed position and role. Once a man masters the rules of the social "games," what then? He plays the games so long as they yield meaningful rewards and the rewards of meaning. Ultimately, the games become confining, boring, even strangling. The man may then wish to opt out, but he cannot—there are no other games to play. So he may become sick. Then, he is patched up by doctors who pronounce him healed, and they send him back into the game. If he seeks to transcend the given, for new realms of experience, he threatens the sleep of the unawakened. They condemn and invalidate him. So he gives up and becomes "normal," or else seeks a richer experience in private, the wile impersonating a typical person.

Since time immemorial, each society has secretly harbored "gurus." These wise men have been sought by sufferers, who may have been rich in goods but poor in spirit. The gurus have taught the seekers to let go their attachments in this world, the better to concentrate on spiritual purification. The intimated rewards have not been wealth, fame, or power; but rather enlightenment and liberation, an enriched, more meaningful experience of oneself and one's world. The gurus have helped seekers attain liberation from entrapment in their culture. They have invited the experience and disclosure of individuality that had hitherto been concealed under the trappings of conformity to roles.

*With apologies to Koestler whose book* The yogi and the commissar *suggested the title for this section.*

The society that would not fall must locate and treasure its gurus, protect them, and not deny seekers access to them. The gurus and their ways are not for everyone. Gurus cannot be hired or bought; they can only be *deserved!* A society without gurus is stagnant, and will perish as did the dinosaurs, unable to change ways to cope with changing conditions.

In America, I think we are experiencing an absence in our midst, an absence of gurus. We have myriad commissars, but no one to lead beyond their ways. The commissars insure that everyone conforms to existing ways, to the image of man that is current, that is synonymous with goodness and sanity. Commissars use bribery, guile, and threats of force to get people to follow the prescribed ways, the ways that keep the society and its existing power-structure intact. Who are the commissars? Most of our teachers are commissars. So are our parents. And our policemen, our psychiatrists and psychologists, and even our neighbors. Radio, TV, and the press function as commissars. All commissars collude with one another to keep us wanting what we are supposed to want and doing what we are supposed to do. Conform, and be rewarded. Dissent, and be damned—or unpopular, our current synonym for damnation. If someone begins to depart from the ways deemed sane or good, he meets a graduated barrage of pressure aiming to bring him back in line. First, the person will experience twinges of guilt and anxiety if he even *thinks* of stepping out of line. If this built-in regulation fails, there is the threat of graded punishment from without. If the person will not yield to parental or family criticism, rejection, or threats, the solid wall of community invalidation will confront him, to threaten exile or imprisonment. If the dissenter—who embodies a protest against ways to live that he *cannot* live—persists in his dissent, he may finally be condemned as mad and be banished to a mental hospital where he is shocked, drugged, frozen, or operated upon, to get him in line or out of the way. And so, the majority of people, young and old, stay in the roles to which they have been trained. The commissars win out. In the ultimate victory of the commissar, each man becomes the unchallenged commissar over himself! I think this time is close at hand.*

Behavioral scientists help commissars at their task. Teachers, parents, and psychiatrists are all informed about ever new, more effortless and automatic ways to bring people into line. School curricula are scientifically broken down into units. These are administered in palatable doses by scientifically informed trainers, who employ the latest form of programmed instructions. Counseling centers, audio-visual aid depots, and a barrage of books and pamphlets are all available to help commissars carry out their assigned task of turning pupils *off* themselves and on to ways they are supposed to follow. The result is that we turn out more graduates from our training institutes than has ever before been true in human history. But we are discovering, we who have graduated from such institutes, that something is missing. The something is *ourselves*. Somewhere along the line, we have lost ourselves, our capacity to *experience* in new modes and qualities. If we are at all sensitive, we notice the absence and become concerned. We start to seek ourselves and our lost capacity for experiencing. I hope we find us.

If present trends in American training continue, the existing gurus, wherever they are, may become extinct, like Dodos; or, if they are cunning, they will hide underground. Then, a giant manhunt will be mounted as soon as the Public Health Service and the Department of Health, Education, and Welfare discover that they are having to cope with a nation of ninnies. Gurus, true teachers who challenge and stretch men's imaginations and souls, will be asked to preside over universities and kindergartens. If this doesn't happen, then one day the Red Chinese will short-circuit our electric power stations; the air-conditioning will break down and so will the computers and the teaching-machines. Our nation will sit stunned, the people having forgotten how to live for themselves, knowing only how to live for the system and for things. An era will have ended.

* See H. Marcuse, One-dimensional man *(London: Routledge and Kegan Paul, 1964) for an account of the ways in which dissent is invalidated.*

Then, it will be the turn of the Asiatic and Africans to follow the American Way, until they too reach the end of their tether. Finally, men of Mars will land on earth and have their turn.

## Beyond the Tether

We *created* the problem of independent learning by the way we taught and trained people to the social roles awaiting them in a social structure that resists change. Pedagogues, parents, people in general, invalidated the experience of learners and shut down their capacity to experience wonder and fascination. We created the problem, and it haunts us, not because "behavioral scientists have expanded our conceptions of human potential by recasting the image of man"; no, the problem haunts us because we find ourselves *at the end of our tether*. We are running in circles at its limit. The tether is firmly fixed to a peculiar debasement of a once magnificent image— the American Way of Life. Originally revolutionary and dynamic in conception, the American Way of Life is now a design for living that more and more Americans cannot live, without the aid of tranquilizers and the threats of the ubiquitous commissars. Yet, all the time, we advertise this way of life abroad, and try to sell it as we sell toilet paper and Buicks, with "hidden persuaders."

What is independent learning? No authoritative definitions are available, and so I shall offer a provisional specification. I shall look at this phenomenon from the standpoint of the learner. What an observer might call independent learning—learning for oneself—the learner experiences as fascination with some aspect of the world, envisioned in the mode of possibility, that is in *imagination* (cf. Sartre[88]). Independent learning is the embodiment and implementation of imaginative fascination. Some aspect of the world discloses itself to a person. He "flips" from the experiential mode of perception to an imaginative consciousness; and he experiences himself as beckoned, challenged, invited, fascinated, by the possibility. The transmutation of this possibility into an actuality then becomes the dominant project of his life. He lives it, and he lives for it.

The person in whom fascination has been turned on, or awakened, suffers a divine discontent, a magnificent obsession (Shaw[94]). He will wallow in his obsession if others leave him alone. He will forget to eat, sleep, play, socialize, or do anything else until he has brought his image of possibility into actuality, or lies nurturing the wounds from his fumbling, awaiting recovery to renew the onslaught. Then, he may again show an interest in other kinds of doing. But, in the midst of his learning rampage, he is far from being "well-rounded," "socially adjusted"; in fact he departs hugely from current images of how people should be. Indeed, the "turned-on learner" *needs to be protected from other people*, from self-consciousness, from the need to conform to images, from distraction, and from serious self-destruction as he contemplates and absorbs himself in the encounter with his fetish—the mystery or the missing skill. When he is thus turned on, no badly-written text, no stuttering teacher can be an obstacle or a deterrent, so long as they embody some of the knowledge that has become the life quest just then. "This book or that teacher has something I want just now. I'll get it out of them somehow!"

Independent learning arises when our present existence has reached an impasse, when our experience has gone stale. The project of "staying the same" has lost its meaning, and so the person seeks "a new interest in life." If he finds one, and he lets himself be addressed by it, he becomes possessed of the divine madness. The burden and dilemma that were his existence have now been thrown off. His existence is now *the quest*. He is turned on. He will not be diverted. He may appear ruthless as he pursues his quest. He cannot be bored by it though he may bore others by his talk of it.

This state of being, of being involved, of experiencing new possibilities of meaning for one's life, and being engaged in their fulfillment—this is what I am construing as independent learning. It entails transcending the past—past involvements and interests, social pressure; in short, it is a matter of detachment and liberation from the momentum and inertia of previous ways of being, behaving, and experiencing.

The fascinated questing of which I speak can be evoked in a number of ways. It may occur of itself in someone who is desperate enough (like the illumination of the Buddha), whose life has been like a Zen *Koan* that he has broken through. *It seems to occur spontaneously in young children before they have been socialized.* More commonly, when it does occur, it happens through a relationship between an entrapped person and some other who functions as his guru and exemplar—someone who releases his imagination, who expands his consciousness; someone who offers a "psychedelic encounter."

Indeed, the guru may aid the process of liberation from previous attachments by helping the person experience more keenly the degree to which he feels trapped. The capacity to become fascinated may be impossible until some level of disengagement from usual concerns, ways, and commitments has been reached.

Or, the one who is to be the guru may function as a tempter—his way of life may excite envy and admiration. His serenity or his enthusiasm may evoke curiosity. He may appear to be having more fun, living more fully, experiencing more. Or he may disclose images of possibility that attract the attention of the bored, unfulfilled seeker, who then becomes fascinated and subsequently experiences his previous involvements as obstacles to his pursuit of new meaning and experience.

Whatever the occasion for being thus turned on, it is this fascinated engagement with an image of possibility that I define as independent learning. We might call it "awakening" or "inspiration," but it is always *intentional* (Husserl,[34] pp. 36, 84; May[64])—that is, it is always related to something in the world; it is always awakening *to something*, being inspirited *by* and *for something*, fascinated *with something*. And it is embodied (Laing[54]); that is, the person lives and acts his experience of awakening. In principle, the turned-on state, which is experienced by the person as different from his usual, repetitive experience, should appear different *to the other person*. We thus have the possibility of a psychology, a physiology, even an epidemiology and sociology, of "being turned on." It is to part of this possibility, an exploration of relationships between personality factors and being turned on, that I shall now turn.

## Personality: Procrustean Bed or "To-Be-Transcended"

Now I no longer believe that there are dimensions of personality that exist "in-themselves." Id, ego, super-ego; self-concept, self-ideal, public selves; traits; drives and needs—these are the terms in which we have long thought of and described "personality": "This individual is highly authoritarian or egalitarian; he has a strong ego or a weak one; his MMPI scores are thus and such, etc." This way of conceptualizing a person, whether as a whole or just some part of him, is no longer relevant or valid for me. After having tried out psychoanalytic, trait-theory, self-theory, and other kinds of theoretical models of man, I have opted for a model that is no model, or is a meta-model. It is one implicitly in the philosophical tradition of existential phenomenology (Luijpen[59]). According to this perspective, man is the being such that in his being, his being is in question. His being is inextricably linked with the world he experiences as real. Other people are part of this world. The being he discloses, shows to me, when I am in one mode of my being—impersonality, formality, and distant, reserved, playing the role of hard-nosed scientist—is different from the being he will show me when I am with him in the mode of invitational dialogue. In short, his experience of his being and the being that he discloses will differ with the context. His being-for-me will differ from his being-for-himself, his being-for-his-dog, his teacher, his mother, the experimenter who studies him, and the guru whose help he may seek to transcend his personality traits or structure. There is a problem here: to dimensionalize and discover hierarchy here, a hierarchy of being. I suspect it is measurable objectively and subjectively in terms of "degrees of freedom." That is, a person may experience his being-for-his-dog as a freer, more authentic and expressive being than his being-for-his-boss, or his wife.

In the last analysis, a person chooses all modes and manifestations of his being. He cannot choose the initial impact on his experiential field of a shout, a blow, a promise, a sunset, a caress—all these things just affect him. But he can effect various actions upon his experience once it has happened. He can blot it out, reconstrue it, project it, distort it, try to preserve it, or let it flow. His personality-for-others and his personality-for-himself can embody a resolve to confine his experience and action to the limits of a procrustean mold. He can regard his experience as being without value and importance or as rich in value. If so, he is impersonating a robot; and he may experience himself as such.

A person can choose *what* of his experience he will disclose in words or behavior (behavior is meaningful disclosure, too) to whoever is nearby. Indeed, we have begun to explore what he chooses to disclose to others, in words, behavior, or even in physiological messages; under what conditions; and to which others (Jourard[41]). In light of this research, I now suspect and challenge the validity (or at least generalizability) of all published psychology, including the psychology of human learning and human personality. I suspect their validity, because the original data (which after all are disclosures) may have been gathered under conditions in which the person being studied neither knew nor trusted the experimenter to whom he showed his learning or his traits. The experimenter doesn't know what experience of the subjects is embodied in the subjects' behavior. What the psychological scientist calls "data" is actually one mode in which the subjects disclose part of their being. There is a growing body of empirical data now to confirm the assertion that a person's being for psychologist A may differ from his being for psychologist B (cf. Rosenthal[85]). Perhaps we should subtitle each report of a research: "*Ss*' disclosure of learning, of traits, etc., for Dr. So-and-So."

In what follows, we shall actually be talking more about *interpersonal* conditions of independent learning, than about personality factors. The capacity to "go out of one's mind" (to

transcend one's personality) seems to be one of the necessary conditions for independent learning, for learning-for-one-
self. And so we are interested in *who* is able to invite a person
out of his mind: who are the "psychedelic people," and who is
willing to accept the invitation? There may well be a stable trait
that could be isolated, that we might call "transcendence-readi-
ness," or "readiness to leave one's personality." Perhaps it persists in people, beyond childhood, through failures on the part
of the commissars to get the child fully socialized. Maslow[62]
referred, in this connection, to "resistance to enculturation" as
one of the general traits of his "self-actualizing" subjects, in
whom "peak experiences" were not a rare occurrence. The peak
experience, of course, entails a leaving of one's mind, one's
usual personality.

## A Kind of Death and a Kind of Rebirth

Now, a hypotheses. I believe that independent learning,
the embodiment of the state of being fascinated, involves six
stages. The first is the experience of the impasse. The next
stage we will provisionally call the stage of detachment, a kind
of dying. The third is immersion in oneself—an entry into one's
center, one's source of experiencing. Next is an emergence, or
rebirth. Fifth is the experience of new possibilities. Sixth is the
selection and pursuit of one of these. I shall attempt to illustrate this hypothesis with examples from several realms: religious conversion, brainwashing, research in psychedelic drugs,
psychotherapy, and dialogue.

I base my hypothesis upon personal experience, but-
tressed by reading that has seemed related, and the reported
experience of others. It appears to me that fascination-with-
something, the process of being turned on, has a certain "natural" history in adults. It is the natural state with healthy children
who have not yet been "turned off." The "turning off" begins
with the experience of despair, boredom, or meaninglessness
as one continues his habitual way of life—acting in one's roles,
doing one's work, being one's public self. Friendships grow stale.
Work becomes meaningless and pointless. One feels dead, or

deadened. The world looks stale, and music loses its savor. Nothing changes. *Plus ça change, plus c'est la même chose.* I'm doing something for everybody, and nothing for me. One feels trapped. No way out seems apparent. Each step out of the circle encounters dread or a sense of hopelessness and futility. One tries new hobbies, new friends, new work, changes of scenery; but it's just a case of changing the ambience within which one feels like a robot. The depression deepens. One becomes afraid he is losing his mind. It is at this point that one's friends, family, conventional psychiatry, and religion may enter. They try, and too often they succeed in halting a natural growth process. The person in this state gradually "loses interest," "stops caring about things." He is regarded as sick, in need of "treatment" to stop him from going out of his mind. Actually, the "not-caring" is a self-initiated process of detachment from previous concerns, a phase in the death-rebirth process we are concerned with. If nothing stops the process, the person gradually enters his own experience more and more. His self-structure dissolves. He detaches himself from his image of himself, from previous friendships—which, after all, have been stabilizing him, keeping him in sameness, which is not the same as sanity. The person may become panicky, as the process of detachment continues; and he finds himself experiencing emotions, fantasies and memories, that ordinarily have been repressed. He surely needs reassurance here, to let the process unfold rather than shut it off. He is encountering his possibilities. *If he lets go enough*, he will fully enter the realm of experiencing that mystics have described as "transcendental," like a homecoming, a visit to the source, rather than a hell to be avoided. It is, in fact, the way of experiencing that we all shared as children, before we were wholly engulfed by the culture.

One cannot, and does not long stay in this realm. One re-enters his ego, but with a new perspective. The self-structure is redefined. I choose a new identity for myself and present it to others who may confirm it or not. The world doesn't look the same now. It is not the same because I am not the same, and it is my world. I look at the old things and the old people; and new features, new possibilities disclose themselves to me. I commit myself to some of these, and I am renewed, until some later time; when the new fascinations, values, and projects go stale, I must begin the process again. When I am reborn and awakened, I experience the world and the people in it as a constant and varied *calling*, a constant source of invitations to become involved. The calls and invitations that were always there, but I never heard them before. The sky called to be looked at. A person clamored for love and attention but I did not hear. Mysteries whispered their presence, but I didn't notice; I thought what was mysterious was actually known and understood. In short, I begin once again to *encounter* the world, and the people in it. In the encounter, I let myself experience the varied reality of the world, a reality that I did not experience so richly, or in so many dimensions, as I now do. Renewed by the plunge into the depths of my own experiencing, I survey the world that I am encountering. Some invitation, some call, some challenge, fascinates me more than the others. Nobody can predict what will now fascinate or repel me, not even me. I commit myself to this one, and off I go until I become deadened once again by a new set of habits.

It has just occurred to me, after completing a year of sabbatical leave in England, that the process I just described is a sabbatical leave of one's mind, of one's personality structure. The academic sabbatical is a removal from one's usual surroundings, but I discovered it is easier to get out of one's surroundings than to get them out of oneself so that new surroundings can invite one into encounter. Many of my American colleagues in England successfully shielded themselves from fascination with and involvement in the English experience, because of the panic they felt when invited to let go their usual preoccupations. They carried America with them. Indeed, the phenomenon of "culture shock," long noted by anthropologists, is another dimension of the experience of leaving, not just one's country, but one's mind. One has to let the American in one die in order to become a participant in a new experience, to be reborn.

Indeed, initiation ceremonies of all kinds recognize this, like fraternity initiation rites or Marine boot-camp training. The hazing, in whatever form, is a symbolic killing-off of a previous incarnation, to abet the reincarnation in the new way of being.

But we are as afraid of dying as we are of leaving our minds. We equate habitual ways of valuing, construing, and acting with life itself. Therefore, to stop these, even when they cease to yield satisfaction and meaning, is experienced as the end of life. It is equated with death. We are afraid to explore the possible experience beyond the tether.

In the act of love, the climax is frequently experienced as a "dying." And after the successful act of love, a person feels himself reborn, ready to respond anew to new dimensions of the world that suddenly, magically, have disclosed themselves to the person. But many acts of love are climaxed not by ego-shattering orgasm; but only by localized, pleasurable twitching. Evidently one has to be ready to go out of one's mind to make love, the love that renews and revivifies.

In the psychedelic-drug experience a person ingests a substance; and then, if he lets go, he commences a voyage into depths of experiencing of which he never would have dreamed himself capable. Later he will re-enter his ego, but again with the experience of being reborn. He will experience the world as if, hitherto, he had looked at it through a fogged-up window, with only a tiny spot wiped clear. With the rebirth, the whole window is wiped clean; and the world stands forth. The world will disclose itself to him in different dimensions than it had disclosed itself hitherto, and he will select some aspect of it with which to involve himself (Leary[58]).

Brainwashing is a corruption of the death and rebirth theme. There, the commissars, who know what they want a person to do and be, convince him that he (his old self) is dead. Under the regime of torture, a person may indeed enter the transcendental realm, but he re-enters a new "robot," into new roles that have been ready-made for him. Doubtless, they seem as real and meaningful to the brainwashee as did his previous incarnation which had been made untenable and unlivable for him by his captors.

In religious conversion, the common denominator seems to be the despair at continuing in the old way (James[36]). The person enters his experience after leaving the world. If his background and present associates are appropriate, then, like the brainwashee, he enters a new way of being that is more or less ready-made for him.

In good psychotherapy, the therapist lets his patient enter his experience deeply. He remains present to help the patient cope with the terrors that arise as he lets go and experiences feelings, memories, and the like that have been long suppressed. With his interpretations, the therapist may aid the process of symbolic dying and facilitate the onset of the therapeutic despair, or the therapeutic psychosis which is part of every effective psychotherapy sequence (Whitaker[111]). Then the person is reborn, and he faces the world with the capacity to respond to its invitations in new ways.

In good teaching, after the fashion of Socrates, the skilled and compassionate dialectician will challenge every assertion and belief of his pupil until the pupil feels he is going to go out of his mind. He may balk at this point. But he may also flip into a realization of infinite possibility, and be thus turned on.

This is my hypothesis restated: independent learning entails the experience of fascination. Fascination is a response to an invitation or challenge disclosed by the world. The invitation and challenge were always there, but the person could not experience them so long as he remained "hung up" or fixated in his usual roles, self-structure, and preoccupations. It is necessary that the usual attachments be suspended, and raw experiencing be turned on (Gendlin[24]). This disengagement from usual concerns is fostered by entrapment and despair (it can be fostered in dialogue); and it may be experienced with dread, as a going out of one's mind, or a dying, followed by rebirth or re-entry into an enlarged self-structure. In the reborn state, the person is now more open to his experience of the world. While he is in this "open" condition, a challenge appears, and the person responds. He may or may not be confirmed by others in his new being. I would propose that something like this happens repeatedly in those healthier personalities for whom independent learning is no problem. I would propose further that a variety of factors militate against this complete process of death and rebirth. I shall classify these under two headings, the social and the personal. Then I shall discuss some factors that foster independent learning.

### *Social Deterrents to Independent Learning*

Each society has a vested interest in maintaining a status quo; or, at the least, it will tolerate only a slow rate of social change. The entire socialization and training process, which includes our schools and universities, aims at producing a modal personality of some specified kind. This is a programmed person, interchangeable, a "behavior package"; one who is stable, predictable, and wants what he must want and does what he must do to keep the social system functioning. Once the person is ensconced in some group, everyone in the group "gets used to him" and constrains him to keep to the ways of being that identify him for *them*. If his identity is an alienated one, if the only being he and they recognize is his being-for-others, he will not likely change. Any challenges or fascinations likely to jeopardize his identity-for-others will be experienced by him as a threat to his status, and even to his existence (Laing[54]). So long as a person remains in his group, he is likely to accede to the pressures to conform to others' definitions of his being.

If the "well-adjusted" group member experiences in himself a protest against his identity-for-others and attempts to change it, he encounters the barrage of resistance I mentioned earlier. It takes courage of heroic proportions to redefine oneself in the face of such invalidation, and such courage is rare. So, apparently, is independent learning.

## Personality Deterrents to Independent Learning

I have spoken before of the commissars. In a sense, we can regard the existing personality structure of the individual as an internalized commissar. The introjected family, teachers, and others comprise a kind of portable Big Brother who watches what I do; and when I experience anything counter to his rules, I feel guilt and dread. These affects are unpleasant enough to steer me back into sameness so that I can again recognize myself as the person I had always (desperately) believed, or at least hoped, I was. If I ignore my guilt and anxiety and persist in experiencing in the forbidden ways, I may feel, with horror, that I am becoming insane. The incipient birth of my unique possibilities is dreaded more than death itself, and so I kill myself (my possibilities) in order to live as a robot. I cling more desperately to my roles, my self-structure, and try to impersonate to myself and to others the one we thought I was. But I hope I have made it clear that, unless I let go, unless I follow my experiencing and enter right into it, I shall remain the same person, the one who has found his goals and values meaningless, his life a charade and a gesture.

## Mystification and the Destruction of Autonomous Being: A Dyadic Deterrent

When the Other is in "bad faith" in his relationship to me, he confuses me. I never know what he is up to, because he does not mean what he says, and his actions belie his stated intentions. That same Other, if he is in a position of power over me, as a parent or teacher, may disconfirm my expressions of interest, of feelings, of intentions: "You don't really like to do that, now do you?", or, "I know you *must* be glad to be here," etc. If a child has been unsure of his own experience and its meaning, he may allow his being to be thus construed for him. He will eventually be mystified (Laing[56]) as to who he is and what his true interests are. These are replaced by a pseudo-self, a set of interests and habits and experiencings which may serve *someone's* interests and freedom, but not his. Such a mystified person is hardly likely to discover the fascinations which proclaim the beginning of independent learning.

When a teacher, parent, or therapist is unaware of being a servant of some ideology or some social system, or when they deny that this is what in fact they are: when they insist that what they do to and with the child is "for your own good," they confuse and mystify the child. They contribute to his sense of ontological insecurity (Laing[54]) and certainly thereby impede independent learning.

### Some Factors That Facilitate Independent Learning

The capacity to become fascinated anew, after old fascinations have worn out, is abetted by numerous factors; but it is the *interpersonal* factor I shall focus upon. Since each of us is an Other to somebody, we can perhaps do something to foster independent learning in the others for whom we are the Other. The basic factors in fostering independent learning, including the processes that underlie it and make it emerge as a response to invitation and challenge, are the human responses of challenge and invitations, stimulation of imagination, confirmation, "letting be," honest disclosure, and willingness to enter into dialogue.

### Confirmation

Buber has said that each man wishes to be confirmed by his fellow, and each has the capacity to confirm his fellow. To confirm the other in his being means to stand back and let his being "happen," let it disclose itself, and to view it with respect, to acknowledge its reality and authenticity. Confirmation does not mean wishy-washy, insincere permissiveness; because often the most direct confirmation is to take a stand in opposition to the disclosure of the other. But the confirmation, the meeting, even in opposition, confirms for the other that he is the one he is. It lets him know that he exists. Confirmation means that I recognize the other *person* as the author of his acts and his utterances. I attribute them to him and his freedom. I confirm him as a free agent who chooses his existence and is responsible for it. The opposite of confirmation is invalidation and disconfirmation. There are many ways to invalidate another person, and they all have the net effect of weakening his sense of his own identity and worth, his sense of being a source of experience and action. One can ignore the other—pretend he doesn't exist, except as a doll, a thing, a nobody, or just another body. One can attribute his actions and utterances to some source other than his free intentionality; e.g., "You don't mean that; it's your illness that is speaking, not you." One can disconfirm all action and utterances save those that are compatible with one's concept of the other. Everything else that doesn't fit these expectations "is not him." Under a sufficiently sustained regime of such disconfirmation, a person will indeed come to doubt his own existence, lose his identity-for-himself, and try to confine his experience and conduct only to that range consistent with his identity-for-the-other.

Confirmation is, in a sense, an act of love. One is acknowledging that other as one who exists in his own peculiar form, with the right to do so. One recognizes that one's *concept* of his being *is only that*—a concept, and not his being. One recognizes that it is *for him* to reveal and define himself to us in this way, at his pace, thus reinforming and altering our experience and concept of him. It is not only not our duty, it is an outright sin to define another's being. Our concept of each other is always out of date. Yet, if he has a weak sense of his identity for himself, if he is ontologically insecure, he may let us do this, or even ask us to.

When I let the other person be and confirm him in his being as he discloses it to me, I am creating an ambiance within which he can dare to *let go of his previous concepts and presentations of himself*. They are not binding upon him. My suspension of my preconceptions of his being invites him to let go while he is in my presence. He can drop yesterday's self-presentations, commitments, interests and goals, and explore the possibilities of new ones. He can weep, regress, enter into himself while he is with me, and feel assured that I am waiting, perhaps with a hand holding his, until he emerges to tell me who he is. And I confirm him, at each instant of the journey, as being the one he is—John searching; John in despair; John emerged, with new goals and values.

### Disclosure and Dialogue

After a person has abandoned his previous incarnation, entered his experiencing, and then emerged, he experiences the world as disclosing new possibilities, new dimensions of its being for him. But I am a part of his world, and I have the capacity to disclose myself to him even while he is embodied in his usual fixed roles and self-definitions. When I am with him, I can disclose to him how I experience him. I can enter into dialogue with him; and with each of his utterances or acts, I can respond out of my experience and disclose to him what it is that I am experiencing. If I remain in contact with him, consistently in dialogue, I may actually lead him to the edge of going out of his mind, thus clearing the way for the emergence of a new self. I ask you to consider dialogue. You say something from your being—let us employ a jazz combo to illustrate. I blow a phrase on my trumpet, and you respond with a passage on your saxophone. Your response is both a reply and a question and a challenge, and so I reply. And so it goes until one of us loses his nerve and dares not let spontaneous, true disclosure out. Dialogue has ended for the time. Now switch to the dialogue in psychotherapy. The patient says something to me. I reply, in honesty. My reply evokes experiencing in him, and he utters this. This evokes a reply from me. We continue in this way until one of us has tripped off panic in the other; at this point, insincerity, dissemblance intrudes, and dialogue has ceased. One of the participants does not wish to be known, and he holds back. In dialogue at its best, the participants remain in contact and let their reciprocal disclosures affect one another. If the dialogue occurs in the context of letting be and confirmation, then the weaker of the two may indeed flip into raw experiencing, find it safe, and emerge in a more awakened state.

Authentic disclosure of self is a likely factor in the promotion of awakening, of authentication and validation of the other, and the emergence of independent learning. But authentic disclosure is rare. More common is semblance, role-playing, impersonation of the other one wishes to *seem* to the Other. Hence, the other person seldom truly encounters a person-in-process. He meets a pledge of consistency, a world of people who do not invite him into new possibilities. If I am in your world, and I do not grow and change, then you are in a world that obstructs and impedes your growth! In true encounter, there is a collapse of roles and self-concepts. No one emerges from an encounter the same as he entered. My willingness to disclose myself to you, to drop my mask, is a factor in your trusting me and daring then to disclose yourself to me. This disclosure of yourself to me aids the process of your disengagement from your previous ways of being. And as I disclose myself to you, I am your world, and this word discloses new possibilities to you—it evokes new challenges and invitations that may stir you and enliven your imagination.

### Challenge: Turning On Other's Imagination

If independent learning is the implementation of fascination with imagined possibilities, then we must be concerned with the imaginative mode of experiencing. We already know much about the perceptual mode of experiencing, but imagining, the "imaginative consciousness," is less fully understood. To imagine means to transcend the here-and-now, to shut off the perceptual mode and invent new possibilities that thus far cannot be *perceived* by anyone (Sartre[88]). The possibilities exist in the imaginative consciousness of the experiencer, and it is for him to "real-ize" these and make it possible for him and others to perceive in actuality what before existed only as his image. The free imagination, like freedom itself, is a threat to all status quo. The free imagination appears to make intentional learning (rather than passive, associative conditioning) possible. The learner, even in a schoolroom, is animated by an image of a future, possible being that is not yet attained. A good pedagogue will seek to vivify and intensify this image—the image of what it will be like when one can read, or count, or play the piano. "Can you see yourself as the life of the party? Would you like to be? Then enroll now...." The dull child, the one who resists teacher's efforts to teach, is often the one whose imagination has been turned off because the possible being it could disclose is frightening. Or his world is so threatening he must stay in the mode of perception, lest a danger appear. Imagining is dangerous because it means a cessation of vigilant scanning. The teacher who turns on the dull pupil, the coach who elicits a magnificent performance from someone of whom it could not have been expected, are people who *themselves* have an image of the *pupils' possibilities*; and they are effective in realizing their images. Good leaders, who have a vivid image of possibility, produce followers in whom this image is awakened; and the followers achieve remarkable feats, on their own. The art of challenge needs to be better understood, but it does seem to entail the ability to awaken a sleeping imagination to fascinating possibility and the possibility of becoming fascinated. Good pornographers are able to awaken the erotic consciousness with images of sexual possibilities. Good gurus are able to awaken the imagination of possibilities in the experience of their followers. Beyond awakening the image of the possibility, the good guru is effective at challenging a person to commit himself to realizing the possibility.

### Encouragement

It is often a long and discouraging voyage, to make an envisioned possibility actual. A friend, parent, teacher, or guru may help the independent learner make his way by offering courage, encouragement, and support in the face of blind alleys, setbacks and failures. Many people have the capacity to imagine possibilities, even fascinating possibilities; but they stop their pursuit after a failure or two. The helper will offer the support which keeps the seeker seeking and trying. The seeking is what is applauded, not solely the "successful attainment."* Many people will neither imagine nor try, because they cannot be guaranteed a visible success.

### Where Are the Gurus?

People who relate to others in a confirming, authentic, challenging, and encouraging way seem to be agents in fostering independent learning in others. Likely, too, they are themselves independent learners, animated by images of possibility that they are themselves actualizing. Imitation of admired role-models (hero worship) is certainly an influential factor in everyone's development, and we shouldn't underrate the importance of this in our deliberations. Indeed, how admirable, heroic, growing, and seeking in fascination are the available Others in society? Who wants to be like his father? His mother? His schoolteacher? If the young people of today are any illustration, they seem to be hell-bent on pursuing an image of a possible being that is portrayed for them by the publisher of *Playboy*. The man who plays with the Bunnies and the Bunnies who are the playmates of the playboys seem more to inspire independent learning (of how to look like one and behave like one) than do the professors of introductory psychology, or the teachers of third-grade social studies. The playboy jack-rabbit is a false messiah, a corrupt kind of guru; but he turns people on. So, of course, did Hitler—but Jesus awakened people too! (Reich[78]).

I wonder if the Establishments in society can tolerate gurus? I wonder if schools, homes, industry, politics, and business will permit people to be turned on to projects of their choosing? Independent learners rock the boat. True education, as opposed to training (which is essential), is by definition subversive. Education liberates individuality: it frees and strengthens autonomy. Training constricts: it reduces variance; it diminishes freedom and lessens autonomy. We cannot ignore the fact that education is a political act, or, better, the embodiment of the political stance of the anarchist.

* *In Kazantzakis'[47] Odyssey, a modern sequel Odysseus says, "Your voyages, O my soul, are my native land."*

Yet, every society needs its anarchists, its gurus; or it will shatter from its own rigidity. Do we have any? Do we have enough? And are they honest?

### The Psychophysics of Being Turned On (or Off)—Each Man His Own Scale

How might we conduct research into the phenomenon of independent learning; or fascination; or being turned on, to or by something? A method exists, one that has a history as long as that of experimental psychology—the psychophysical method, or an adaptation of it. In the psychophysical methods, a subject is asked to report his experience of a difference in weight, or size, or odor. This is the being of the phenomenon for the person. The experimenter then looks at the stimuli and notes their being-for-him or their being-for-his-measuring-devices. Systematic research into independent learning might proceed by devising schemes for self-rating and ratings by an experimenter as to when a person has been turned on, or fascinated. Then, one inquires into the structure of that turned-on person's world, as it exists for him and as it may be "objectively" recorded by the *E*—how he experiences certain other people in his world, himself, his body, etc. The relationship of these other people with the *S* can be explored by interviews with these others—how they experience the *S*, what they wish for him, how they implement their wishes for him, etc. The techniques employed by Ronald Laing and Aaron Esterson[56] in their magnificent studies of the families of schizophrenics are quite germane here. They were able to show, with incredible vividness, how the "symptoms" of the patient made sense as intelligible reactions to the behavior of the others in the patient's world. They would interview the patient alone; then the patient with mother, with father, with mother and father; then mother alone, father alone, and mother with father. The interviewers were skilled. The interviewees revealed, dramatically, how they changed their being in each context; and overall, it became clear how the one designated as the patient could do little else than go mad. Duplicity, disconfirmation, annihilation of the patient's autonomy—all were lucidly disclosed in these interviews, together with mystification of the patient as to what was going on. Why would it not be possible to study the significant people in the world of a turned-on person in similar ways? We might find that both the turned-off, dependent-learning state and the turned-on, fascinated, autonomous questing become quite intelligible as the reasonable and intelligible praxis of a person *in the world that exists for him.* And since all of the participants in such studies would *be* personalities, ample opportunity would be afforded for shedding more light on the facilitating or inhibiting effects of various personality structures on independent learning. ✦

[1968]

# *I-3*   *An Odyssey Within**

Whenever Western man has felt stalemated, at the end of his tether, his first impulse has been to burst through and out and push farther west. He has searched the outside world for freedom, resources, love, distraction, and fulfillment. He has found many of these, but inevitably, no matter where his voyage led him, he has then found himself again experiencing entrapment. Like Homer's Odysseus, or like the boll weevil, he has been looking for a home, but once he finds it, he finds it a trap. Then he may try to drink himself out of boredom, blast himself into orbit out of this world, or consult psychotherapists for help in finding out what is wrong with him.

Now when this man or woman was en route, on his *quest* for a home, he was magnificent—vital, alive, eyes snapping and dancing, sexy, fit, cunning, inspirited. The man had only to stand in the presence of the woman, or she in his, and they turned one another on. He paused in his quest, perhaps confusing her with his quest, and married her; together they made a home and eventually had it made. Once ensconced in Ithaca, or the suburbs of Ithaca, they began to die a spiritual death, even a physical death. There seemed nothing more to quest for. The outside world seemed stagnant, and so did they. They might have traveled abroad, only to find they couldn't leave the suburbs behind them. They carried them within and compared everything they saw abroad with the way they were at home.

*\*Presented as a talk at the Language and Life Seminar, University of Florida, 1966.*

This is a caricature of a kind of modern western man (I've seen him here and in Britain and in a few places on the continent), but it's not entirely inaccurate. He always looks *outside* when his life becomes stagnant within.

Now Koestler has observed that, whenever western man is *really*, desperately trapped, he looks east. He consults the writings of the yogas, Zen monks, the Sufis—and there he finds the advice to search *within*. Without a teacher to guide him, and without the resolve to abandon all his attachments to material things, and his family, he looks inside as a western man does—searchingly, as with a pen-light in a light-tight closet. The thin beam darts here and there, but reveals no new vistas or expanses. Only terrifying ghosts, or dry dust and ashes. Yet, the advice I think is sound. There is an Odyssey to be commenced, and Odyssey within, a quest for one's source, one's home, one's self. *Only* this source, one's self, one's experience, is not stagnant, stifling, encapsulating when it is released from the crust of habits and concepts. It appears that when one reaches it, he is able to stay in his physical home and yet find an immense variety of sights, sounds, smells, challenges, delights in what before looked only stale and stagnant. When a man finds his self, his core, when he gets out of his mind, a new universe of possibilities begins to disclose itself to him from his own embodied being and from the world outside. The old people in his life disclose different facets of their being to him; trees show him new colors, faces, possibilities. The world is full of fascinations and possibilities, as a candy store is for a child with 15¢ to spend. He need only choose something to spend himself on. His inner impoverishment is at an end.

When a man breaks out of his mind, new possibilities disclose themselves to him from his embodied being and from the world outside. Why did they not show themselves before he left his mind? I have come to believe, on the basis a variety of personal experiences and evidence from other sources that it is because "being in one's usual mind" is, in essence, *a pledge to tune out the disclosure of the world*. Everything in the world, every person, every tree, every bird, every car, sewing-machine and typewriter is a source of transmission or disclosure of its changing being, like myriad radio or television transmission stations. But the signals, of course, are sent in a variety of channels, frequencies, and modes. The transmission is incessant, so long as the being exists. But we do not receive it incessantly, in its possible variety. We have goals and projects to fulfill—make a living, get status, paint the house, cut the grass, diaper the baby—and these projects require us to *order* the possibly chaotic world of beings which disclose their being to us. Our projects, what we are "hung up on," as the beatnik puts it, structure and congeal our world. We categorize things, form concepts, crystallize our behavior into habits. We do this because we can't help it, and because we *must*, or else face the prospect of failure at our projects. Indeed, even if we have conceptualized the beings of the world, we might fail in our projects. Our concepts have to be reasonably accurate, and our habits efficient. If they are, we psychologists say the person is "in contact with reality" and is competent, well-adjusted, in his mind (but not in his experience).

Each concept is a pledge to stop noticing anything about the disclosed being of the thing conceptualized. Each habit is an assertion that there is no change in the world. If I have an idea of what and who you are—a husband or wife, John or Bill, a dog, a car—then I look at you each time we meet long enough to be sure it's you, then I stop noticing the endless disclosure of your being that you embody. So long as I remain pledged to pursue my present projects, I note only those aspects of the disclosed world that are related and relevant to these goals. When I am trying to get some work done, and you are nearby, I don't notice anything more of your being than your capacity to help or hinder me. I don't see the color of your eyes, the spring in your gait. I don't hear the tremor in your voice that, to someone less preoccupied, signifies sadness or loneliness. As fast as I change projects—I might do so a hundred times a day—I reorder my world, so that the same world turns a hundred faces to me, and while I note one face, I'm blind to the other 99. And

I switch from one set of habits to another, to cope with this frozen world.

But we soon reach an end to the number and variety of the projects we mount. We seek a certain income, a certain reputation, a certain concept of ourselves, a certain arrangement of our work or property, and "kicks." These projects embody the meaning of our lives. We turn from one to the other, and experience enough variety, and perhaps fulfillment and meaning, to keep us going through each day. In time, for good reasons, our projects wear out, they lose magnetism, pursuit of them loses zest, and attainment of them loses satisfaction. We have stayed too long in Ithaca. But we don't know where to go.

Kazantzakis picks up Odysseus where Homer leaves him: returning from Troy, he conquers and masters the externalized versions of his own, and all human possibilities that would distract him from his true goal, Ithaca. He has arrived there to establish dominion over his kingdom.

He marries off his son, reminds his wife he is home, buries his father (not necessarily in that order), and then takes off again. With a hardy band of men companions he leaves on a spiritual pursuit, the transmutation of flesh into spirit, the quest for freedom, the continuing fulfillment of his possibilities. He says, "Your voyages, O my soul, are my native land." The *quest* is Ithaca, but Ithaca was not his quest. Odysseus wants to say, when he meets Death, "Take me, I'm ready, there's nothing left of me to take; I've consume my flesh, transubstantiated it into spirit."

I think the true Odyssey is the Odyssey within. Into experience—of self and world. I think Odysseus' travels, while apparently in the geographical world, depict man's quest for himself and his possibilities in his experience, which is neither inside nor outside, but between.

Let us go back now to modern man, who may be starting to discover that his work has become efficient and uninvolving. His wife and children are apparently known quantities, and perhaps even boring, or distracting in ways he would rather not be distracted. His hobbies have lost their savor. There is an end to the changes he can make in the appearance of his house. His friends have begun to be predictable, and to his horror, so is he. He is very much *in* his Ithaca, he is solidly ensconced in his *mind*—in his concepts—and he finds it like a bottle that encloses him and barely lets him breathe. He may leave Ithaca—perhaps he'll take a better job at Antioch—but he soon finds it's not so different, he hasn't really left Cornell. To really leave Ithaca, he has to leave his mind, his concepts, and this terrifies him. In fact, he may find himself plotting all kinds of breakouts—run off with a coed and leave all behind; find himself loathing friends, family and colleagues, and run to a psychotherapist, who may ease him back into his mind with the help of a few tranquilizers to numb him to the pinch of the narrow walls. However, to resume his ultimate Odyssey, he must leave his mind and go into his experience. This is where his Odyssey resumes.

At this point, I want to give a brief account of a "trip" to Ithaca taken by a person with whom I am well acquainted.

On the occasion of which I write, I was in the company of a physician, who had himself, many times, taken the psychedelic trip. He was my guide and teacher. I took the dose of the drug in a shot glass of water, and sat chatting with the others, fellow-travelers. Before long, I began laughing—it was a gigantic joke, a hoax—but the laugh was on me. Everything I could see or hear or think seemed so arbitrary and unnecessary and it could have so easily been different. I could have been somebody else. There seemed no necessary reason why things fell when they were dropped; why not float, or scoot off sideways? Then, I noticed the wire of the telephone receiver, close to my hand. A dim beam of light fell upon it, and it had an exquisite and fascinating iridescence. It seemed to give off a ruby glow. (Ordinarily, I am rather color-blind, or insensitive to subtle variations in hues.) I spent what seemed eons of time holding the cord, dangling and twisting it, fascinated with each new configuration that was produced. I felt as if veils had been lifted from my eyes, ears, nose, skin, and my sense of my own body. Sounds from the street would catch my attention, and it was as if I was truly hearing for the first time, as if wax stoppers had been removed from my ears. Everything was as important as everything else. I would note the feel of the chair against my backside, or the texture of a desk-top, and nothing else existed. Odors, tastes, the sight of the flames in the gas fire— each of these presented itself to me, and I would note them, become them: my consciousness *was* these things and was *of* these things.

Perhaps an hour might have passed, by earthly time. I found myself flipping from the perceptual mode of experiencing to the imaginary mode. I could imagine something, and my image was as real as any perception. At a whim, I could transform my image of a person into a dog, cat, or locomotive; and each was as real as any perception.

Then I was truly swept away on a journey back through time. I experienced the sound of the song, "Ramona, I see you by a waterfall." Peculiar faces I couldn't then recognize, of very demure dandies, with fedora hat, bow tie, and devilish looks in their eyes, appeared and then disappeared. A phrase was uttered by somebody, some baby-talk gibberish I couldn't decipher. I experienced a period of my childhood, perhaps when I was two—a precocious peanut of a child, sentient, but regarded as a doll, like the midget in Gunter Grass' novel, *The Tin Drum*. The dandies were the teen-agers of the late 1920s—my older brother and his friends and an older cousin, who, when praised for their neat garb, would make a certain coy gesture. The song, "Ramona": my mother would put me on the counter of our store and ask me to sing that song, "Ramona, I preshoo kanishiks"— and that was the baby talk. The elephants' legs: fat women in the store, me reaching to their knees, they in short dresses, stocking-tops turned down. The sounds like Bronx cheers? To a lady out shopping, a two-year-old dwarf is not an existent being, so why shouldn't they make them if they were uncomfortable.

But I didn't stop there—I meaning my experience. From time to time, I would experience what I thought was the universe—a spiral wave of nothingness that would move in a spiral path, cast itself into a configuration that I felt was the being of a whole millennium; then it would fold back on itself, only to flow again to cast out another, higher way for the world, the people, to be. I heard a ghostly laughter, howling about what a joke it was to end one configuration—that everyone in it thought was God's plan—only to have it washed out of existence to be replaced by another.

In one of these moments of the universe's movement, I became a lion. I felt my claws tense—front paws and back; my mouth curled involuntarily into a snarl, that became a strangled gargle, finally to be released as a full-throated roar. The release of the roar was one of the most satisfying, and I think integrating, experiences of my life. I felt myself extending from my center right out to the edges of my body, perhaps filling it and living it for the first time. It is, I can assure you, a magnificent experience to feel your toes as your own, like talons, and as an integral part of yourself, rather than those little nubs experienced as "way down there."

From time to time, I would flip back into the mode of perception, and experience the world outside my own skin. It was constantly changing appearance, as if the edges of things—which ordinarily confined and contained their being—became waxy or actually ruptured, so that the insides were disclosed.

Several hours later, I and my fellow voyagers began to surface. It was like an experience of being reborn or reincarnated. At midnight, we went to a nearby Cypriot restaurant—a psychiatrist, a social worker, a writer, a young physician, and myself. We ate as if for the first time. The feel of jaws and teeth rending meat and bread was exquisite.

By several days later, I had the feeling of having lived a dream, but a dream of possibilities that seem more accessible.

This is the experience, that I have barely outlined, that I had in mind when I first agreed to talk to this group. This was an inward Odyssey, a marvelous voyage out of mind and concepts and into raw experiencing. This experiencing, which runs like a subterranean stream under the layer of our usual, concept-cluttered consciousness, is our source. It is the source of our changing being. Access to it permits us to transcend or undercut the usual polarities of inner-outer, subject-object, person-environment. When we are able to enter our experience, we are, virtually, "turned on."

To what are we "turned on?" To intentional experience. Concepts and projects are indeed suspended, bracketed, as in Husserl's *epoché*, and being, consciousness of the being of the world, is permitted to disclose itself. To be turned on means to turn off analytic thinking and reason, conceptualizing, searching, trying. It is, rather, an experience of being enlivened from what one experiences as "within," of flowing from one's center. It is a valuable experience, and it appears to be the basis of personal growth. To be out of one's mind and into one's unprejudged, unsearching experiencing, to be in the mode of "letting-be and letting-happen" calls for moments of nonattachment and liberation from projects. An immersion in one's experiencing, with the dissolution of the ego, gives one an acute realization and raw feel of the "game" nature of much of our everyday life, of our falseness and deadness and inauthenticity in ordinary existence.

But the intimation of what is possible, when induced by drugs can be, I believe, a false and possibly dangerous path to liberation, to fulfillment, to Ithaca. It is like cheap grace, effortless nonattachment.

Actually, if Ithaca is our quest, and our quest is Ithaca, then growth must entail an endless dialectic of being in one's mind, pursuing projects, outgrowing concepts and projects, re-entering experience, emerging again, responding to new invitations disclosed by the world, re-conceptualizing, forming new habits, and so on until death.

To avoid the re-entry into experience is to equate our present being as the final answer to the question, "Who am I and what can I be?" To stay in raw experiencing, never incarnating oneself into a given identity, is to be no-where, no-one, with no-body.

I am now fascinated with the possibilities of abetting everyman's Odyssey without drugs. I'm grateful for my drug-induced experience of my usually repressed possibilities, but I can also see some danger in reliance upon drugs for liberation. In fact, I now believe that repeated doses of LSD destroys a person's ability to commit himself to projects that take longer than 5 minutes to complete. Such a person becomes project-less, and hence world-less. I've had a number of acid-heads consult with me, as part of their effort to find values worth committing to, to make a world for themselves that has futurity. It's a challenging task—I don't think Tim Leary has been an entirely responsible messiah.

I know that it is possible to go out of one's mind, to let oneself enter his experiencing, in everyday contexts. Indeed, we are all, always, one decision away from access to our possibilities. Every time we are engaged in authentic dialogue, we reach a point where we can either let the next disclosure happen, or close it off in semblance. If we let it happen, we permit our experiencing to happen. It is usually terrifying for the insecure. He finds safety in the stifling confines of his roles, self-concept, and ego.

Meditation upon a mandala, a navel, a tree, or a rose can, if one lets it, if one can let go, flip one out of his mind, to experience new possibilities.

Committing oneself wholeheartedly to some project, to the point of failure, then persisting to struggle with it—then giving up: at the moment of giving up, the solution presents itself. This too is a momentary letting-go which permits experiencing to happen.

Indeed, fulfillment of a project, rich gratification of a need, a quest for love, contact, confirmation, can release a person from the world-structure imposed by the project.

But the Odyssey is never complete. An Odysseyan cycle is complete when a person has existed in his mind to the point of despair and boredom, gone out of it, to let new possibilities be disclosed by his own being and the being of the world, then re-conceptualized the world, and transacted with it in pursuit of new projects. But then it must happen again. And again.

Indeed, the average man who lives out of his experience and wholly in his mind seldom grows but instead gets sick. The schizophrenics, the Outsiders described by Colin Wilson, have gotten lost in their experiencing and couldn't make it back into the world lived in by their peers. I suspect that love for a loving person may be the necessary condition for making a successful Odyssey of the sort I've been describing. The loving and beloved person who knows he will be confirmed by his loved one dares let go his clutch on his present identity and self-concept to go out of the safe but dull region of the known into realms of possibility, then to redefine his identity. I suspect artists and writers and dancers and poets who dry up have lacked the luck or inner faith of Blake. I hope that some of my colleagues and I will, in time, learn more, not how to produce instant liberation and integration, but rather how to become better guides, servants and leaders of individuals and not peddlers of knowledge (as to how to confine and limit man, so he can the better be controlled) to social, political and military institutions. The Odyssey of an institution is not mine. ✦

# *I-4* Healthy Personality and Self-Disclosure*

For a long time, health and well-being have been taken for granted as "givens," and disease has been viewed as the problem for man to solve. Today, however, increasing numbers of scientists have begun to adopt a reverse point of view: Disease and trouble are coming to be viewed as the givens, and specification of positive health and its conditions as the important goal. Physical, mental, and social health are values representing restrictions on the total variance of being. The scientific problem here consists in arriving at a definition of health, determining its relevant dimensions, and then identifying the independent variables of which these are a function.

Scientists, however, are supposed to be hard-boiled, and they insist that phenomena, in order to be counted "real," must be public. Hence, many behavioral scientists ignore man's self, or soul, since it is essentially a private phenomenon. Others, however, are not so quick to allocate man's self to the limbo of the unimportant, and they insist that we cannot understand man and his lot until we take his self into account.

I probably fall into the camp of these investigators who want to explore health as a positive problem in its own right and who, further, take man's self seriously—as a reality to be explained and as a variable which produces consequences for weal or woe. In this [essay], I would like more fully to explore the connection between positive health and the disclosure of self. Let me commence with some sociological truisms.

* From *The Transparent Self* by Sidney Jourard. Bibliographic notes in this chapter can be found in the complete bibliography from *The Transparent Self*, Appendix Chapter V-2.

Social systems require their members to play certain roles. Unless the roles are adequately played, the social systems will not produce the results for which they have been organized. This flat statement applies to social systems as simple as one developed by an engaged couple and to those as complex as a total nation among nations.

Societies have socialization "factories" and "mills"—families and schools—which serve the function of training people to play the age, sex, and occupational roles which they shall be obliged to play throughout their life in the social system. Broadly speaking, if a person plays his roles suitably, he can be regarded as a more or less normal personality. *Normal personalities, however, are not necessarily healthy personalities* (Jourard, 1958, pp. 16-18).

Healthy personalities are people who play their roles satisfactorily and at the same time derive personal satisfaction from role enactment; more, they keep growing and they maintain high-level physical wellness (Dunn, 1959). It is probable enough, speaking from the standpoint of a stable social system, for people to be normal personalities. But it is possible to be a normal personality and be absolutely miserable. We would count such a normal personality unhealthy. In fact, normality in some social systems—successful acculturation to them—reliably produces ulcers, piles, paranoia, or compulsiveness. We also have to regard as unhealthy those people who have never been able to enact the roles that legitimately can be expected from them.

Counselors, guidance workers, and psychotherapists are obliged to treat—with both patterns of unhealthy personality—those people who have been unable to learn their roles and those who play their roles quite well, but suffer the agonies of boredom, frustration, anxiety, or stultification. If our clients are to be helped, they must change, and change in *valued* directions. A change in a valued direction may arbitrarily be called growth. We have yet to give explicit statement to these valued directions for growth, though a beginning has been made

(Fromm, 1947; Jahoda, 1958; Jourard, 1958; Maslow, 1954; Rogers, 1958). We who are professionally concerned with the happiness, growth, and well-being of our clients may be regarded as professional lovers, not unlike the Cyprian sisterhood. It would be fascinating to pursue this parallel further, but for the moment let us ask instead what this has to do with self-disclosure.

To answer this question, let's tune in on an imaginary interview between a client and his counselor. The client says, "I have never told this to a soul, doctor, but I can't stand my wife, my mother is a nag, my father is a bore, and my boss is an absolutely hateful and despicable tyrant. I have been carrying on an affair for the past 10 years with the lady next door, and at the same time I am a deacon in the church." The counselor says, showing great understanding and empathy, "Mm-Humm!"

If we listened for a long enough period of time, we would find that the client talks and talks about himself to this highly sympathetic and empathic listener. At some later time, the client may eventually say, "Gosh, you have helped me a lot. I see what I must do and I will go ahead and do it."

Now this talking about oneself to another person is what I call self-disclosure. It would appear, without assuming anything, that self-disclosure is a factor in the process of effective counseling or psychotherapy. Would it be too arbitrary an assumption to propose that people become clients *because they have not disclosed themselves in some optimum degree to the people in their life?*

An historical digression: Toward the end of the 19th century, Joseph Breuer, a Viennese physician, discovered (probably accidentally) that when his hysterical patients talked about themselves, disclosing not only the verbal content of their memories, but also the feelings that they had suppressed at the time of assorted "traumatic" experiences, their hysterical symptoms disappeared. Somewhere along the line, Breuer withdrew from a situation which would have made him Freud's peer in history's hall of fame. When Breuer permitted his patients "to be," it scared him, one gathers, because some of his female patients disclosed themselves to be quite sexy, and what was probably worse, they felt quite sexy toward him. Freud, however, did not flinch. He made the momentous discovery that the neurotic people of his time were struggling like mad to avoid "being," to avoid being known and, in Allport's (1955) terms, to avoid "becoming." He learned that his patients, when they were given the opportunity to "be"—which free association on a couch is nicely designed to do—would disclose that they had all manner of horrendous thoughts and feelings which they did not even dare disclose to themselves, much less express in the presence of another person. Freud learned to permit his patients to be, through permitting them to disclose themselves utterly to another human. He evidently did not trust anyone enough to be willing to disclose himself vis-à-vis; so he disclosed himself to himself on paper (Freud, 1955) and learned the extent to which he was himself self-alienated. Roles for people in Victorian days were even more restrictive than today, and Freud discovered that when people struggled to avoid being and knowing themselves, they got sick. They could only become well and stay relatively well when they came to know themselves through self-disclosure to another person. This makes me think of Georg Groddeck's magni-ficent *Book of the It (Id)* in which, in the guise of letters to a naive young woman, Groddeck shows the contrast between the *public self* pretentious role playing—and the warded off but highly dynamic *id*—which I here very loosely translate as "real self."

Let me at this point draw a distinction between role relationships and interpersonal relationships—a distinction which is often overlooked in the current spate of literature that has to do with human relations. Roles are inescapable. They must be played or else the social system will not work. A role by definition is a repertoire of behavior patterns which must be rattled off in appropriate contexts, and all behavior which is irrelevant to the role must be suppressed. But what we often forget is the fact that it is a *person* who is playing the role. This person has a self, or I should say he *is* a self. All too often the roles that a person plays do not do justice to all of his self. In fact, there may be nowhere that he may just *be* himself. Even more, the person may not *know* his self. He may, in Horney's (1950) terms, be self-alienated. This fascinating term, "self-alienation," means that an individual is estranged from his real self. His real self becomes a stranger, a feared and distrusted stranger. Estrangement, alienation from one's real self, is at the root of the "neurotic personality of our time" so eloquently described by Horney (1936). Fromm (1947) referred to the same phenomenon as a socially patterned defect. Self-alienation is a sickness which is so widely shared that no one recognizes it. We may take it for granted that all the clients whom we encounter are self-alienated to a greater or lesser extent. If you ask anyone to answer the questions, "Who are you?" the answer will generally be, "I am a psychologist," "a businessman," a "teacher," or what have you. The respondent will probably tell you the name of the role with which he feels most closely identified. As a matter of fact, the respondent spends a great part of his life trying to discover who he is, and once he has made some such discovery, he spends the rest of his life trying to play the part. Of course, some of the roles—age, sex, family, or occupational roles—may be so restrictive that they fit a person in a manner not too different from the girdle of a 200-pound lady who is struggling to look like Brigitte Bardot. There is Faustian drama all about us in this world of role playing. Everywhere we see people who have sold their soul, or their real self, if you wish, in order to be a psychologist, a businessman, a nurse, a physician, a this or a that.

Now, I have suggested that no social system can exist unless the members play their roles and play them with precision and elegance. But here is an odd observation, and yet one which you can all corroborate just by thinking back over your own experience. It is possible to be involved in a social group such as a family or a work setting for years and years, playing one's roles nicely with the other members—and never getting to know the *persons* who are playing the other roles. Roles can be played personally and impersonally, as we are beginning to discover. A husband can be married to his wife for 15 years and never come to know her. He knows her as "the wife." This is the paradox of the "*lonely* crowd" (Riesman, 1950). It is the loneliness which people try to counter with "togetherness." But much of today's "togetherness" is like the "parallel play" of two-year-old children, or like the professors in Stringfellow Barr's (1958) novel who, when together socially, lecture *past* one another alternately and sometimes simultaneously. There is no real self-to-self or person-to-person meeting in such transactions. Now what does it mean to know a person, or, more accurately, a person's self? I don't mean anything mysterious by "self." All I mean is the person's subjective side—what he thinks, feels, believes, wants, worries about—the kind of thing which one could never know unless one were told. *We get to know the other person's self when he discloses it to us.*

Self-disclosure, letting another person know what you think, feel, or want is the most direct means (though not the only means) by which an individual can make himself known to another person. Personality hygienists place great emphasis upon the importance for mental health of what they call "real-self being," "self-realization," "discovering oneself," and so on. An operational analysis of what goes on in counseling and therapy shows that the patients and clients discover themselves through self-disclosure to the counselor. They talk, and to their shock and amazement, the counselor listens.

I venture to say that there is probably no experience more horrifying and terrifying than that of self-disclosure to "significant others" whose probable reactions are assumed, but not known. Hence the phenomenon of "resistance." This is what makes psychotherapy so difficult to take and so difficult to administer. If there is any skill to be learned in the art of counseling and psychotherapy, it is the art of coping with the terrors which attend self-disclosure and the art of decoding the language, verbal and nonverbal, in which a person speaks about his inner experience.

Now what is the connection between self-disclosure and healthy personality? Self-disclosure, or should I say "real" self-disclosure, is both a symptom of personality health (Jourard, 1958, pp. 218-21) and at the same time a means of ultimately achieving healthy personality. The discloser of self is an animated "real-self be-er." This, of course, takes courage—the "courage to be." I have known people who would rather die than become known. In fact, some did die when it appeared that the chances were great that they would become known. When I say that self-disclosure is a symptom of personality health, what I mean really is that a person who displays many of the other characteristics that betoken healthy personality (Jourard, 1958; Maslow, 1954) *will also display the ability to make himself fully known to at least one other significant human being.* When I say that self-disclosure is a means by which one achieves personality health, I mean something like the following: It is not until I *am* my real self and I act my real self that my real self is in a position to grow. One's self grows from the *consequence of being.* People's selves stop growing when they repress them. This growth arrest in the self is what helps to account for the surprising paradox of finding an infant inside the skin of someone who is playing the role of an adult. In a fascinating analysis of mental disease, Jurgen Ruesch (1957) describes assorted neurotics, psychotics, and psychosomatic patients as persons with selective atrophy and overspecialization in various aspects of the process of communication. This culminates in a foul-up of the processes of knowing others and of becoming known to others. Neurotic and psychotic symptoms might be viewed as smoke screens interposed between the patient's real self and the gaze of the onlooker. We might call the symptoms "devices to avoid becoming known." A new theory of schizophrenia has been proposed by a former patient (Anonymous, 1958) who "was there," and he makes such a point.

Alienation from one's real self not only arrests one's growth as a person; it also tends to make a farce out of one's relationships with people. As the ex-patient mentioned above observed, the crucial "break" in schizophrenia is with *sincerity*, not reality (Anonymous, 1958). A self-alienated person—one who does not disclose himself truthfully and fully—can never love another person nor can he be loved by the other person. Effective loving calls for knowledge of the object (Fromm, 1956; Jourard, 1958). How can I love a person whom I do not know? How can the other person love me if he does not know me?

Hans Selye (1950) proposed and documented the hypothesis that illness as we know it arises in consequence of stress applied to the organism. Now I rather think that unhealthy *personality* has a similar root cause, and one which is related to Selye's concept of stress. It is this. Every maladjusted person is a person who has not made himself known to another human being and in consequence does not know himself. Nor can he be himself. More than that, *he struggles actively to avoid becoming known by another human being. He works* at it ceaselessly, 24 hours daily, and it is work! The fact that resisting becoming known is *work* offers us a research opening, incidentally (*cf.* Dittes, 1957; Davis and Malmo, 1950). I believe that in the effort to avoid becoming known, a person provides for himself a cancerous kind of stress which is subtle and unrecognized but none the less effective in producing, not only the assorted patterns of unhealthy personality which psychiatry talks about, but also the wide array of physical ills that have come to be recognized as the stock in trade of psychosomatic medicine. Stated another way, I believe that *other people come to be stressors to an individual in direct proportion to his degree of self-alienation.*

If I am struggling to avoid becoming known by other persons then, of course, I must construct a false public self (Jourard, 1958 pp. 301-2). The greater discrepancy between my unexpurgated real self and the version of myself that I present to others, then the more dangerous will other people be for me. If becoming known by another person is threatening, then the very presence of another person can serve as a stimulus to evoke anxiety, heightened muscle tension, and all the assorted visceral changes which occur when a person is under stress. A beginning already has been made, demonstrating the tension-evoking powers of the other person, through the use of such instruments as are employed in the lie detector, through the measurement of muscle tensions with electromyographic apparatus, and so on (Davis and Malmo, 1950; Dittes, 1957).

Students of psychosomatic medicine have been intimating something of what I have just finished saying explicitly. They say (*cf.* Alexander, 1950) the ulcer patients, asthmatic patients, patients suffering from colitis, migraine, and the like, are chronic *repressors* of certain needs and emotions, especially hostility and dependency. Now when you repress something, you are not only withholding awareness of this something from yourself, you are also withholding it from the scrutiny of the other person. In fact, the means by which repressions are overcome in the therapeutic situation is through relentless disclosure of self to the therapist. When a patient is finally able to follow the fundamental rule in psychoanalysis and disclose everything which passes through his mind, he is generally shocked and dismayed to observe the breadth, depth, range, and diversity of thoughts, memories, and emotions which pass out of his "unconscious" into overt disclosure. Incidentally, by the time a person is that free to disclose in the presence of another human being, he has doubtless completed much of his therapeutic sequence.

Self-disclosure then, appears to be one of the means by which a person engages in that elegant activity which we call real-self-being. But is real-self-being synonymous with healthy personality? Not in and of itself. I would say that real-self-being is a necessary but not a sufficient condition for healthy personality. Indeed, an authentic person may not be very "nice." In fact, he may seem much "nicer" socially and appear more mature and healthy when he is *not* being his real self than when he is his real self. But an individual's "obnoxious" but authentic self can never grow in the direction of greater maturity until the person has become acquainted with it and begins to *be* it. Real-self-being produces consequences which, in accordance with well-known principles of behavior (*cf.* Skinner, 1953), produce changes in the real self. Thus, there can be no real growth of the self without real-self-being. Full disclosure of the self to at least one other significant human being appears to be one means by which a person discovers not only the breadth and depth of his needs and feelings, but also the nature of his own self-affirmed values. There is no necessary conflict, incidentally, between real-self-being and being an ethical or nice person, because for the average member of our society, self-owned ethics are generally acquired during the process of growing up. All too often, however, the self-owned ethics are buried under authoritarian morals (Fromm, 1947).

If self-disclosure is one of the means by which healthy personality is both achieved and maintained, we can also note that such activities as loving, psychotherapy, counseling, teaching, and nursing are impossible of achievement without the disclosure of the client. It is through self-disclosure that an individual reveals to himself and to the other party just exactly who, what, and where he is. Just as thermometers and sphygmomanometers disclose information about the real state of the body, self-disclosure reveals the real nature of the soul, or self. Such information is vital in order to conduct intelligent evaluations. All I mean by evaluation is comparing how a person is with some concept of optimum. You never really discover how truly sick your psychotherapy patient is until he discloses himself utterly to you. You cannot help your client in vocational guidance until he has disclosed to you something of the impasse in which he finds himself. You cannot love your spouse or your child or your friend unless those persons have permitted you to know them and to know what they need in order to move toward greater health and well-being. Nurses cannot nurse patients in any meaningful way unless they have permitted the patients to disclose their needs, wants, worries, anxieties, and doubts, and so forth. Teachers cannot be very helpful to their students until they have permitted the students to disclose how utterly ignorant and misinformed they presently are. Teachers cannot even provide helpful information to the students until they have permitted the students to disclose exactly what they are interested in.

I believe we should reserve the term inter*personal* relationships to refer to transactions between "I and thou" (Buber, 1937), between *person* and *person*, not between role and role. A truly personal relationship between two people involves disclosure of self one to the other in full and spontaneous honesty. The data that we have collected up to the present time have shown us some rather interesting phenomena. We found (Jourard and Lasakow, 1958), for example, that the women we tested in universities in the Southeast were consistently higher self-disclosers than men; they seem to have a greater capacity for establishing person-to-person relationships, inter*personal* relationships, than men. This characteristic of women seems to be a socially patterned phenomenon which sociologists (Parsons and Bales, 1955) refer to as the *expressive* role of women in contradistinction to the instrumental role which men universally are obliged to adopt. Men seem to be much more skilled at *im*personal, *instrumental* role playing. But public health officials, very concerned about the sex differential in mortality rates, have been wondering what it is about being a man which makes males die younger than females. Do you suppose that there is any connection whatsoever between the disclosure patterns of men and women and their differential death rates? I have already intimated that withholding self-disclosure seems to impose a certain stress on people. Maybe "being manly," whatever that means, is slow suicide!

I think there is a very general way of stating the relationship between self-disclosure and assorted values such as healthy personality, physical health, group effectiveness, successful marriage, effective teaching, and effective nursing. It is this. A person's self is known to be the immediate determiner of his overt behavior. This is a paraphrase of the phenomenological point of view in psychology (Combs and Snygg, 1959). Now, if we want to understand anything, explain it, control it, or predict it, it is helpful if we have available as much pertinent information as we possibly can. Self-disclosure provides a source of information which is relevant. This information has often been overlooked. Where it has not been overlooked, it has often been misinterpreted by observers and practitioners through such devices as projection or attribution. *It seems to be difficult for people to accept the fact that they do not know the very person whom they are confronting at any given moment.* We all seem to assume that we are expert psychologists and that we know the other person, when in fact we have only constructed a more or less autistic concept of him in our mind. If we are to learn more about man's self, then we must learn more about self-disclosure—its conditions, dimensions, and consequences. Beginning evidence (*cf.* Rogers, 1958) shows that actively accepting, empathic, loving, non-punitive response—in short, love—provides the optimum conditions under which man will disclose, or expose, his naked quivering self to our gaze. It follows that if we would be helpful (or should I say *human*) we must grow to loving stature and learn, in Buber's terms, to confirm our fellow man in his very being. Probably, this presumes that we must *first* confirm our *own* being. ✦

[1974]

# *I-5* Reality, Perception, and Healthy Personality

## Introduction

If one knows how to function effectively, one has a sound basis for the development of a healthy personality. The ability to perceive reality as it "really is" is, therefore, fundamental to effective functioning. It is considered one of two preconditions to the development of the beautiful and noble person. Our need systems heavily affect our ability to perceive reality—we often perceive what we want to see rather than what is really there.

Our behavior is always undertaken with reference to the world as we believe it to be. We can hardly make sense out of anybody's behavior unless we somehow learn from individuals how the world appears to them—what they are paying attention to, how they interpret the things they see and hear, and what their expectations are regarding the world about them, according to Combs[1] and others. We will be puzzled if we see someone run in terror from an automobile engine as it starts up, because to us the automobile is simply something to get us from place to place. However, if the person is a primitive who has never seen an automobile, that person may perceive it as a punishing instrument of the gods that is about to engulf someone. If we know how the person perceives the situation, we can understand the situation better and offer help.

A person's perceptions and beliefs will be inaccurate or distorted unless the person takes steps to verify them. Reality contact is not a given; it is an achievement! Efficient contact with reality must be worked for, because there are powerful forces at work at all times, tending to distort perception, thinking, and recall.

## Some Influences on Perception of the World

In the first place, the content of our field of perception is necessarily selective; it cannot include all inner and outer reality that exists at a given moment. Only part of the ongoing flow of feelings, thoughts, and external events is detected by our sense organs and represented in our field of awareness. Our sense organs resemble TV or radio receivers, in that they are differently sensitive to stimuli of different intensities and qualities. But even within the receptive range of our senses, we still notice only a fraction of all the sensory information reaching our brain. Some of the important determiners of *figure*, that is, of our focus of attention, are unfulfilled needs.

Our feelings and our needs direct our perception, thinking, remembering, and fantasy, so that the figure will be that perception, thought, or memory most relevant to our needs of the moment. Our cognitive processes are thus servants of our needs. When we are hungry, we think and dream about food, we search for it, and we tend to ingnore everything in the world that is inedible or that will not help us to get food. If we are sexually deprived, we tend to have fantasies with erotic themes, we find it difficult to think about other things, and we look at the world from the standpoint of the sexual gratification and frustrations it is likely to afford. If we are anxious because of some threat to our security, we are unlikely to notice the beauties of nature; we are too busy seeking the source of danger so that we might escape from it. There have been many experiments conducted to demonstrate how needs determine our attention and the content of our consciousness, and so we need not dwell further upon this point. More germane to our discussion is the manner in which emotions and unfulfilled needs operate to distort our perceptions and beliefs.

## Influence of Immediate Needs Upon Perception

Perception is perhaps one of the most important processes in psychology and is essential in understanding human behavior. According to Combs and Snygg,[2] *all behavior* is related to perception. A student attends a university because she perceives it as being helpful to her career or because a parent perceives it to be helpful to her offspring's development. A thief robs a bank because he perceives it as the source of money, according to Willie Sutton, one of the most famous of bank robbers. A child cries when seeing a clown because he sees it as a monster rather than as a funny creature.

The most important influence upon perception and misperception is the perceiver's own needs. At about noontime, if you are driving through a strange city, should you see painted on a store window the name of the owner, *Sandwharf*, you are likely to perceive it as *Sandwich*. If you are embarrassed by sex-laden words and are asked to read a list quickly, you are likely to misread *breast* as *beast*. In a passionate political or personal argument, one's need is so great to win that we may avoid perceiving the other person's position at all.

The presumption, of course, is that since we are all human, others would perceive things the same way we would. A healthy personality is by no means exempt from this law. These persons too may momentarily see only themselves as "right" in their perceptions of complex political situations, for example, but they are able to look back upon themselves, their arguments, and their behavior and recognize when their needs are causing them to misperceive reality—or at least to miss other possible realities. This capacity for reflection back upon self is a uniquely human characteristic and is exceedingly valuable in keeping a certain openness to new ideas, new friends, and new joys. If someone perceives all new sports or new challenges as producing probable failure, that person will avoid tackling new, exciting experiences.

The perception principle is useful also in understanding the behavior of others, particularly of those whose cultural backgrounds may be different. The Russians see our election system as inefficient because it enables popular rather than competent persons to be elected to office on the basis of the amount they spend for advertisements. We see their system of nominating only one candidate as a farce. Some of the most cherished beliefs may rest upon doubtful perceptions of reality. The need to be right is so strong that we will defend our perceptions most vigorously and violently when we are least sure of them. A child who perceives a kitten as something warm, soft, and playful will run to play with it on a visit to a friend's home. Another child who sees a kitten as something that will bite and scratch you will run in terror from the animal. Any effort on the part of an adult to force contact with the kitten can only increase the terror unless the child's perception is gradually helped to change. A young (or old) man who has great need to prove his uncertain manliness will perceive every date as a challenge to conquest rather than to relationship and may be expected to display himself, posture, and go to all lengths to seduce or conquer rather than to relate.

This viewpoint is often termed a *phenomenological* or *perceptual* point of view. It suggests that we would better understand our associates and children through knowing how they and we perceive reality.

Our needs and emotions not only make us believe things that are untrue; they also blind us to truth. If a perception gives rise to devastating depression or hopelessness, there is a tendency for people simply to ignore the disquieting truth. Anyone who has suffered the death of a loved one will know how difficult it is to realize that the deceased will not be seen any more. People tend to forget, or more accurately, to repress the memory of painful or humiliating events.

Many needs can be gratified only through relationships with other people. This means that strong emotions are mobilized in our interpersonal relationships. Reliable information about another person is difficult to obtain, because much of that person's behavior goes on at times when we cannot see it. Furthermore, the person's consciousness of the world is not accessible to our direct vision. We can only learn the subjective side of another person if he or she confides in us, and the person may not be willing to entrust us with personal information.[3] Often we are obliged to form our concept of another person on the basis of overt behavior alone. We infer, as accurately as possible, what an individual's perception might have been, so that we can predict his or her behavior in similar situations in the future.

## Other People's Influence on Our Sense of Reality

Reality is what we take to be real. This, in turn, is powerfully influenced by what significant other people have told us is true, real, and important in the world. We are continuously told by newspapers, comics, friends and family members, movies and television programs about the way things are. Sometimes this influence is subtle; someone merely describes some aspect of the world to us, and we find that this description impels us to see the world as we were told it is. One teacher played a classroom game; she asked the children to pretend that blonde, blue-eyed children were evil. In time, the black-haired children came to loathe the blondes, who in turn felt inferior.[4]

Other people, then, can so influence one's ways of perceiving, and of attaching meaning and value, that one loses one's own autonomous perspective. If other people are strong, with high status, they may invalidate one's own perspective on reality; the weaker person accepts the perspective of the stronger.

For example, when high school seniors in the minority are confronted by perceptions or judgments from a majority identified as college students, the high schoolers conform to the perceptions of the higher status college student.[5]

A person may need to disengage from other people and go into solitude, in order to separate other people's perspectives on reality from one that is more truly individual.[6]

## Language and Ontic Projection

*Ontic projection* is Thomas Hanna's[7] term to describe what a person takes to be real—attributions of reality. Each language provides words that sensitize a person to those aspects of the world that are most important for survival in that place. Thus, we have only one word for snow, whereas Eskimos have many, corresponding with different qualities of snow, which indicate whether hunting or igloo building are possible.[8] We do not see the world; rather, we "read" the meanings of what we see, just as we read the words in a book. These meanings are provided for us as we grow up by the person who teaches us to speak our "mother tongue." It is our mothers who give the first meanings to our world, who give the world the "voices" with which it tells us of dangers and gratifications. In developing countries like Indonesia or India, each child learns three languages, each of which highlights some aspects of the world more than others, and which gives different meanings and emotional qualities to the perceived world. Thus, a child will learn the language of the village from his or her mother; in India or Indonesia, it will be one of the several hundred local languages, which differ so much that people fifty miles apart cannot understand one another's mother tongues. At school an Indonesian child will learn Malay, and an Indian child will learn Hindi—both languages are the national tongue, which facilitates communication throughout the country. Finally, both Indonesians and Indians may learn English, which makes communication beyond national boundaries possible.

In each case, the language that is spoken affects perception. In order really to perceive what is there in the world, a person will have to suspend language and really look and listen, to discern the reality *beyond* language (pp. 67-69).

**Reality Testing**

Our chances of behaving effectively are increased if we perceive the world accurately and form valid beliefs about it. But we know that unfulfilled needs and strong emotions can so shape our experience that we misinterpret facts, arrive at erroneous conclusions, and, indeed, frequently fail to see and hear what is there. How does a person go about increasing the efficiency of perception and thinking? How does a person carry out reality testing? Indeed, why would a person seek the truth when unreality is often more pleasant in the short run?

*Reality testing* means applying the rules of logic and scientific inquiry to everyday life. When we engage in reality testing, we are systematically doubting our own initial perceptions and beliefs until we have scrutinized them more carefully and checked them against further evidence. We do this when we have learned that truth, ultimately, is the best servant of our needs and is a value in itself.

## An Example of Reality Testing

A nineteen-year-old woman once consulted me, seeking help with a problem that was bothering her. She believed her roommate was stealing her money, jewelry, and even stationery. She noticed various items missing from her dresser from time to time, and she concluded her roommate was guilty. However, she dared not confront the roommate with her suspicion. Instead, she felt distrust and resentment and struggled to conceal these feelings from her. Their relationship gradually deteriorated to one of formality, forced politeness, and false expressions of friendship.

I asked the young woman why she didn't bring the whole issue out into the open. She stated that if she did this, her roommate would hate her, and she couldn't stand this. I asked if there were any other possible way of interpreting the loss of her money and jewelry. She replied that she hadn't thought of any. Rather, she had concluded that if her things were missing, they must have been stolen by the person closest to her. When I suggested that her roommate might be saddened at the way their friendship had deteriorated and that she might welcome some frank talk to settle things, the young woman admitted that this might be possible, but she was afraid to talk about the problem. However, she agreed to broach the subject.

The next time I saw her, she was happy to report that she had discussed the whole affair. She learned that her roommate was puzzled by the way their relationship had changed. Moreover, she was glad to discuss the loss of the articles with her and she was able to clear herself of any blame. In fact, the roommate too had been missing some money, and investigation by the dormitory counselor brought forth the fact that other women had been robbed and that the guilty party was a cleaning woman, who was promptly discharged.

The example illustrates how some initial, untested beliefs that one person forms about some aspect of the world—in this case, about another person—can lead to misunderstanding in interpersonal relationships and to considerable unhappiness.[9] At first, the woman was afraid to carry out any efforts at reality testing to see if her assumption of the guilt of her roommate was warranted. This illustrates another aspect of reality testing; frequently, people may be reluctant to go after the information that is crucial to the formation of accurate beliefs. Yet if a person gives in to the fear of getting at the truth, that person is almost sure to become increasingly out of touch with reality.

## Rules For Reality Testing

The search for the "real" reality in contrast to the perceived reality is a difficult one even for the scientist. Here are some rules that may help you become far more effective in reality testing:

1. State the belief clearly.
2. Ask, "What evidence is there to support this belief?"
3. Ask, "Is there any other way of interpreting this evidence?"
4. Try to determine how consistent the belief is with other beliefs that are known to be valid.

## Living in the "Raw World": The Return to Experience

It is probably the lot of human beings that once they have learned speech, then perceptions of reality are always filtered through, and guided by, their *concepts* of reality. For example, if you learn the concept *gun* and then look at a gun, you probably see something entirely different from what a primitive savage might: guns have no place, nor even a word to describe them, in his or her culture.[10]

Words limit what a person will actually experience in a concrete situation. Once a concept has been learned, a person will look at a given object long enough to place it in its proper category or to assign an appropriate name to it. The person may then ignore much of what is actually there. We are all familiar with the bigoted person who, once he or she has determined that a person is a Jew or a black, never looks further at the person. The bigot "knows" the properties of all members who fall into those classes. In reality, the bigot fails to observe the enormous amount of variation among members of any class.[11]

The ability to break down categories and discern uniqueness is as essential for healthy personality as the ability to classify. But the ability to see what is there, to transcend labels and classes and apprehend the thing before one's view, is a means of enriching one's knowledge of the world and of deepening one's contact with reality. Fritz Perls[12] would have his patients in Gestalt therapy go through exercises of simply looking at something or somebody, in order to discern the reality beyond the concept. To be able to sense the "raw world" involves the ability to abandon presently held concepts and categories. This ability is possessed by the productive scientist who deliberately ignores the orthodoxies, and looks ever afresh at the raw data that prompted the formation of present- day concepts and categories. The artist probably possesses to a marked degree the ability to apprehend the unique, the individual object.

The ability to set conventional categories and concepts aside and to look fully at the world with minimal preconceptions seems to be a trait that facilitates scientific discovery, art, human relations, and, more generally, an enrichment of the sensory experiences of living.

The capacity to let oneself see or perceive what is there seems to entail the *temporary cessation of an active, searching, or critical attitude*.[13] Need-directed perception is a highly focused searchlight darting here and there, seeking the objects that will satisfy needs, ignoring everything irrelevant to the need. Being-cognition, as Maslow has called it, refers to a more passive mode of perceiving. It involves letting oneself be reached, touched, or affected by what is there so that the perception is richer. In Maslow's own words,[14]

*The most efficient way to perceive the intrinsic nature of the world is to be more passive than active, determined as much as possible by the intrinsic organization of that which is perceived and as little as possible by the nature of the perceiver. This kind of detached, Taoist, passive, non-interfering awareness of all the simultaneously existing aspects of the concrete, has much in common with some descriptions of the aesthetic experience and of the mystic experience. The stress is the same. Do we see the real, concrete world, or do we see our own system of rubrics, motives, expectations and abstractions which we have projected onto the real world? Or, to put it very bluntly, do we see or are we blind?* [p. 38]

This mode of cognition, however, seems to be possible only at those times when we have adequately fulfilled the basic needs. When we are anxious, sexually deprived, or hungry, it is as if our organs of perceiving and of knowing have been "commandeered" to find the means of gratification. Our consciousness seems most free to play, to be most receptive to new impressions, when the urgency of needs is diminished. The implication is clear—if we want to know hitherto unnoticed features of the world that confronts us, our chances of so doing are increased when our basic needs are satisfied.

The direction of our cognition by needs has adaptive value, because it increases our chances of finding the things that will satisfy our needs and it permits us to avoid dangers in our environment. However, if persons are *always* perceiving the world under the direction of their needs, they will simply not perceive much that exists. The aesthetic, appreciative contemplation of reality, with no purpose other than the delight of looking at it, or experiencing it, lends a dimension of richness to an existence that is ordinarily characterized by the search for satisfaction.

Competence at gratifying one's needs frees one from time to time of the necessity to be forever struggling and permits one the luxury of aesthetic sensing.

## Some Existential Suggestions

The next time a friend does something that puzzles you, try thinking about how he or she has perceived the situation and see if you can understand the behavior better. To really exercise this principle, try inferring the perception of someone who is quite distant from you ethnically and make a real effort to understand the person.

The experience of being in a minority is an extremely healthy one, provided you can stalwartly resist efforts of those of higher status or authority to make you change your mind. Be sure, of course, that you are taking the position because of your genuine perception of what is the right thing to do, rather than merely to be inflexible. This is the kind of experience that makes for true intellectual integrity—an important component of the high-level functioner.

One of the exercises Gestalt therapists ask their patients to engage in is really looking at someone familiar to them. This is a way to break up one's concepts so that one really sees what is there, not what is *said* to be there.

Try bracketing off previous knowledge about yourself and really look at yourself naively.

Be careful what you believe to be true, because as long as you believe it, then for you it is true. But your beliefs about reality, your *attributions of reality* or your *ontic projections*, profoundly influence your life. Of especial importance for healthy personality are those beliefs about limits, about your weaknesses and lack of aptitude. If you believe you cannot learn to play a musical instrument because you lack talent, get a musical instrument and learn to play it. If you believe you cannot do without food for three days, go on a five-day fast. Challenge your own beliefs, especially about yourself and others, because what you believe to be true about self and others functions more as persuasion than as description.

## Summary

Healthy personality depends upon accurate perception of and knowledge about the world. One of the best ways to help understand another person's behavior is to know how that person has perceived the situation. Our perception and our thinking is subject to influence by needs and emotions, and we are vulnerable to confusion of perception with imagination. Consequently, our perception may be very selective and distorted, and our beliefs unfounded. Reality testing is the technique of verifying our perceptions and beliefs by seeking further information and by engaging in rational thinking about the implications of our perceptions. Other people can influence our perspective, even to the point of replacing it with their own. Reality testing entails disengaging oneself from action and querying one's views of a situation to discern whether they are compatible with fresh perceptions and with reason.

The "return to experience" involves viewing the world afresh, uninfluenced by language and ongoing needs and projects. This basic perception is what Maslow described as B-cognition and appears to be the aim of the enlightening disciplines, such as Zen, Taoism, Sufism, and as the Yaqui sorcerer Don Juan called it, "stopping the [speech of] the world," so that one can really see it. ✦

### Notes and References

1. *The phenomenological or perceptual approach to understanding behavior was developed by Arthur W. Combs and Don Snygg. A recent revision of their text is A. W. Combs, F. Richards, and A. Richards,* Perceptual Psychology *(New York: Harper, 1978).*

2. *A. W. Combs and D. Snygg,* Individual Behavior, *2nd ed. (New York: Harper, 1959).*

3. *S. M. Jourard,* Self-Disclosure: An Experimental Analysis of the Transparent Self *(New York: Wiley-Interscience, 1971) provides a review of Jourard's research into factors in self-disclosure.*

4. *This experiment was carried out by Ms. Jane Elliott and is reported in the documentary film,* Eye of the Storm.

5. *D. L. Wiesenthal, N. S. Endler, T. R. Coward, J. Edwards, "Reversibility of Relative Competence as a Determinant of Conformity Across Different Perceptual Tasks," paper presented at the meeting of the Eastern Psychological Association, Chicago, May 1973.*

6. *See R. D. Laing and A. Esterson,* Sanity, Madness and the Family *(London: Tavistock, 1964) for dramatic illustrations of the way the perspective of one member of a family is invalidated by others.*

7. *T. Hanna,* The Other "Is", *unpublished manuscript, University of Florida, 1973.*

8. *B. L. Whorf,* Language, Thought and Reality, *J. B. Carroll (Ed.) (Cambridge, Mass.: M.I.T., 1956). Also see S. Hayakawa,* Language in Action *(New York: Harcourt, 1941). See also H. Werner,* Comparative Psychology of Mental Development *(Chicago: Follett, 1948), Chapters 9 and 12; R. Brown,* Words and Things *(New York: Free Press, 1958).*

9. *G. Ichheiser,* Appearances and Realities: Misunderstandings in Human Relations *(San Francisco: Jossey-Bass, 1970), pp. 1-120.*

10. *See note 8.*

11. *G. W. Allport,* The Nature of Prejudice *(Reading, Mass.: Addison-Wesley, 1954), especially Chapter 2.*

12. *See F. Perls, P. Goodman, and R. Hefferline,* Gestalt Therapy: Excitement and Growth in the Human Personality *(New York: Dell, 1951), Chapters 2-4, for examples of these exercises.*

13. *This difficult art is central to classical phenomenological philosophy and is known as the Epoche; it requires bracketing off one's previous knowledge of the object or phenomena perceived. Developed by E. Husserl,* Ideas: General Introduction to Pure Phenomenology *(London: Allen & Unwin, 1931).*

14. *Maslow, op. cit., pp. 67-96. See also E. Schachtel,* Metamorphosis: On the Development of Affect, Perception, Attention and Memory *(New York: Basic, 1959), pp. 220 ff.*

# II Roots of Holistic Psychology: Humanistic/ Cognitive/ In-spiriting

# *II-1* On Being Persuaded Who You Are

## Introduction

Man is a mystery, not a problem. The proper stance before a mystery is to open oneself respectfully to its disclosure. A problem is only to be solved. Man is not a problem to be solved, though there are those who view him as such. A mystery is indefinable. So is man. But there are those who seek to define and describe man's "essence." The peculiarity of man is that, whatever his "essence" might be, it does not determine what he can do with it. Human beings stand before their own substance in the way an artist encounters his paint and canvas—it is up to him to create something of original beauty, or of banality, out of the material at hand. A person will make of his situation what he *believes* is possible.

Belief is the outcome of having been convinced that something is the case. Human beings believe they can and cannot do, can and cannot overcome, can and cannot become, what *someone* has persuaded them is their nature.

## On Being Shaped to Conform to an Image

When we come into the world we are the embodiment of incredible possibilities. The various "agencies of socialization," family, school, mass media, shape our growth and development, so that at any given moment in time, like right now, each of us is involved in a repertoire of social roles—sex, age, family and occupational roles—which fits the social system.

Spokesmen for the ruling minority try to persuade the majority into believing that they are living in a utopia. This utopia, this good society, this best of all possible societies in the history of mankind, the one in which we are living right now, is not seen as a utopia by blacks, nor women, or by young people between the ages of 14 and 22. It turns out to be a utopia primarily for men in positions of power, who have been schooled in the world outlook of Orange County, California, who are over the age of 40. Orange County is a state of mind rather than a geographical site. White South Africa is like that—not a utopia for most of its citizens. How do you persuade the people for whom a place is not a utopia that it is a utopia? There are three techniques—lying or mystification, bribery, and threats. I will discuss some of the ways in which these techniques have been used to maintain the status quo.

Organized religion has traditionally functioned to bribe people with promises of a better life in the hereafter, and to somehow persuade them that you render unto Caesar the things that are Caesar's and that you render unto God the things that are God's. One of the things that you are not supposed to do is to criticize the way your society is organized. Hardly any of the organized Protestant, Catholic or other churches have been at the vanguard in the history of the western world's liberal or revolutionary movements. It's much more common for the churches to be in direct collusion with the power structure, the military, and with the large economic interests. I remember in May, in the *Gainesville Sun*, a small town university newspaper, there was a little article explaining that over 300 million dollars of the endowments of the four or five major Protestant churches of the United States were invested in stocks, in prime war industries, and nobody seemed to bat an eye. Of course, the Vietnam war was on. As I reviewed the situation, I realized we've got to broaden our conceptions of space and time, and ways to live life.

Billions of dollars are spent every year in the U.S. for elementary schools, colleges and universities. These schools exist to induce a respect, a love, and a passion for truth, justice and beauty in the people who go through them. But all that happens is that you socialize Americans. There's a difference between a typical product of our school systems and someone who is committed, passionately, to truth, beauty and justice.

If we spend $8 billion on these institutions, considerably more billions are spent on advertising, the aim of which is to get people to be functionally decorticated so that they can't tell the difference between real value and sham. I consider this absurd. It's almost like the scene in *Catch-22* where a patient was encased in plaster; the nurses would pour fluids in at the top and drain them out at the bottom, and then change the bottles around without even recognizing that the man had been dead for some time. Television, radio and movies also mystify us. Even Dick Tracy and Little Orphan Annie tell their readers how to be. We have been *persuaded* to become, and then be, the kind of person we now are.

## On Being Persuaded and Convinced

How have you been persuaded to be you? I mentioned two ways. Bribes of affection and material goods from parents and other agents of socialization. And threats: if you don't stay the way you now are, something awful will happen to you— criticism, prison or mental hospital.

Hypnosis is a kind of persuasion. I actually prefer words like persuasion, convincing and rhetoric, because those terms belong in everyday life. Hypnosis is thought to be an esoteric practice, or a highly specialized medical technique. But there is a sense in which conventional medical healing with drugs and surgery is a kind of convincing. All psychotherapies are a kind of persuasion, as are education and socialization. There are obvious and subtle ways of getting you *to be* in the way that *somebody* thinks you are. And so we push the question right back: Where did you ever get the idea that you are who you now are? How were you persuaded, seduced and bribed to be that way? The subtlest way in which we are convinced of our identity is other people's views of us, the attributions that they make. The descriptions that are laid on you are a very subtle kind of hypnosis. Here is another kind of hypnosis: Your mother says, "Be sure you have one bowel movement a day or else you'll feel sluggish. Be very sure you always put on rubbers when it rains because you know you are vulnerable to colds." You then miss going to the toilet, and feel sluggish. Every time it rains, if you don't wear a scarf and rubbers you come down with a terrible cold. Your physiology has been invented by your mother. There is a sense then, in which we are *somebody's* invention. It is very illuminating, and sometimes shocking, sometimes hilarious, to reflect on yourself and your situation and raise the question anew: "Where did I ever get the idea that I had to be this way, or that my situation is this way?" You discover that the script for your action and physiology was written by your mother, your father, a school teacher, and your younger brother. They defined you, and here you are.

## On Being Convinced One Is Sick and/or Crazy

We are who somebody persuaded us to be. If you are persuaded that you are out of your mind, you may begin to believe that you are mentally sick. If you believe you are mentally sick, you feel you must go to an expert on mental sickness. Consider a college student, a young man 20 years old. He discovers his father is a bore and something of a pompous ass. His mother is a silly chatterbox and he decides to spend little time in their company because it's not very rewarding. He learns Transcendental Meditation and begins to practice it. He starts to smoke marijuana, in secret with some classmates. His parents then say, "You're really acting strangely. Let's take you to the doctor. You haven't had a checkup for quite some time." (Everybody is persuaded that if they do not consult a doctor twice a year, they may have contracted a terminal illness. A child is taken to the pediatrician every two weeks to weighed; if he's got an ear, nose or throat infection, he's got to get penicillin. He becomes hooked. He becomes a doctor addict, very early, and he gets withdrawal symptoms.) The student is sent to a psychiatrist, who says, "What originally was a schizoid tendency, a tendency to withdraw, has now escalated into a full-blown episode of catatonic schizophrenia. For his own good the lad ought to be taken to a state hospital." He is sent there and given electroshock and thorazine. By the time he comes out, his kidneys are ruined, he has a haircut, he has put on weight, he starts drinking beer again and he no longer sits in that frightening way in his room all alone, silent.

Every perspective other than the one regarded as sane and proper is regarded as sick and crazy. Sanity and propriety in people are defined by people in power. So that, in a sense, if a person does not share the orthodox view of the good society and of how men, women, children ought to be, then he is in-validated, not listened to. Martha Mitchell was possibly one of the most honest persons in direct touch with the Watergate scandals, but an effort was made to regard her as mentally ill in order to discredit her testimony. The perspective or testi-mony of a child about adults is usually discredited. For a long time the perspective and testimony of blacks about our racism was discredited. The view of women was long discredited. When the discredited people consented to be ignored, the social sys-tem did not change. Because it was a utopia for its leaders.

## On Being a Prophet

In the midst of the darkness and suffering which is the experience of the majority of the people and other living crea-tures around the world, there arise prophets, people who envi-sion another way for the human situation to be. Life itself, in the present and in the times that follow, is the test of prophecy and the prophet. By prophets I don't mean people who foretell the future, but people who see the connections between present ways in which life is lived and society is organized and conse-quences that everybody agrees are bad, such as war, physical disease, psychological breakdown, emptiness of existence, suffering, exploitation, destruction of the environment, and so on. It takes a prophet to disengage, in order to see the con-nection between the way life is lived and those consequences. And it then calls for imagination—the ability to envision, to break the hypnotic spell of now, in order to be a prophet. I'll mention some people whom I have regarded as prophets, so as to clarify any definitions of the prophetic function. The Old Testament prophets like Moses, Isaiah, Jeremiah, Amos, fit my criteria of a prophet. Karl Marx, Sigmund Freud and Ronald Laing are all prophets. B.F. Skinner is a prophet in so far as he envisioned *Walden Two*, a kind of utopia organized on the principles of operant conditioning. Hugh Hefner, founder of the Playboy empire, is in some ways a prophet. A.H. Maslow was a prophet, as were Jung and Reich. The founders of Black Liberation and Women's Liberation can be regarded as prophets. The founders of Synanon, Alcoholics Anonymous and Weight Watchers likewise have served a prophetic function in modern times. A question I ask of any prophet is, Does he or she enlighten other people? Does this prophet challenge people to grow, to make the most out of the flexibility that inheres in man and his situation, or do these prophets invite passivity, stupidity, stupefaction and blind faith? Does following the prophet's way increase capacity for dialogue, empathy, love? Is life enhanced in the person and all whom he contacts?

## On Getting Out

When man finds his situation intolerable, he seeks ways to alter it. This calls for a perspective which usually is difficult to obtain. So compelling and hypnotic is the present definition of the situation, that for millennia man left his situation, either literally, by a voyage, or metaphorically through assorted disengagement disciplines. Why? In order to get a fresh perspective on the intolerable situation that he left. Throughout history there are many myths that express this way to a new life. One of my favorite myths is the *Odyssey*, which I see as an allegory of personal growth. It is about a situation that was once life-giving but became stifling and stagnant. In order to make it fit to live in, the hero had to leave, open himself up, enlarge his awareness of human possibilities and possibilities of the world, and then to return. It is most peculiar that in this society, to transcend one's situation, to get out of one's situation, is one of the worst crimes against the status quo; everything is done to prevent it. When people do disengage, they frequently become terrified. A role affects not only your action, but also your experience. And in order to feel like a son, a mother, or a father, you have to repress most of your possibilities of imagining, thinking, remembering, feeling and perceiving. To disengage from the role is to unrepress those possibilities of experiencing. If you have been led to believe that deeply buried in every man is a sewer of filth, rape and murder, that is exactly what you will find when you unrepress.

Powerful pressures prevent a person from getting out, but there are other ways. A voyage is a good way to disengage from your roles in your situation. Yoga and all of the other meditative disciplines are likewise ways of disengagement. In order to truly get *into* meditation, you've got to get *out* of your roles. You can't get into a Hatha yoga posture until you can disengage and uncommit your musculature from the way it has been committed to allow you to be in your usual roles in your daily situations.

Religious ritual, when it is authentic, is a way to disengage a person from his secular roles and activities in order to transform consciousness. The *way of being* that is described in the Old Testament and to some extent in the New Testament, and the way of the Buddha are all "ways out." If a person lives in those ways, he will indeed change his consciousness of his situation, and he will change his body, because to get *into* those ways means getting *out* of your usual roles. An encounter with death, to realize that you are finite, can yield new ways to see one's situation. Professor Bill Soskin believes that John the Baptist nearly drowned those whom he submerged; the encounter with death made it possible for his disciples to feel reborn. Psychotherapy can be a way out. It can invite a person out of his roles into new experience which can be both enthralling and seductive. There are some people who never leave psychotherapy. And it is also terrifying for many, for a good psychotherapist invites a person, at his own pace, to disengage from his usual way of being himself. And as I say, it's exhilarating or seductive. Encounter groups at growth centers where for a weekend, a week or a month you are bombarded with honesty, but more important, acceptance, can make a person get out of his usual roles in a way that is almost exhilarating. It produces a "high" that is astonishing. And, then, so there are people who go to growth centers and they never leave. And I suspect that something of the same sort has happened in eastern ashrams where you go and you never want to leave, for your way of being there seems so much more safe, meaningful, lifegiving and enlivening than your life back home. But I'm biased; I take that to be undialectical, a kind of idolatry. Anything that is idolatrously pursued is destructive of life. To hang on to a high is destructive. Trying to stay out is destructive, just as trying to stay in is destructive. Idolatry of the status quo is destructive. Then comes the hard part; the hard part is the return.

## The Return

Personal growth, and fulfillment of life-giving possibilities in the human situation, calls for new, more viable visions of the good world, the good society, and the good life. This fulfillment of the possibilities in the human situation requires a *return* to what one takes to be his home, to make it fit for life. Where is home? Home is not only a piece of geography; it is the roles that you have left. On returning home changed, a voyager may find himself invited to be the person he was when he left. The others may refuse to accept and confirm the changes. To accept this invitation is to invalidate one's growth. Odysseus returned to Ithaca and, to make his home fit for him, he slaughtered his wife's suitors and buried his father. He married off his son and established dominion over his kingdom. This is an allegorical way of saying he had grown. He was a bit bloody, but he had grown larger. The return is hardly ever easy. ✦

[1973]

# II-2 The Laugh That Heals, A Case Study

At one time, I believed man was free. I thought he chose his existence, and enjoyed or suffered the consequences of his choices. Then I started University, and began the study of psychology, sociology, and anthropology. My aim was to help produce a better world for man. There I was shattered to learn that freedom was an illusion. Man lived his life along grooves worn by his predecessors. His choices were determined by drives, habit, emotion, and stimuli arising in his milieu. The only hope I could see for bettering man's lot was that offered by my teachers—learn the determiners of man's condition and his action, and seek to gain control over them. This program conquered Nature's mastery over man, and there was no reason why it couldn't enable man to comprehend and master man, to understand, predict, and control him, to shape and to reshape him (and myself) in almost any image. It took a number of years to discover that this approach to a study of man is an option one need not accept, that I could be as a psychologist and a psychotherapist without reducing man to the level of an object, and myself to the status of a manipulator of my being and that of my fellows.

In my work as a researcher, I have by now come to believe that my colleagues and I have had a joke played on us by the "Subjects" in our research (a better word is "Objects," because we either ask them or force them to renounce their freedom, and play the part of a "determined" being). We have tested and interviewed thousands upon thousands of people without realizing that they *are* people who are unlikely to reveal the truth of their being to impersonal, high status strangers like us.

I now suspect that the "Subjects" (Objects) of our scientific study have told or shown us what they think we want them to tell or show. If they disclose the truth of their experience in the research setting to anyone, it is to their closest friends, not to the experimenter. They collude with the investigator by presenting themselves to him as he requests—as determined beings. The researcher perpetuates the myth that man is unfree by describing what he observes, what his "Subjects" (Objects) show him. Researchers into human behavior and experience will be obliged, I am now convinced, to become as involved in dialogue with their "Subjects" as psychotherapists must with their "Patients," if a more valid image of man is to be obtained, an image that shows man's possibilities to transcend determiners of his condition as well as his better-known option to be the passive victim or object of determiners.

I began my practise of psychotherapy in a scientific spirit: I had been taught the view that people become "ill" in consequence of determiners, and it was my job to ascertain these determiners, comprehend them through my theory, and neutralize them by correct application of therapeutic "techniques." Gradually I came to an alternate view, as the report will disclose.

The case I shall discuss is neither extraordinary nor dramatic as cases go. However, the experience was world-changing for my patient, and the "successful" outcome of the relationship confirmed me at a time when I was myself in a process of growth. I was changing from a well-trained psychotherapeutic technician—a suave novice practitioner of therapeutic *technique*—into a person seeking to transcend technique, in expression of my commitment to help another person grow, that is, transcend *his* ways of being and behaving in the world.

My report will include:

(a) An introduction to the patient;
(b) A portrayal of my situation at the time I met him;
(c) An account of our relationship;
(d) My interpretation of what happened; with

(e) Some reflections on training for, and growth in psychotherapists.

## The Patient Briefly Introduced

Robert Smith* was homosexual. He was a smiling, baby-faced man, 28 years old, of medium height and build, well-groomed, carefully dressed to seem casual in shirt and tie, sports jacket and slacks. He was employed at a salaried position, and was simultaneously working to complete his dissertation for the doctorate from a university in another state. He was unmarried, but was going with a woman he thought he loved. She knew nothing of his homosexual background, nor of his current liaisons with men. The previous night he had been with a man, and it disgusted him. He told me he was fed up with being "queer," but couldn't get sexually involved with women. Though he had an "ideal relationship" with this girl Jane, he had never been to bed with her, nor had he petted or kissed her passionately. He said she thought of him as shy, or prudish. Their friendship up to then had been one of shared interests and values, but he knew she wanted more. If he was ever to marry, he thought Jane would be an ideal wife for him. He couldn't bring himself to reveal his homosexuality to her, but he was afraid that she would soon find out. She was a passionate woman and he didn't want to deprive her of a full sexual life. He wanted to know if he could overcome his "condition," and become "sexually normal." I agreed to explore this with him, to see what might evolve.

## The Situation of the Psychotherapist

I was carrying out a part-time private practise in psychotherapy, my main job being a teacher of courses in clinical psychology. There was neither clinic nor training program at my university, and I had to do a private practise to sustain my growth as a clinician, and unfortunately, to make a living, as my university salary was appallingly low.

---

* Of course, all details that might identify the person behind this pseudonym have been altered.

Robert Smith contacted me after I had been in practise for two years. I had begun my work with a spirit of confidence in the excellent caliber of my training, which was along neo-psychoanalytic lines. A fair description of my outlook would be to say I felt well-armed with theory, and with a repertoire of technical ways of responding that I was sure would dissolve symptoms, and permit growth to resume in stultified patients. Indeed, with some of my patients I enjoyed signal success, and I thought myself a promising therapist. Those patients whom I thought I couldn't help, and those with whom I fell into an impasse after a trial period, I would refer elsewhere. My finesse, accuracy and timing in interpreting and reflecting my patients' disclosures were all progressing nicely, I thought.

But as time unfolded, I found increasingly that my patients were not responding to the weaponry in my psychotherapeutic arsenal. I had been doing what one was expected to do at such times—I discussed difficult cases with several trusted colleagues. I examined my countertransference attitudes. I went over tape-recordings of sessions, to see what I might be concealing from myself, and to try to discern technical errors I might be committing without awareness. So near as I and my colleagues could discern, I was well-nigh faultless in my conduct of therapy. I honestly felt that it must be the "strain" of patients I was receiving. In truth, the majority of these were people who had been "rejected" by other psychotherapists in town, but some were having their first experience at psychotherapy. It was tempting for me to surmise that the unresponsive patients were all ambulatory schizophrenics, and hence inaccessible to outpatient psychotherapy.

However, I was in a bind. I needed to practise therapy for various pressing reasons, and yet I felt increasingly ineffective as a therapist. I had either to go out of practise, or learn and grow. I opted for the latter.

I began to see that, after qualifying as a psychotherapist, my way of being with patients did not so much help them grow as advertise the school in which I trained. It was as if, in sitting with a patient, my responses to him said redundantly, "I was trained at Buffalo. I was trained at Buffalo." The patients didn't give a damn about my "orientation," they wanted help. I assigned them a job—they were to relate whatever they experienced during the hour. My task was to listen, and confine my responses to reflections and interpretations that I felt were appropriate, and that would convey my acceptance and understanding, and that would foster insight in the patient. Some patients complained of my impersonality, of my "clinical manner," but I would construe these complaints as resistance, as indeed, in a way, they were. Many patients found my behavior strange and unnatural, especially those who had not received a college education, and who had never encountered psychotherapists before. For my part, I experienced the psycho-therapeutic role as a sort of monastic discipline, an ontological tightrope that one must balance upon with great care. If one permitted himself to be tempted off it by a patient's imprecations to "be more human," or jolted from it by some impulse or current of feeling, then the game would be lost. This was a curious kind of obsession, I see in retrospect, and it was accompanied by the expected compulsions and rigidity in my deportment with patients. I rigidly avoided answering questions. I eschewed any form of physical contact, like shaking hands, or holding a weeping patient's hand. My very speech, as it could be heard on a tape-recording, sounded radically different from my usual way of being with people. I sounded as if I was trying to impersonate someone—Freud perhaps, or some of my mentors. Certainly I didn't sound "natural" to myself, and I must have appeared strange to my patients, like a robot, or maybe some kind of an actor.

To be sure, I *could* answer a question if I had first reflected the feeling that it embodied, or construed the defensive implications of it to my satisfaction. But I discouraged questions. If the patient asked me anything about my experience, I would sidestep in most adept fashion. I even subtly trained my patients to be embarrassed about asking me anything about myself. I was a mirror that reflected back what was there, and sometimes even more, with my incisive interpretations. And my experience was that of a fast-thinking, analyzing computer, looking for connections, hints from the unconscious, etc. But psychotherapy, so practised, was not only increasingly ineffective, as I was finding out; it was positively exhausting. After some sessions, I would find myself with a headache, as must hypocritical sinners who have had to spend a polite hour with their minister, trying to seem righteous.

It was in this setting, or bind, that I resolved to find a way out. With great anxiety, and even more guilt, I began to permit myself to violate some of what I defined as essential rules for the conduct of therapy. I justified my deviationism by seeing myself as an explorer, a researcher whose job in a university obliged him to push back frontiers of knowledge. And so, I began to answer patients' questions. I let myself either respond to some of my own feelings, like compassion (I would hold someone's hand, or put an arm around a shoulder if the person was weeping), or to disclose my feelings when they existed, to let the patient know what I was experiencing. And I let myself *experience* in many modes: thinking and reasoning, but also fantasy, remembering, feeling. I would laugh, tell a joke, give advice, express anger or annoyance, disclose fantasies, but all within a context of seeking to help the patient discover and disclose more of his being, and to experience a relationship that was safe and illuminating. In short, I began to let myself be, experience and disclose myself as "more human" in my therapeutic encounters. I did not exclude "technical" experience or responses from repertoire, I still reflected and interpreted silently and aloud. But I did not *confine* myself to an incisively analytic mode of experience, or a scrupulously "clinical" way of behaving. I included the technical responses in a broader context of a sincere effort to be a helpful human being to another person seeking help.

I felt lonely and afraid in my venturesomeness. However, I found some comfort from the fact that Carl Whitaker and his associates were reputed to be even more "wild" than I knew myself to be in relation with patients, and Carl was a responsible chairman and Professor of a Psychiatry Department. (Later, I became better acquainted with him and his colleagues; I had also met some former patients who were bewildered by their experience in therapy with these men, but who had manifestly benefited from the treatment. Still later, I consulted with Whitaker and Tom Malone when I was in need of personal aid.)

At around this time, I came across Martin Buber's *I and Thou*. This book was as much of an illumination for me as I had earlier found Freud, when I sneakily read him during my undergraduate days at the University of Toronto. There, Freud and psychoanalysis were mentioned unexeceptionably by my professors with a sneer, or with the revulsion of a member of the League for Decency in Literature toward the books of D.H. Lawrence or Henry Miller.

And so, feeling partly like an unruly disciple (which was odd, because I had no master, and none of my mentors had told me *explicitly* to be as rigid as I had been) and partly like a bold explorer, I gradually humanized my relationships with patients. It was a revelation. I no longer had to be chronically self-conscious, in order to strip my being of unconscious "sewage," and insure that none leaked out to befoul me, my patient, or our relationship. My patients could no longer predict my responses to their disclosures. I could let myself be transparently affected by my patients, and I didn't have to talk to them in such stilted fashion, choosing my words with the care of the Delphic oracle. I dared to experience and disclose myself, and I felt that, somehow, this needn't be devastating for either my patient or myself. My patients responded with greater openness, and I felt myself confirmed. I was beginning, belatedly, to change from a priggish, impersonal technician to a transparently real person who was qualified and more important committed to helping another person grow. I saw that earlier I was committed in good faith to the ways that earned me good grades, and membership in the psychotherapeutic elite. But retrospection showed me that, when a patient was asking for help, I was offering acoustic badges and sophisticated gestures. I had been more concerned with the fidelity of my responses to my theory than with their authentic fitness as the expression of my being this person intending to help that very person potentiate himself. In short, *I* was beginning to grow.

## The Relationship Unfolded

I began seeing Robert, my new homosexual patient, three times weekly, explaining that as we progressed we would reduce the frequency of our meetings. He mentioned that he was familiar with the way therapists worked, because he had already had something like 500 hours of therapy over the past four years. He had been in analysis with a qualified psychoanalyst of some reputation for about 300 hours, had been through "non-directive counseling" with a VA psychologist, and had about 100 hours with a professor of psychology at his alma mater. I wondered what the outcome of all this experience was for him. He said that he had found each of his therapists very helpful and kind, but his homosexuality persisted in spite of their efforts to help him overcome it. However, he found the experience invaluable, because he was keenly interested in the theory of psychotherapy and his sample of therapists' technique was now quite extensive. He wondered what technique I followed. I reasoned to myself that if he had managed to slough off the effects of therapy transacted according to some technique, that I had better not add to his string of victories. I told him I had no technique, or that I didn't follow any prescribed method—which at the time was increasingly true. He said, "Oh, you follow the sincerity technique, the 'honesty bit.' I don't know if that will work." I said that I didn't know either, but that we might try meeting several times, to see what developed.

I liked him at our first meeting, in spite of the fact that I could see he was a polished ingratiator. He was terribly intellectual and "objective" about his "case," and when I pointed this out to him he mentioned that he was glad I could see this so quickly. It gave him confidence that my impressions agreed with those of his earlier therapist.

He devoted the next dozen or so meetings to narrating his life history to me, though I hadn't asked him to do so. It was as if he knew what was expected of him, and obligingly complied, like a good boy. One time he asked me if I was interested in his dreams, since I hadn't made any point about inquiring into them. I said that I was, whenever he chose to tell them to me. He promptly began outlining dream after dream, and asked me if I would care to see both his life history, and his dream file, which he then removed from his briefcase. He had prepared these documents for one of his previous therapists, the analyst. The dreams were typed on 5 x 8-inch cards, dated, classified according to theme, and with "the interpretation" typed beneath each. I declined his offer to read either the life history (a bulky typescript) or his dream cards, preferring that he tell me things himself, and narrate dreams whenever they came up in the course of our conversations. He was somewhat crestfallen at this refusal, and felt that a lot of time might be saved if he didn't have to go over the ground again. I told him there was no definite ground to go over, but that I hoped it would be possible for him to be less planful and controlled in his conversation with me. He became panicked at this, saying that he was afraid to be spontaneous. Unless he kept his feelings under tight control, he would get very sexy, as he was beginning to feel toward me. He flushed, and became silent. I asked him what he was experiencing. He said he wanted to come over to me and kiss me.

This was a crisis for me, because I had no "pat" responses to offer him, as I had hitherto, such as reflecting his feeling, or trying to interpret the hidden meanings underlying such a disclosure. I remained silent, and he asked, "Would you like me to? Would you let me?" I said, in some anxiety, for I was afraid he might "act out," "Look, Robert, I wouldn't enjoy it if you did kiss me; and let me remind you that you're supposedly seeing me to find out if you can go beyond homosexuality, and make it with women."

He was crestfallen, and at the same time relieved. He told me that he was introduced to homosexuality by an army psychiatrist whom he had met during his service overseas, not as a patient, but as a friend. Up to that time, when he was 22, he had had numerous homosexual fantasies, but no actual sexual relations with men. He liked to kiss and be kissed, and to have fellatio performed on him, but in numerous affairs he found himself attractive to men who "used" him for anal intercourse, or to perform fellatio, without really meeting his wishes in the matter. He would experience a climax during the sexual acts, but he told me that he was always revolted by the whole procedure, once his passion had died down.

I wondered about his experience with women. He said that he had been with a prostitute several times in Germany, but went only to see if he could "make it." He couldn't. He found that he would be passionate enough before penetration, but he would deflate as soon as he was about to enter. He told me that this was the theme of his experience with women: he could be attracted to them, and even pet with them up to a point. But with the several girlfriends that he had had at college, who clearly wanted him to go "all the way," he could never get over the feeling that if he entered them, it would hurt them. And he also had a feeling, an obsession, really, that intercourse with a woman was somehow dangerous. All this narration proceeded in a detached, almost clinical way. It was material he had gone over many times with his previous therapists. He wondered if I wanted him to "go over old ground" again—after all, it would be needless if only I would read his life history. I still declined to read this opus, and confined myself largely to listening to his narrative, and to my own reactions to his presence.

## II

By this time, we had met for about 20 sessions. He had disclosed himself to me as a defensive, passive, ingratiating man, highly intellectual, and somehow, very childish, in that his discussion of women reminded me of the fantasies I used to share with my chums when I was about 12 or 14 years of age, and we were very naive—we wondered if girls "liked it," did "it" hurt them, etc. At various points in our conversations, he asked me about my experiences in learning about women, he wondered whether I had ever been actively homosexual, or even passively, imaginatively homosexual. I answered his questions straightforwardly and in honesty, and discovered that he had never talked about sex, on a personal level, with anyone. Not with his parents, not with male friends, not with female friends. He knew everything there was to be read about sexuality, but he could only talk about it as a biological phenomenon, or as an act that varied cross-culturally and between social classes.

### III

My readiness to disclose some of my experiences—only those which I felt comfortable sharing with him—in the context of our increasingly open dialogue, brought something else to light. He discovered and revealed to me that he had never been able to trust or confide in *anyone*, throughout his life. His present girlfriend was the closest confidante he had ever had, but even with her, he felt it necessary to conceal much of his experience and his feelings. He came to experience himself as an actor, always on stage, with everyone including me, but much less with me than had ever before been true. He was at first dumbfounded that I answered some of the personal questions he addressed to me—therapists don"t do that! And he tried many times to inveigle me into talking about myself just because he would like to get to know me better. Whenever this happened, I was able to realize it, and point out how I thought he was evading his job of exploring and revealing his experience. He smirked every time I caught him "playing" the game of "trap the therapist." As the sessions proceeded, he evidently discovered that I meant business about wanting to be of some help to him—not necessarily in overcoming his homosexuality, but rather in helping him to discover, or re-discover his experiencing, and to be more authentic at least in his relationship with me. Frequently, in our meetings, the dialogue would be so rapid that he abandoned his usual, smiling, contrived and self-observing manner of being with me. We sometimes had arguments about matters in psychology. Sometimes, my comments about how he was presenting himself in our session, or something he had said or done in the past would evoke a response from him, of anger, or laughter, and his role of "the good patient" would evaporate, and an unself-conscious, frightened person would be revealed.

## IV

During the time we were meeting, he was continuing to see his girlfriend. He would visit her apartment, and she would spend time at his flat. Occasionally, they would spend the night together, in the same bed, hugging and kissing, but Robert always stopped short of the point where he would become impassioned. He noted that she was getting impatient with him, and moreover, was making hints from time to time about married life. He always joked these away, in talking with her, but to me he confessed that the idea frightened him and appealed to him. He reported that he was becoming much less controlled and contrived with Jane, and some his acquaintances noticed that he seemed less tense and brittle when he was with them. I noted, too, that I felt more at ease with him, and he would switch in and out of what I started to think of as "the authentic mode" during our sessions. He was more often in the authentic mode than in that of "the cool, friendly, intellectual" with me. He mentioned, too, that he had not had any homosexual experiences since he began therapy with me. His initial consultation with me came the day after he had, as he put it, "disgusted himself by letting myself be picked up by some fellow in a 'queer' bar, and going home with him." He still felt attracted to men whom he deemed handsome, and had occasional fantasies and reveries of sexual activity with these passing strangers. He told me he felt sexy toward me from time to time, both in the sessions, and between sessions, but it didn't bother him so much.

I told him I could usually note when he was in a sexual reverie, during sessions, and it didn't bother me; and moreover, I began to see that his homosexuality was not an active quest for sex so much as it was a seduction, a bid for affection from someone who was either big brotherly, or kind-fatherly.

When I told him what I thought about the meaning of his seductive self-presentation, he was startled. He hadn't thought
of it that way, but he was a frightened and lonely person, and
did not feel very manly. He found it difficult to make friends, the
more so because men he might like as friends were not homosexual, and he was afraid to cultivate personal friendships out
of the fear his homoerotic tendencies would be revealed, and
the sought-after friendship would be destroyed. He experienced
himself as a sissy and a coward.

## V

We were in about the thirtieth session at this time. He had
spoken of his earlier childhood, and of his parents, but always
in a clinical, objectified way. In the context of his discussion of
friendships, or the lack thereof, I inquired about his earlier childhood. He started to give me his by then typical narrative of his
upbringing, as if he were a psychiatrist giving a report at a staff
conference about "the patient," and I told him, "Look, Robert,
cut it out, and let me know what it was like for you." He unex-
pectedly wept for a brief interval, silently. He would look up
from between his fingers, note that I was sitting quietly, give an
embarrassed grin, or grimace, and then weep more wholeheartedly. When he finished, he said, "It was hellish," and proceeded
to portray what his life was like as he was growing up in his
parents' home. I should mention that Robert spoke without any
trace of a Southern accent, and gave the impression of a culti-
vated, cultured, well-spoken man, which indeed he was. But in
beginning to speak of his childhood, some vestiges of an accent
that I could easily place as rural Southern appeared. Robert was
a self-made man, albeit not very manly by his own standards.

He grew up as an only child on a small farm, about 15
miles from the nearest town. His mother had taught in a grade
school before marrying his father who continued to teach,
among other things, physical education. The father was something of a narcissist, a man who took considerable pride in his
physique, his strength, his appearance. I gathered from Robert's
account that empathy was not one of his father's long suits. He

admired athletic prowess and physical strength in boys, and Robert had neither as a child. His mother hated the farm where they lived, and longed for a more genteel way of life, with a man more genteel than her husband proved to be. She introduced Robert to music, art and poetry, and used him as her confidant. Robert remembered, with fury, the innumerable times his mother would sigh deeply, and say, "Oh, what a bull your father is," and, "Oh, what I have to put up with." In the small house in which they lived, Robert knew when the marital ritual was enacted. His father evidently lacked finesse as a lover, and his mother was not very responsive to him as she did her wifely duty. But the father would prove himself several nights weekly, as Robert recalled. He received the indelible impression that sexual intercourse hurt women, from his mother's frequent allusions to her lot and burden.

Robert's father regarded the boy as a loss and a disappointment. He couldn't or wouldn't play football at high school, he didn't date girls, he wasn't very wholehearted about farm chores—the father delighted in pitting his muscles against a manure pile, or a sack of feed. When Robert was in high school—a substantial bus-ride away—the father would enjoin his son to date, be a man, go out with girls, and then tell the youth about the dangers of women: "You can never tell whether they're clean. V.D. is dangerous. A girl who gets frightened will seize up on you," etc. From conversations like this, painfully embarrassing to Robert, he acquired the image of a vagina as some kind of cesspool, effulgent with plague, with a hair-trigger bear-trap at the portal. He told me that this was the first time he had ever really re-experienced his father's and mother's voice and manner and their impact on him. He was undergoing a fine abreaction, with full emotional wallop. And he naturally saw how his obsessive, only half-formulated fears of intimacy with women were related to the family nexus within which he grew up. I attributed the emergence of this fully lived memory to the fact that our relationship had evolved, by this time, to one of considerable mutual openness and trust. He saw me as interested, concerned, and committed, and I was. I saw him, and experienced him at a fantasy level, as a rather bewildered young brother of mine. I don't know whether my experience of myself as a quasi big-brother was in response to his nonverbal plea to me to be as a brother (he had never had a brother) or whether I slid into the role because it is easy for me. I rather think it was the former.

Sometime after this breakthrough, perhaps three meetings, Robert appeared in his former brittle, detached, sophisticated, smiling mode—in short, defensive.

## VI

I asked him what he was concealing. He told me it was something he had forgotten long ago, but raking up his past brought this memory to fruition. He didn't want to tell me because it was horrible, and though I accepted him as a homosexual, he was certain I would have nothing to do with him when I knew the awful truth. I said I didn't know either but I was willing to gamble if he was. He wasn't, and he spent that session in intellectual chit-chat. The next session, he appeared, grim as death, mouth clenched, actually looking no longer like a boy, but like a man. He said, "I'm going to tell you," and he proceeded to do so:

During his teens, he spent a lot of time alone on the farm. He was friendless, and did not stay around the school to take part in games, or to socialize with the boys and girls. Though his father and mother both had convinced him that sex with females was agonizingly painful for the girl and deadly dangerous for the boy, he was not without urges. He would masturbate often—sometimes two or three times a day, once seven times. I listened with interest and without comment. But masturbation was not all. "There were the animals..." and at the mention of the animals he blanched, stammered, tears came to his eyes. I sat quietly. He said, "I had relations with animals." I said, without much surprise, because I was surmising that this was what he was about to disclose, "Oh, which ones?" He then told how, over a period of about two years, beginning when he was 14, he had intercourse with just about every species of animal on the farm—with the mare, with the sheep, (not with the sow), with a turkey. As he told me this, I was imagining the scenes, trying to picture the teen-age boy in the postures that must have been called for, and trying to imagine his anguish, his passion, his self-hate. Then, in completing the list of his conquests, he mentioned that the family milch-cow was his favored partner. I asked him how he went about coitus with his bovine paramour, and he said he stood on a stool. His face, as he was recounting this story, was filled with self-loathing and guilt. I was in a mode of compassion, ready to offer him support, and approval for finding the courage to uncover a long-buried aspect of his past. Before I could say anything, the ludicrousness of the image in my mind triggered off gales of laughter in me. I tried to stifle it, and then gave way to guffaws. Robert asked if I had gone out of my mind. Finally, in response to his half-frightened, half-angry question, "What in God's name are you laughing at? It's not funny!" I said, "Forgive me, I'm not laughing at you. But here you've been telling me you're afraid to make love with a pretty, gentle, soft woman, and yet you were that close to a cow, a highly dangerous beast!" And I had to laugh again. There was something infectious about my laughing, because Robert smiled, then let out a snicker, and then laughed and laughed and laughed, and I was laughing, and the scene was of two men howling with laughter, eyes gushing tears.

## VII

I know why I laughed, and why I said that phrase, "a highly dangerous beast." One doesn't usually think of cows in those terms. I explained to Robert that when I was in my junior year in high school in Canada, schoolboys from the cities would spend summers on farms to help bring in the harvest. World War II was on, and the only people left to run farms were schoolboys and old men past the age of military service. On the farm at which I was employed—16 years of age, completely ignorant of farms and farming—an old hired man had the job of introducing me to my various chores. These included removing fresh manure from the gutter behind the cattle, attaching the milking machine to the cows' udders, and then stripping the milk from the udders after the milking machines were removed. The hired man, like many country folks, liked his joke, and especially one played on a lad from the city. One is supposed (I later learned) to approach a cow's udder for the purpose of attaching the leads from a milking machine, or for manual milking, from the left (or right—I forgot which. It doesn't matter, because this episode concerns one particular neurotic cow). The hired man said, "Sid, put the machine on Bassie (the first cow in the row)." I said, "How?" He told me, "Just go behind her, push her tail to one side, reach under, and put the leads on." I followed instructions, and as soon as I reached with one of the leads of the machine, I received a hoof in my stomach that sent me asprawl into the well-manured gutter. The hired man had his laugh, and the owner bawled him out, ordering him to instruct me properly. I was bruised and filthy, and learned a respect for the kicking powers of cattle.

Robert's agonized narrative had evoked my recollection of my sudden tumble into a stable gutter, and I laughed. My account of my farming adventure sent Robert into fresh convulsions of laughter.

## VIII

After the laughing orgy, I felt somewhat uneasy, that I had gone too far, and violated principles of therapeutic technique in a dangerous way. Our session ended amiably enough, but I discussed the episode with a colleague, and looked at it within the context of transference-countertransference dynamics, what it might mean to the patient, what it meant to me, etc. I had never reacted this way before in a psychotherapeutic session. However, I felt that my patient and I had a good relationship, and that no harm was done, no rejection was felt by him, and I knew I felt compassion and understanding for him. When Robert returned for his next session, he confirmed that he did not feel rejected. We got on to other things.

## IX

Evidently, a turning point had arrived. Robert saw me as much more human than he had ever seen me, or his previous therapists heretofore. Moreover, he saw me as a source of help that he felt free to ask for without his previous reserve, which in his then defensive and inauthentic mode of being, meant *he* wasn't really asking *me*. Rather, in asking for help, it was a case of him watching himself ask for help from someone whom he saw in a professional role who didn't mean what he said, and who wasn't the person he seemed to be. Robert said, "I'd like to ask some advice about women." It was clear he meant business. There was nothing of his previous, half-cynical, depersonalized manner about him as he asked. It appeared that things were coming to a head in his relationship with his girlfriend. He wanted to be as a man to her; he understood the origins of his previously inhibiting obsessions about the danger of sexual intercourse, and the inescapable hurt that it does the woman. He felt more passionate toward Jane, and she was obviously interested. I invited him to ask me questions, and I promised to answer them as helpfully as I could (like a big brother). He cross-examined me about a number of matters— in a man of his age and intellectual stature, it was somewhat pathetic to learn how naive he was. His questions were of the same order that one gets when one gives a talk on sex and love to freshmen in a dorm. He was embarrassed to reveal his genuine naivete—he had read many books, but somehow, what he had read did not apply to him. In our discussion, I acknowledged his embarrassment, and told him honestly that I respected his courage in asking the questions he did. He appreciated the support, but said he didn't need it anymore, he wanted information. And so it went.

## X

The next day, at 8:00 a.m., I received an urgent phone call from Robert, asking for an emergency session. We were not to meet for four days, but I told him I'd see him at 9:30 that morning. I was anxious, and afraid that some panic had overtaken him. I reached my office about 5 minutes before his knock, and he came in with a huge, smug grin on his face, and rings under his eyes. He said, "Shake my hand, Sid!" I did so. He said, "Three times I did it last night. It was marvelous, and it didn't *hurt* her."

## XI

This happened at about the time of our 40th session. We discovered we were about finished with therapy. We spent another 6 or 7 meetings trying to work through and understand what had occurred throughout our relationship. He said that my laughing, which got him laughing from the belly for the first time in his life, was very important. Much of the intellectual insight he had gotten in his psychoanalytic sessions of several years earlier took on meaning for him. He found new energy in himself. He had asked Jane to marry him, and she accepted with alacrity. He decided not to tell her of his homosexuality of the past, though she knew he was in therapy. He overcame a number of snags in his doctoral research, and proceeded to complete it. We had ended.

## XII

About six months after our formal ending of sessions, we met again, at his request. He told me how his life had been going. He looked different, more definite, less self-observant, less brittle, stronger. More like what we usually think of as a man, or perhaps what we thought of as a man. He said he got twinges of attraction toward men who caught his fancy, but no longer felt it signified his damnation and perversion. He didn't feel compelled to follow up such twinges into action. He had become friends with several men, on the basis of mutual interests, and even though he liked one fellow especially—at one time he would have explored to see if the chap would seduce him—he was not troubled with his feelings, but only acknowledged them to himself. He was delighted with Jane, and I met her at a later meeting. She seemed most pleased with him. Later, I received a wedding announcement.

## Reflections on the Experience

Robert lived in a narrow, frightening world. He had early become estranged from authentic being, I assume because he had been disconfirmed by both parents. To survive with any integrity at all, he had to conceal his impulsivity, first from his parents and other people, and then from himself. He learned to present an intellectual facade to the world. He postured his way through life. His presenting "symptom" was homosexuality, but more fundamental was his alienation from a unified experience of himself, the experience of his freedom, and from new possibilities of being. Heterosexual contact was experienced by him as dangerous and sadistic. His adolescent experiences at bestiality had proved so repulsive to him that he repressed all recollection of the events. He could ultimately only present himself as the person he chose to *seem*—a scholar, an intellectual, an aesthete, with a secret stigma, homosexuality—only by dint of keeping a distance between himself and other people. If he permitted others to come too close to him, they might see through his imposture, and recognize his stigma. If he dropped his guard, and behaved spontaneously, especially among men, he might experience uprushes of transparent, uncontrollable homoerotic feeling. Women were not to be regarded as anything but platonic companions, with whom one might discuss the finer things of life, and share an appreciation of art and music. He could not experience himself as fully a man, in the social world he inhabited, because he found himself timid, passive, and without experience of love and intimacy with women. He could not successfully rationalize his feelings of inadequacy on this account. A relationship with a woman had begun, against a context of underworld, transient homosexual promiscuity. The woman was his intellectual peer, and was evidently unfrightening to him, perhaps warmly maternal with obvious potentialities for adult passion. She saw possibilities in Robert of his becoming a husband and lover. She invited these possibilities into being. This invitation, experienced by him over a period of time, was terrifying, but tempting enough to induce him to seek yet another bout of psychotherapy. His previous encounters (or lack of encounter) with professional psychotherapists had been little more than prolonged theatrical gestures on his part—charades carried out with fellow actors, he in the role of patient, they in the role of therapist.

I said that Robert lived in a narrow, frightened world. I also had been living in a narrow, frightening world, the world of the technical psychotherapist. He was estranged from his being, and his presenting "symptom" was homosexuality. I had been estranged from my being while practising psychotherapy, and my symptoms as a therapist were rigid, technical impersonality in my presentation of self, and impoverished experience of myself—permitting myself to experience only in the mode of calculation and analytic reasoning. When Robert came to me for help, I had *begun* to free myself from this trap that I had made for myself out of my experience in training. My preceptors had not intentionally impressed this stereotype on me, but on leaving "home base," I evidently persisted in it for the protection it provided me. But it was also stifling to me.

I was able to offer Robert a relationship that for him was dramatically different from previous relationships with therapists, and more ultimately, his relationships with *anyone*. It evolved gradually into a relationship of increasing trust, such that he was able to realize the dissolution of his defenses, and the uprush of usually repressed experiencing. He felt confirmation, not only of what he had been and was, but of his tenuous gropings toward new possibilities, the gradually emerging experience of freedom. He felt safe enough to risk disclosing more of his actual being to me than he had to anyone, and he found my responses to him humanly confirming rather than clinically dissecting. I related to him as a *person*, and as it were, invited him to be as a person with me rather than as a member of the depersonalized categories "homosexual," and "patient," the embodiment of a disease process to be shown to an impersonal curer, one whose task it was to neutralize or extirpate the "pathology."

From a technical point of view, I don't believe I discovered or invented any new formula for clinical practise that can be taught in books or seminars—viz: new ways to interpret, or reflect, or advise. Instead, I believe that, in being with him as a person, I presented Robert with a variety of expressions of my commitment to be helpful. These included interpretations, reflections, advice, information, but also less technical expressions, ordinary conversation presented in a context of immediate relevance to the dialogue that was going on. By being myself freed from the necessity to restrict my being, and enact or impersonate a rigidly defined therapeutic role, I was more whole, natural, free-flowing, imaginative, inventive, and spontaneous. I attributed person-hood and freedom to him, not disease-process. The relationship became dialogue, not for its own sake, but for the sake of helping another person seek his way in the world. There were limits to the freedom I allowed myself and the patient in this dialogue, because of the purpose for which it was undertaken. But I have since come to believe that the limits of any theory, approach or technique must always be tested and even pushed (within the bounds of law, ethics, and human decency) if the needs of patient and therapist alike for growth-opportunities are to be met, and if the relationship is not to crystallize into some game, with each player "hung up" on his part.

If there is a lesson to be learned from this case, I think it is this: our training, at institutes and graduate schools, is probably necessary to wean us from previously unexamined ways of being with people, and to introduce us to ways of implementing our desire to be helpful. Listening, interpreting, reflecting, fantasy sharing, etc., all may be helpful techniques, but I suspect that many therapists find that, from their trainers, they have unwittingly absorbed a kind of orthodoxy that takes the form of restriction on their ways of being as therapists. What is called for in training institutions is encouragement and exploration of ways to *transcend* one's teaching and one's theories, as new experience is encountered in therapeutic practise. Too often, I feel, therapists evolve a repertoire of behavior that constitutes their "couch-side manner," and they will not extend themselves or involve themselves with a patient beyond this fixed repertoire. If the patient doesn't respond, they refer him to another therapist, or keep him for interminable therapy, or rather boredom and expense. This is tantamount to a pledge not to grow. Ideally, I think that after some period at active therapeutic practise, one should not be able to recognize the school or theory in which the therapist has been trained. If one can, it may mean that he has not surpassed his previous techniques, or, it may mean that he has not permitted himself to be affected by his experience with each new patient he encounters.

The theory, jargon, and technique in which a therapist has been indoctrinated can best be regarded as an *idiom* in which one person discloses his *intention* and *commitment* to be helpful to another. When a relationship in which this idiom is spoken or acted out reaches an impasse, as inevitably it will, the therapist must make a choice: either to keep uttering the same messages over and over, thereby maintaining himself in the same existential position, or dare to leap into the unknown, and respond in new ways. These new ways express his commitment to "stick" with his patient until the invitation to growth is accepted.

I have even come to suspect that authentic psychotherapists, those who have transcended their techniques and theories, represent one of the few sources in today's alienated society of championship for individual liberty. I define an authentic psychotherapist as one who commits himself to the release of possibilities in himself and in others. He is a man of goodwill and trustworthiness. It will take time for his patient to experience him as such, and he must *be* such a person in his heart, in his "being for himself." He offers his good will and his trustworthiness in the medium of a dialogue, and it naturally takes time for his patient to run out of the projections and inappropriate attributions. Ultimately, however, the patient will experience the goodwill, the trustworthiness, the confirmation, and the commitment to wholeness and fuller functioning. When this happens, then the "healing reflex," a dissolution of old ways of being and the emergence of a more integrated and authentic way to be commences in the patient. It is more helpful, even essential that the therapist not be "hung up," or at least be less hung up on stereotyped concepts of himself, therapy, disease, or of the being of his patient. If he is free to experience himself and the world in many modes, and free to respond in the therapeutic dialogue in diverse ways, with fantasy, expression of feeling, jokes, debate, instruction, interpretation, movement (why not, at some point, dance with the patient?), physical contact— his very being there with his patient, in dialogue, cannot help but evoke new possibilities of being in him. Surely a therapist should be the embodiment of more freedom and courage to be that than those who consult with him. Earlier, I said that the jargon and technique in which I was trained was a message, an idiom that proclaimed like a badge the school in which I was trained. This is not to say that jargon and technique are essentially that. They can also be the embodiment, in language, of the commitment to be of assistance in the project of personal growth. But they will only be experienced as such by a patient if that is truly what the therapist *means* by such curious ways of expressing himself. In due time, a patient will find out or experience what his therapist is "up to"—getting rich, or famous, or protecting himself, or defending the social order, no matter how the commitments are concealed. At least the patient will feel from the therapist's impact on him, whether or not the latter is *for* him, and not for some other aim.

Each institution in society has its defenders, and the defenders have access to "experts" with whom they can consult, in order to preserve the hegemony of the institution over the individual. Indeed, psychologists and psychiatrists have often served in consultative capacities to those who seek to make men more amenable to group pressure or administrative edict. This role for students and healers of men is, I believe, a betrayal and an expression of bad faith. A more suitable role for psychologists and psychiatrists is that of exploring and understanding the determiners of man's condition and action, *not* to "use" this knowledge the better to predict, control and manipulate men (i.e. reduce their freedom); and *not* to sell this knowledge of determiners to others who would invalidate and "use" men against their interests. Rather, the proper aim for psychologists, psychiatrists, and other students of the human condition is to learn of "determiners" so as to discover means of transcending them, so that man can experience more of his freedom than he presently does. To do less than this is to be in bad faith to the very people who offer themselves as "Subjects" (Objects) in human research. These people give their time and confidence and trust (when they don't dissemble during the investigation) in the assumption that the knowledge of their being they have offered will be of ultimate help to them. Instead, this knowledge is often used against them, to reduce them to manipulada in the hands of advertisers, businessmen, politicians, and others who consult psychologists and buy knowledge about man.

The psychotherapist can be the defender of individual liberty, of the right to be who one is, and to fulfill new possibilities of being. He can awaken people to the experience of freedom and to their freedom to experience. I believe that the existential-phenomenological challenge to our discipline can, if accepted, enable researchers among us to produce a more valid image of man, and psychotherapists to be more efficient healers.

## A Post-Script: On Laughing

People who consult psychotherapists are notoriously lacking in a sense of humor, and if my sample of experience with my colleagues is at all representative (it probably isn't), I would say that therapists seldom laugh with their patients. This is a pity, because I suspect that laughter can heal. Indeed, the ability to see the humor in situations betokens man's transcendent capacities. At one time, if I found something funny in a psychotherapy session, I would have scrutinized myself thoroughly, in order to analyze it away, the better to maintain myself in the neutral therapist mien. It is quite liberating to feel one can laugh in therapy, when there is something to laugh at, and someone to laugh with. ✦

# II-3 Growing Personality, Not "Adjustment," Is the Goal in Counseling and Psychotherapy*

People seek the help of a psychotherapist when their lives have reached an impasse. The symptoms of the impasse are diverse, including physical suffering, inability to concentrate, anxiety, depression, boredom or guilt, inability to love another or to make love, loneliness, obsessions, antisocial behavior—the entire gamut of psychopathology as we know it.

Diverse though the symptoms of misery might be, they share one feature. They are the inexorable outcome of "adjusting" to a way of life, a way of existing and behaving in the world, which an informed common sense would tell us *must* lead to a breakdown, to a "checking out" or a refusal to carry on further in that way. We know now that the elaborate schemes for classifying "symptoms" of mental "illness" into neat categories is unprofitable for would-be helpers of others. When we label someone "a schizophrenic" or "a neurotic," we lull ourselves into thinking that we understand him before we actually do. The impasses in existence are only superficially described as illness, a term which at best is a metaphor, not an explanation. We spent centuries regarding people who "don't fit," whose behavior we could neither understand nor accept as "evil," as "possessed by demons." It was indeed an advance toward greater compassion among men when the illness-metaphor was applied to the people who would not play the game of social existence as it was "supposed" to be played. But not all who, though physically intact, cannot play the game are sick. Per-

*The bibliographic notations in this chapter refer to the complete bibliography from Disclosing Man to Himself, which can be found in Chapter V-1.*

haps none are. As Szasz[100] has graphically stated it, "mental illness" is a myth, one that had an historical purpose, but which no longer helps man regard and treat deviants as his brothers. Now, the persistent belief that people who "check out" are "mentally ill" and need to be "cured" of their disease symptoms beclouds understanding. Indeed, the belief that one's "patient" or "client" or "counselee" is an exemplar of some category of disapproved humanity—viz.: schizophrenic, delinquent, neurotic, etc.—leads the would-be helper to treat him as less than a full human being, less than a fellow traveler through this life. Anyone who has been treated by another, not as the very one he is but as the embodiment of some category—a Negro, a Jew, a professor, a psychotic—knows that *he* is not being addressed by the person who so regards him. If I am regarded as "a patient" by "the doctor," and neither he nor I ever become acquainted with one another, we are doubtless both cheated; and it is questionable whether any enduring help can come out of so impersonal a transaction.

It is more apt to regard the one in need of help as a *fellow seeker*. He seeks relief from his suffering, to be sure, and more fundamentally (whether or not he can verbalize the ultimate goal of his quest), he is seeking a way to be in the world, a way to live with others, and a way of being for himself that is meaningful and rewarding; a way that produces satisfactions, hope, and meaning in expanding experience rather than pain, misery, stultification, and impotence. These latter outcomes are *cries for help*. They are, as well, proof that the seeker's way of life up to the point of breakdown was not compatible with wellness. It seems futile for a physician, psychotherapist, or "growth counselor" to "treat" a symptom by anesthetizing the person with assorted drugs, or by reducing him in some way, and then to send him back to the very way of life that was inimical to truly human being. What is called for in addition to cure is to help the seeker find some way that will permit him to function more fully, more authentically, with a more liberating focus to his existence. The counselor must aim to seek *with* his client and persist in the search until they jointly *discover* what changes in the client's self and world will permit him to live a life compatible with wellness. The helper, if he is to be more than a "first-aid technician," must grope with his client, to find healthy personality for him: that is, *a healthy way of being a person in the world* (the literal meaning of "personality").

## What Is Healthy Personality?

Healthy personality is growing personality. It is a way for a person to function in his world, a way that yields growth without placing other important values in jeopardy.[39] People commit themselves to a repertoire of values; they live *for* them. One who is a healthy personality seeks to fulfill them, and he defends them when they are under threat. A healthy personality is to himself as a dedicated farmer is to his farm—he does everything in its time. The abundance of the crops, the state of his livestock, and the condition of his outbuildings are testimony to the farmer's alert and responsive care. The healthy personality likewise shows evidence, in his very being and presence, of his alert and responsive care for himself. He finds his life meaningful, with satisfactions and some accepted suffering; he loves and is loved; he can fulfill reasonable social demands upon him. And he is in no doubt as to who he is, what his feelings and convictions are. He does not apologize for being the very person he is. He can look out on the world and see it from the standpoint of how it presently *is* (according to social consensus); but he can also see himself, the world, and the people in it from the standpoint of *possibility*. He can regard the world as a place in which he can bring into being some possibilities that exist only in his imagination. The world, the other person, and himself—none of these are seen by a healthy personality as sclerosed, frozen, finished, or defined once for all.

Such a person has free access to a dimension of human being much neglected by the "square," the hyper-conformist, the modal personality. I am referring here to something that has been called "the unconscious," "experiencing,"[24,25] "transcendental experiences," "mystic experience." This hidden dimension of the self, sought for centuries by men who have longed for personal fulfillment beyond rationalism, is usually dreaded by the average person. It could be called "experiencing *possibility*." It sometimes "peeps out" when one permits himself to be unfocused and aimless, unintegrated, not going anywhere or doing anything; but it is "tamped back" in anxious haste, for it is experienced like the contents of Pandora's box. When his unconscious threatens to speak, when direct experience of self or world invades his consciousness, he becomes overwhelmed with anxiety and may temporarily feel he is losing his mind and sanity. Indeed, he is on the point of "going out of his ego." His present self-concept and concepts of things and people are shattered by implosions and explosions of raw experience from within and without. He experiences his being in dimensions presently unfamiliar to him, hence frightening. But a healthier personality recognizes that his unconscious, this persistent but usually drowned out "dream," this source of new truth, is the voice of his true, real self—a statement of how he has mistreated himself (if the message is dysphoric) or an invitation to new possibilities of being for which he has become sufficiently grown and secretly, unconsciously prepared.

Wise men have always known that when the unconscious speaks, when fresh, transconceptual experience reaches awareness, it is better to pay attention. The breakdowns or check-outs that we have referred to are final outcomes of not listening. The symptoms and suffering are but the voice of the real self, the voice of human being protesting in a voice so loud it can no longer be neglected. Before the breakdown, the voice murmured softly from time to time; but its murmurings were in a code, a forgotten language[23] that could not be understood. And so the person persisted in the ways of behaving, the ways of construing himself and other people, that had become increasingly good neither for his own growth nor for his well-being. The healthier personality listens to his boredom, his anxiety, his dreams and fantasies and gropes for changes in ways

of meeting the world that will permit greater realization of potential self.

Indeed, the healthier personality transcends the contradiction between conscious and unconscious, between being
fully focused and grandly unfocused—he can oscillate between
the extremes and push them further than the less healthy individual. When he focuses, he is fully focused; and when he "lets
go," he really lets go. Healthy personality is manifested by a
mode of being that we can call *authenticity*, or more simply,
honesty. Less healthy personalities, people who function less
than fully, who suffer recurrent breakdowns or chronic impasses,
may usually be found to be *liars*. They say things they do not
mean. Their disclosures have been chosen more for cosmetic
value than for truth. The consequence of a lifetime of lying about
oneself to others, of saying and doing things for their sound
and appearance, is that ultimately the person loses contact with
his real self.

The authentic being manifested by healthier personalities
takes the form of unself-conscious disclosure of self in words,
decisions, and actions. It is a risky way of being, especially in a
social setting that punishes all forms of action and disclosure
that depart from some current stereotype of the ideal or acceptable man. The healthier person will doubtless experience
many a bruise for being and disclosing who he is, but he prefers to accept these blows rather than lose himself or sell himself (his authentic being) for short-run acceptability.

Indeed, there is much reason to suspect that authenticity
before others is the same mode of being that permits a man to
have access to the underground realm of experiencing, the
unconscious. Defensiveness and concealment of self before
others unfortunately are the same modes of being that screen
off a man's unconscious, his preverbal experiencing from himself. The currents of feeling, fantasy, memory, and wish that
would get a man criticism from others also produce anxiety in
himself; so he blocks these from the view of self and others in

the service of self-defense. In time, he succeeds in fooling him-self as much as others into believing he *is* the man he is so expertly *seeming* to be. In truth he is an "invisible man." What-ever is authentic of him, whatever is most spontaneous and alive (his experience of his possibilities), is buried so deep not even he can cognize it. One of the reasons less healthy person-alities are so self-conscious, so deliberate in their choice of word and action before others, is that they dread letting something slip out that truly expresses their being, something which will get them into trouble. They are, as it were, idolaters of the state of artificial grace known as "staying out of trouble." In fact, they have sold their souls and possibilities for a good, but false name.

All this is not to say that healthier personalities are always fully visible, fully transparent, before the gaze of self and oth-ers. Such chronic self-revelation may be itself idolatrous, and is suicidal in certain circumstances. Certainly we would expect a healthier personality to have enough common sense, judg-ment, even cunning, to preserve himself in a hostile environ-ment, dropping his guard only when he is among trusted and loving friends. And, in fact, a healthy personality will have been able to enter into and maintain relationships of trust and love with one or more people, people whom he has let know him and whom he knows and responds to.

Another dimension of healthy personality concerns the realm of values itself. Healthier personalities seek and find meaningful values and challenges in life, such that there is an element of direction, of focus, to their existence.[21] Less healthy personalities, estranged as they are from their real selves, usu-ally pursue only clichéd goals and values current in their present social milieu. These latter goals frequently do not challenge or inspire the average person to the fullest integration and ex-pression of his unique being; they do not "turn him on" or keep him going. The upshot is that he will often feel trapped or, worse, feel that he is "losing his mind." The latter fear is most likely to occur when a person looking at the externals of his present situ-ation finds that he has accomplished or has been given "everything to make a man happy"—but that he, in honesty, is miserable, bored, and doesn't know what to do next. He has "loved ones," a family, material success, a nice house, car, and so on; but he finds his work increasingly boring, more like a treadmill, and his relationships with others empty, formal, and all too predictable; and he entertains fantasies of murdering his loved ones, chucking it all, and going to the South Seas, only to repress these ideas with the anxious thought, "I must be insane to harbor such notions." He might scurry into further "busy-work," commence drinking to excess, create excitement by treading along primrose paths at great risk, or do other searching in the outer world for some new meanings. He looks in the wrong place, the right place being within his own experience. The healthier personality, less estranged and less afraid of his real self, can look within and without and create or find new sources of value, new directions of commitment, even when these elicit some criticism from others in his world. He is freer to invest value in more aspects of the world than his less healthy counterpart.

A healthy personality lives in and with his body, he is an "embodied self."[54] He is not afraid or ashamed to touch his own body or the bodies of other people with whom he is on intimate terms. He is able freely to move his body, which has a look of grace, coordination, and relaxation. "He dances through life," to state this idea in its most extreme but essentially accurate form. By contrast, the less healthy personality is afraid to live in his body. He represses his bodily experiencing and feels his body alternately numb and dead or as a dangerous and stinking cesspool charged with explosive nitroglycerin. He must take care lest an urge, a feeling, an impulse, or a movement break through the tight control. For him, this would be disastrous. One of the most common evidences of disembodiment is muscular tension that reveals itself as stiffness in body posture, awkwardness in gait, the mouth a thin red line, the jaws clenched, and the face an immobile mask, frozen in false smile or anxious frown or counterfeit dignity; the voice emits sounds that are jerky, pressured, constricted. Touch such an average person on the arm or place one's arm around his shoulder, and he will instantly stiffen, experience panic, jump as if stabbed, and perhaps experience a mixture of sexual arousal and guilt or anxiety. The healthier person has a more fully lived and experienced body.[65, 77, 78] His face is mobile and expressive; he speaks in a voice that is free, not one which is fighting off an impulse to say something else at the same moment that the present speech is being emitted. It is no accident that average people receive psychotherapeutic benefit from instruction in vocalization or freely expressive dance and from massage and other forms of direct experience with their bodies. Indeed, the therapists of the future will without doubt be obliged to learn to live gracefully with their own bodies and to learn ways of inviting their clients to get back into theirs.

An important part of bodily experience is sex, the erotic impulse and feeling. Perhaps our puritanical avoidance of body-contact in everyday life expresses our mixed attitudes toward sexuality. A healthier personality is able to experience his erotic feelings without fear; and he is able to express them in a relationship with a chosen partner without needless inhibition, as part of the sexual dialogue. The less healthy person is usually so self-conscious that he cannot "let sexuality happen" in his attempts at loving transaction, and so he tries to force matters. The result may be premature climax, impotence, frigidity, inability to know and to attune oneself to the sexual being of the partner, and so on. Likely, the beginning at a cure of liberation from sexual difficulties is made outside the bedroom, but inside the self.

We alluded above to the ability of healthier personalities to find and maintain relationships of love and friendships in the world. This ability insures that a healthier person will have access to relief from the existential loneliness in which we all live. It will be noted that I used the term "relief." Loneliness is not a disease of which one can be cured; it is instead an inescapable fact of human existence. Less healthy personalities, cut off as they are from the fount of their real selves, find *them-*

*selves* terrible company. They cannot long tolerate solitude, and they run willy-nilly into busy-work, or superficial companionship with others. They do not, however, truly encounter another person and enter into dialogue with him. Hence, the feeling of loneliness, of not being known and understood, chronically nags at them like a boil on the buttocks or a stone in the shoe. The healthier personality, because he is less self-concealing and has readier access to his own fantasy, feelings, and memories, is less afraid of solitude when that is his lot; and when he is with others, he can feel secure enough in his own worth that he can let encounter and dialogue happen. During the process of such dialogue, the shell which encapsulates him as a separate, isolated being ruptures; and his inner world expands to include the received world of experience of the other. When the dialogue ends, he has experienced himself in the new dimensions evoked by the other person, and he has learned of the personal world of another—thus he is enlarged and changed. The less healthy personality defends himself against being so affected and changed in his contacts with others. He "rubs shells," or clinks his character armor against that of the other person, but does not meet the other. There is no encounter.

Just as a healthy personality dares to let himself be the one he is, so does he respect, even cherish and defend, the "suchness," the idiosyncrasy, of the other person in his world. He eschews sneaky efforts to manipulate the feelings, thoughts, and actions of the other; hence he truly experiences the other person as *an other*, as a source of being, different in some respects from himself and similar to him in other ways. The less healthy person dares neither to let himself be, nor to trust the being of the other when he is not trying to control that being. In his transactions, he seeks always to influence the other, if in no other modality than in the way in which he will be *seen* and experienced by the other. In the extreme instances of unhealthy personality, the individual actually (this can only be stated metaphorically) detaches his ego from his body and functions as a spectator and manipulator of his own depersonalized body as "it" transacts with the other person. This depersonalized body is then manipulated before the other, in the hope that the other's experience of and responses toward this counterfeit person can thus be controlled: robots performing before others who are perceived as robots.[54] ✦

[1968]

# II-4 *Somatic Disclosure and Perception of the Soma*

If Laing and Lowen are correct, the average man in the West is not "in" his body. If not in his body, then *where* is he? And *who* is he? To be embodied is to experience one's body as the center of one's existence, to feel alive, to perceive the state of one's body as it changes from pleasure to pain, from energy to fatigue, from vitality and excitement to calm and tranquility. More typically, people repress body-experience and find themselves anesthetic to their bodily states, and not "in" what they are doing. The average state of being, according to this view, is schizoid. This psychiatric jargon means, simply, pretending to be someone, some body whom one *is not*. The schizoid person knows that he is not the way he is trying to appear. He lives a life of pretence and duplicity, which is one interpersonal dimension of unembodiment. For politicians and businessmen, the impersonation of sincerity and altruism, in order to seduce the voter and customer, is the norm.

I would like now to explore some further dimensions of unembodiment, both interpersonal and intrapersonal. One way to unembody oneself is to pretend to be somebody else. In so doing, one is not "in" his acts, or his body. This pretence is abetted if one can obliterate the experience of his own bodily being. Such obliteration, so near as we know, is carried out through acts of repression of unwelcome bodily experience, e.g., sexuality, pleasure, minor pain. This is the intrapersonal dimension of unembodiment.

A person will repress any dimensions of his experience which terrify him, or which have led to unbearable pain and anguish. Thus, there is considerable evidence that children are trained to repress the experience of pleasure in their bodies by being punished with blows, censure, or withdrawal of love when they are seen masturbating. Better to functionally amputate the genitalia than to undergo the horror of living with parents who cannot love a sexual child.

If a person chronically represses the experience of his body, or some dimensions of bodily experience, such repression must manifest itself in some way. It does. Subjectively, repression of bodily experience is experienced as no experience, as a hole in one's experience of being. Objectively, repression of experience manifests itself as character structure, or muscular armor—a peculiar configuration of muscular tonus and flaccidity, which results in a person's characteristic bodily posture, gait, style of movement, and which imposes profound effects upon automatic and autonomic functions of the body, such as breathing, elimination, circulation and rest. The late Wilhelm Reich was adept at looking at a naked body, and reading from it what impulses a person was repressing, what kinds of conflicts the person likely had with parents, and the like. Alexander Lowen is likewise very skilled in this art of "reading" the disclosure of the body—somatic disclosure. There is no magic in this. If a person has been obliged to live a dutiful, unpleasurable life, and dares not experience, much less express his rage and resentment, then he must hold the rage in. One need only clench one's teeth, tighten the neck muscles, shoulders, arms, pinch in one's buttocks and in general be "up tight," and then try to smile, and hold that posture to empathize with someone who chronically is in this way. Not to notice phenomena like this is to be blind and deaf to somatic disclosure.

Another way in which unembodiment manifests itself is in the impact that an unembodied person has upon the consciousness and the body of another person. As I point out later, there may be reason to suspect that bodies communicate directly with bodies, without much direct cortical, or perceptual mediation. A person who has repressed much of his sense of vitality, then, might inhibit the vitality of another person who, before the encounter, felt "full of beans and juices," very much alive. On making contact with the unembodied one, he notices himself feeling diminished in vitality and zest for life. I once had a colleague who affected me in this way. I would arrive in the morning at my desk full of plans and projects, literally dancing with excitement. The colleague would simply appear in my room to discuss his work for the day, and I would notice my zest oozing away, the sense of value that my projects held for me evaporating and losing meaning. This man affected me as an evil witch must have affected her victims. In fact, I became so fascinated with this man's effect on me that I began to observe my bodily states whenever I was involved in conversation or shared activity with all kinds of people. I noted that, when I was with my favorite people, I burst with vitality, I laughed, my life and actions had meaning and worth. When I was with certain others, my sense of life would hemorrhage, leaving me drained, flaccid, and empty. If the favored other was a woman, I would feel erotic and turned on—not necessarily in a sexually excited way; just aware of a certain electric polarity between us. I began to feel that, if the woman and I did not have this spark, there was something wrong with *her*, that her words and her body might disclose contrasting messages: an arrogant thought, and one likely to infuriate my woman's liberation friends, but that was what I thought. I believe we have enough technology available for a physiologist to take various measurements of activation from a person, using GSR, EEG, pulse and blood pressure measurements, etc., in order to record the enlivening-calming-deadening effects of one person upon another, below the threshold of immediate awareness. We need, of course, to record and describe the means, the "language," and the somatic disclosure patterns that produce these effects.

The discipline known as kinesiology likewise enables a person to "read" bodies through characteristic gestures and postures. Thus, Birdwhistell has been able to demonstrate how people's bodily postures may contradict their words. A person may say, "I'm open to your suggestions," the while holding their bodies "closed," with arms folded, legs crossed, buttocks pinched—nothing could budge such a person from his pledge to sameness. They may not be aware of what their body is saying. A person who is unembodied through such acts of chronic repression and suppression thus, literally, tries to be no body, or some body other than what he takes his body to be. If he loses track totally of what his body actually is, then truly we can say he is estranged, his body has become "Other" to his self. His self is unembodied, his body is dehumanized, depersonalized. He experiences himself as being a spirit, a consciousness trapped in a machine or a pile of meat which is *not him.*

This unembodied way of being is not peculiar to psychiatric cases, but has rather become the norm, a kind of normalized madness. Being in the world in a chronically armored and yet unembodied way seems to make it possible for people to endure the boredom, stress and violence of conventional, status-quo-maintaining life styles. If such functional amputation of the body is not successful, and the person still feels the feared vitality, or the unwelcome pain and boredom of conventional life, then he may anesthetize his body with alcohol, or various sedative types of drugs. A part of the entire pharmaceutic industry as well as the food-producing industry (since alcohol is a kind of food) is thus devoted to the amputation of the body from the person. Most peculiar! One seldom thinks of the drug and food industries as counter-revolutionary agencies which foster conformity to the economic and political status quo.

The way in which a person thinks about, and fantasizes his body is another way in which unembodiment, or peculiar ways of being embodied may be revealed. Seymour Fisher and Sidney Cleveland, in a brilliant series of researches with the Rorschach test, were able to show that persons who saw things in the blots that had shells, walls, or definite boundaries, differed from persons who saw objects with blurry or shattered boundaries in styles of behaviour and sickness. Thus, patients with cancer of internal organs had higher "penetration of boundary" scores than persons with skin cancers, and lower "barrier" scores. Fisher and Cleveland propose that the responses to the ink-blot test reveal the way in which a person unconsciously imagines his body to be. However warranted their hypothesis, it does appear that what a person *believes* to be the case about his body becomes a self-fulfilling prophesy. It further appears that we have been grossly unimaginative in our ways of thinking and theorizing about the body. The way of the physician and anatomist and physiologist, who sees the body only from the outside, has become the way in which school children and finally adults experience their bodies. We do not yet have a phenomenological anatomy and physiology which would reveal to us how our body is from the living inside.

A physician and one's own mother can take over the function of detecting one's bodily states, and estimating one's strengths and weaknesses. The child who is told that he is weak, or hungry, or sleepy by his loving, overprotective mother, may lose the ability to construe his bodily states and possibilities. Consequently, he may eat when his mother says he is hungry, and not be allowed to stop eating until that human gauge of his capacity, his mother, says, "You have eaten enough." Such a child may become very fat indeed, if his mother's estimates of his food needs do not coincide with what his body actually needs.

If one underestimates the capacity of one's body to endure stress and hardship, one may sicken, die, or be killed long before it becomes an inexorable, physiological necessity. The "Outward Bound" training teaches young people that they can endure and survive well beyond the limits they had been taught to believe were inflexible. Sir Ernest Shackleton kept his men alive on the open boat ride across the Antarctic waters because he refused to accept the fact they would die.

In short, one's body is very plastic indeed—it does what one expects or demands of it. One should be careful what one expects of one's body, because that, likely, is what one will get from it. Clearly, the Olympic records of endurance and speed, which change annually, show that we seldom expect enough of our bodies, but instead, overestimate their fragility and weakness. Actually, our potential toughness has yet to be put to the ultimate test.

Let me explore more fully this notion of a person's beliefs and expectations relating to his body. If a person believes with utter certainty that he is going to die—for example, if he learns he has "terminal and inoperable cancer," or a fatal heart condition—then he is likely to imagine himself dead, thereby hastening the advent of his physical demise. "Spiritual" death, or imagined non-existence, become prophesies to which the organs and cells of the body respond. There is no way of estimating how many people die, as it were, through being hypnotized by words or symbols that signify, "Your life is finished." I have even argued that cultural expectations about the right age to die function in the same way, almost as hypnotic suggestions or invitations to die; when a person reaches, say, 80 or 95 years of age, there is nothing for him to do, and he is expected to view each day as likely to be his last, thereby hastening his demise. If he remained involved with the pleasures and challenges of life, then death would take him by surprise. Kazantzakis tells of the nonagenarian who would goose and fondle young girls at the village well. When asked, "Grandfather, tell us of life," he replied, "It is a glass of cool water." "Are you still thirsty, then?" "Of course," said the old man, "I want to drink to bursting."

A Nobel prize awaits the scientist who is able to show how inspirited states of being—being engaged in meaningful tasks and projects—are reflected in bodily states such that immunity mechanisms are most efficient, and the nuclei of cells do *not* release cancerous growth, and the mechanisms of wound-healing and recovery from fatigue are most rapid and efficient.

Doctors may not be one's best friend. We know of a person who began to have "epileptic" seizures some years ago. They were intense, grand-mal convulsions, such that the man often broke his hands as he thrashed about during the period of unconsciousness. Over a period of years, the medications given him to control the seizures lost their effectiveness for him, and, moreover, exacerbated his blood pressure elevation, and threatened his kidneys. It appeared he was going to die from kidney failure, or from circulatory failure consequent upon his blood pressure.

A colleague and I, through correspondence, undertook to train this man to recognize his seizure—"auras," and to engage in actions that might abort them. We were able to help the man drastically to reduce the frequency of his losses of consciousness with convulsions, and to all but eliminate his need for sedating, anti-convulsant medications. Our hypothesis was that, once the man had his first seizure, and showed the characteristic "spikes" on his EEG tracing, that he became the subject of an hypnotic, brain-washing onslaught of suggestion, as follows: "Why, you lost consciousness and had a seizure. You are a sufferer from epilepsy. Never mind, there is no shame connected with this. Julius Caesar was an epileptic, Shakespeare and Jesus probably were, and of course Dostoyevsky was. But you are lucky. Advances in medical science have made it possible for us to control seizures with some powerful drugs, if you will trust us, and put yourself in our hands. Of course, you may feel a bit sleepy, and your gums may get puffy, but if you are careful to take your medicine regularly, you can live a normal life." It is difficult to resist such a powerful, even seductive invitation to view oneself as helpless, with no power within one's body to prevent the loss of consciousness and the seizure; in short, to become dependent upon drugs, to become passive in order to let outside agencies control bodily happenings. There is reason to suspect that many people deemed "epileptic" are leading drugged lives, rather than being helped to find ways of mobilizing the strength of their bodies and their wits in order to stay conscious and non-convulsing.

There is another aspect of unembodiment that fascinates me, and that is the notion that one's entire body functions like a canary in a coal mine. Before modern detection devices were invented, miners would take a canary into the mine. If the air was not fit for breathing, the canary would cease singing, and would die before the atmosphere became totally lethal for humans. A number of lines of observation suggest that a person responds bodily to other persons, to landscapes and scenes, such that if he can perceive variations in the state of his bodily being, he can detect when the situation enhances his life, and when it diminishes his sense of zest and vitality. R. D. Laing speaks of the "fantasy" mode of experiencing the world which, typically, is not available to the reflective consciousness but which can be tuned in on if one seeks to. Thus, a person may say, after a transaction with somebody, "I feel full, or empty, or drained, or sucked dry, or shafted, stabbed in the back, strangled, etc., etc." These statements are metaphoric and analogical, but they express something real that was going on., Perhaps the kinesiologist or an ethologist could point to the somatic disclosure that was responsible for these effects. Rather than view fantasy as "the unconscious" of which Freud spoke, I prefer to view the fantasy mode of experiencing as a special kind of perception—using one's body as a canary. Jordan Scher uses the term "vivacious perception" with a similar meaning. He speaks of "life to life communication," referring to the measurable reaction of philodendron leaves when a scientist, Cleve Backster, even thought of setting fire to them. Scher has gathered considerable evidence showing that the fantasy mode of perceiving, or "vivacious" perception is available to children and "primitive" people, and mostly lost in socialized adults. The ability of a child to tell which of the smiling adults do not like him; the ability of a so-called schizophrenic to discern when his therapist is irritated with him, the while trying to seem like a friendly and compassionate healer; the "physiognomic" perception of artists who paint a mountain as huge, ominous; or children who depict a body part as unusually large or small are phenomena related to, but not identical with vivacious perception. In fact, I propose that we use the term, *somatic perception* to subsume what Freud called "the unconscious," Laing calls "fantasy," Werner called Physiognomic" perception, and Scher calls "vivacious perception." The hippies speak, in this connection, of "vibrations." It is fascinating to think that one's body vibrates at various rates and amplitudes; research must develop further in this area. It is probably such somatic perception which enables the African Bushman to sense the approach of animals at a great distance, or who know where water is by consulting the feel of their bodies rather than the sight of the land. Socialization that results in unembodiment annihilates our capacity for "seeing," or testing the world with our bodies. When we repress the experience of our bodies, we not only reduce our experience of being alive, but, in order to protect ourselves from threatening pleasure and pain, we actually create circumstances by which we become stupid, that is, uninformed, in a peculiar, somatic way. We do not know when our daily regimen, our diet, our repressed or inhibited ways of interacting with others, our pattern of rest and exercise, are good for us or destructive. We lose the ability to tell when we like or hate someone. Oddly enough, the destruction of our capacity to perceive somatically probably explains why the James-Lange theory of emotion lost vogue. According to William James and the Danish physiologist Lange, one sees the bear, runs, and then becomes afraid, rather than see the bear, decide it is dangerous, become afraid, and then run. If one is in tune with his body, his body "sees" before, or different from what his eyes see. One tells what he is perceiving, somatically, by the act of reflection—in this instance, receiving the disclosure of his body to his reflective awareness.

Thus far, I have asserted that conventional upbringing in the Western world typically results in unembodiment in the majority of persons so socialized. This unembodiment manifests itself in inter-personal duplicity (play-acting, pretence, role-playing, pseudo-self-disclosure) and in a loss of sensitive awareness of one's own bodily being. I have suggested that unembodiment is the outcome of the repression of the early experiences of pleasure and pain that young children undergo in the process of growing up, and that such repression produces a loss of a very important dimension of consciousness I call *somatic perception*. Somatic perception refers to a person's awareness of the response of his body to the situation in which he finds himself. One perceives the world somatically by "tuning in" on one's bodily states as one goes through life situations. Thus, one's eyes see a person smiling; one's ears hear the person say "I love you," yet the person who sees and hears feels tense and on guard. Somatically, the person is perceiving that all is not well, more information is called for before a less defensive posture will be taken. I will argue that loss of the capacity for somatic perception—perception with, and of the body—is a factor in the self-induction of physical and psychological breakdown. If a person cannot discern how his relationships with others, and his physical regimen are affecting him as an embodied being, then he will continue living lethal or pathological life-styles. He will be anesthetic to the pain and dispiritation which are being generated, which would call upon the person to change what he is doing in some life-and health-saving way. Consequently, the unembodied person behaves his way into situations of stress and entrapment so overpowering, that physical and psychological collapse are the only ways out. Medical care which does not seek to re-embody a person, and sensitize his somatic perception is, at best, only first aid. Any sedating or tranquilizing medical care which further destroys the capacity for somatic perception is ultimately a menace to health, according to this perspective.

If it is true that conventional socialization results in unembodiment in varying degrees, then the salutary functions of certain disciplines and techniques become understandable. I wish briefly to discuss Yoga, massage, dieting and fasting, Rolfing, Gestalt therapy, at least to call attention to some of the features they share in common.

## Some Techniques for Re-Embodiment: Restoring Somatic Perception

Unembodied people live lives of impersonation and charade. They pretend to be who they are not. They maintain the charade by lies to others, and by repression of their awareness of their own bodies and bodily states. By being anesthetic and uncognizant of what is going on with themselves, unembodied people become somatically "blind," and do not "see" how others affect them as vital beings, nor how their own way of life is stressing or dispiriting them. Consequently, they sicken themselves.

The first, and most fundamental healing act is to stop doing and being in the sickening ways. Thus, doing nothing is the primitive act of healing, since it enables a stressed, decompensating organism to become recentered. But Western man finds it difficult to do nothing, and so he usually consults Western-trained physicians to "do something" to heal him so he can return to the sickening way of life. The physician obliges by "doing" with drugs, or by undertaking surgery, both of which practices may so disrupt a person's somatic integrity that he is thereby sickened for the rest of his life with an iatrogenic disease. There is today, an epidemic of drug side-effect diseases.

Increasing numbers of people in the West have begun experimenting with healing techniques originating in Eastern philosophies and religions. All these techniques share one common feature; they entail an abrupt cessation of destructive, anesthesia-producing life styles, and they enliven consciousness in general, and somatic perception in particular. I will discuss each, briefly, in turn.

### Gestalt Therapy

This discipline, created by the late Fritz Perls out of psychoanalysis, phenomenology, existentialism, Zen and Yoga philosophies, involves techniques which invite a person to stop thinking, remembering, imagining, and in other ways "distancing" himself from the perceptual here and now. The person is asked to *perceive*, to receive the disclosure *of* those parts of the world that are most salient to him right now, including perception of what his body is doing and feeling. I have not, myself, been "treated" by Fritz Perls, nor have I been in any of his demonstration workshops, but I have read his writings, and know many people who have changed their ways of life consequent upon experience with a Gestalt therapist. The heightened awareness of the body that Gestalt training produces is, certainly, one of the healing features of this discipline. The person who is helped in and through Gestalt therapy increases the sensitivity of his somatic perception.

### Fasting, and Special Diets

I have tried fasts of varying lengths (five days was the longest), and I have been on a 21-day brown rice and wine diet (my approximation to a macrobiotic purification ritual) and I can report that the stopping of my usual eating and drinking patterns did help me to become more aware of the state of my body, and also heightened my sensory awareness in general. After several days of not eating as I usually did, I became not only more sensitive to the way my body felt, but I also saw, heard, tasted, smelled and felt everything more keenly. It is a worthwhile hypothesis to propose that with decrements in the sensitivity of somatic perception go decrements in sensitivity of vision, hearing, taste, and the other sense modalities. In short, when we repress the capacity for somatic perception, we diminish our capacity for perceptual consciousness in all sensory channels.

### Marijuana, LSD, and Peyote

I have experienced the effects of each of these drugs, and I can report that in each case, they disengage me from my usual ways of being conscious (and unconscious) of my body and my world; and of course, the drugs appear to "open" me up to perceive dimensions of my body-experience and the experience of the world that ordinarily, I ignore, or relegate to the background of my experience. While "stoned" on marijuana, for example, I feel my body from the inside, as it were, and as whole. On becoming unintoxicated, my somatic perception reverts to its (for me) customary diminuendo quality, as I go back to my usual structures of consciousness.

### Hatha Yoga

I practice a repertoire of Hatha Yoga asanas with some regularity, together with slow, deep, regulated breathing. This experience has taught me a great deal about somatic perception, and about muscular armor. In fact, I realized, on trying initially to enter any of the asanas, that there is no *a priori* reason for a person not to be able to bend and twist his body in any of the myriad positions that have been described. Young children have very little difficulty entering even some of the more peculiar postures, whereas adults have to go through prolonged practice to make it. The reason lies in the fact that we all become overspecialized neuromuscular systems, overadapted to the diet, and daily regimen which we live. Our bodies express this overadaptation with chronic patterns of muscular tone and relaxation. To enter a Yoga posture calls for a "letting go" of some chronic way to be in one's body, and this letting go is what makes the entry into an asana so difficult. But as one practices daily, with accompanying slow, deep, paced inspirations, breath-holdings, and releases, one becomes sensitized to one's body in new dimensions, one perceives tension here and there, in short, one becomes more adept at somatic perception. The outcome of a regime of Hatha Yoga is heightened consciousness of the world in general, and of course, more sensitive somatic perception.

### *Massage and "Rolfing"*

I have been massaged many times by masseurs and masseuses who follow the sensuous teachings of Bernard Gunter. This entails being massaged and touched, not with the aims of the medical physiotherapist or the athletic trainer, who wish only to loosen muscles; but rather to heighten sensitivity to one's own body, to feel the pleasures and pains with more keenness. A massage of two to three hours will nearly "stone" a person, and in my experience, heighten his somatic perception.

Rolfing refers to a technique that might be called deep massage invented by Ida Rolf, and now systematized and called "Rolfing." It entails the application of pressure with knuckles, finger tips, elbows and other parts of the body to deep musculature, with a view toward relaxing chronically tense muscles.

The theory holds that, as a person grows up, and undergoes traumas and conflicts, he responds by defensive tensing of muscles which result in postural imbalances. After rolfing, a person stands and moves in a more balanced, co-ordinated way. I can vouch that persons whom I know who have been rolfed not only look, stand and move better, but report intense experience of enlivenment within their bodies, heightened sexual awareness, vitality, and, in general, more somatic perception. ✦

# *II-5* The Mystic Dimension of Self

Through a door, behind a veil, in the underworld, lies a dimension of experience, call it pre-conceptual or primary experience. Freud knew of it and called it "primary process"—it underlies the secondary process or better, the secondary process is an abstraction from, a distancing or emergence from, a selection of those possibilities of unified experiencing which serves the function of surviving in this physical, social, and interpersonal world. When we depart from this primary experience we have, in effect, frozen possibility. The world as mediated by the ego, is a constructed, constricted, artificial world. When we get trapped by our own creations and problems and unsurmountable conflicts arise, we must, perforce, if the problems are to be solved, get behind the door and dip into the fountain of unlimited possibilities of non-habitual construing, perceiving and acting. This plunge into "the other world," then to return, is what we call "creativity." The "other world," the mystic dimension, cannot be named but only (and rarely) experienced. To exist in it without the return is to be mad or to be lost to the possibilities of communication with "squares"—people who confine themselves to the world of shared, frozen, concepts. Both extremes of experience must be viewed as inimical to survival or well-being. To be lost in the world means to live a half-life, to skate on the surface of existence, and to be at a distance from the being of things for themselves. To be lost, out of the communal world, submerged in the sea of primal experience, means one is ill-equipped to cope with "practical" matters, such as physical survival, social acceptance, and the like. There is an extreme cost associated with both extremes in modes of experience.

Now it seems true that the capacity to go *out* of one's ego and into primal experiencing of self-in-world is the source, and the means of growth, release of potentiality, and of creativity. There are doubtless creative people who, protected from danger, live most of their existence "way-out" and come back on summons, to address practical questions from their vantage point and footing on the ground of being. There are likely more who ground themselves in the practical world, but have discovered ways of turning themselves on, or "getting into" their primary experiencing when they encounter impasses. There are likely, too, persons who have reconciled the contradiction between inner and outer and who consistently see the mystic in the real, the infinite in the finite. We might call the latter type of person a "general practitioner" of mysticism and the former two types "specialists"—the first a reality specialist, the second a "mystic" specialist. Neither of the latter two is a "complete man."

But let us postulate that we have entered an age where we can no longer afford to ignore our inner dimension, the capacity for mystic experience—that we are suffering a kind of starvation in our repression of personal mysticism. The current interest among behavior scientists, educators, and public health officials in "human potentialities" attests to the importance of the problem of estrangement from our potential, presently strangulated selves. It is as if the public, aware that something is wrong, that there must be more to existence than filling bellies, is asking for help. The response to the plea takes the form of renewed interest in mysticism—the hypothesis being that the solutions to the riddles of existence is to be found in one's personal being, not by fleeing from it still further into the world, and away from one's experiencing.

Fortunately, there is a record of thousands of years of search-ing the limits of human experiencing for us to draw upon. The mystics of the Jewish and Christian faiths, the Buddhists,

Yogis, alchemists, Sufis, Zen Buddhists; the accounts of madness; the testimony of drug users—all these will be consulted with renewed vigor by experts firmly rooted in the values and goals, theory and practice of this world. They will be seeking knowledge as to how to "enter" the world under, around, and behind the ego and things, and guidance as to the means of construing the experience to be lived in that lost, inner world. We need to learn from ancient teachings how to interpret the experience we undergo in the dream world, the world out of our ego.

But to enter the mystic, preconceptual world takes courage—it is as frightening to the uninitiated as a new land is for a faint-hearted explorer from a safe, familiar, home-base. It is the terror of the unknown "within" oneself which prevents the majority of men from seeking to experience their own fount of possibility, their potential, mystic dimension of their personal experience and existence. The mystic dimension peeps out from time to time in the world of even the "squarest" Babbitt—in dreams, and also in anxiety attacks which signal imminent danger to values in the world, danger from mysticism, from unplumbed potentials for experience and action.

Let it be granted as a worthwhile hypothesis that access to the mystic dimension of one's experience is at once the source of creativity, the means for releasing potentials for knowing, feeling and acting that are valued in the world, and also the occasion for loss of sanity. If this hypothesis is sound, then the mystic dimension is truly a double-edged sword, which, like any source of power, may not be for everybody. By whom should the door to mysticism be opened? By men who have proven their goodwill, their purity of heart, their freedom from dominion by motives of personal aggrandizement or pleasure *per se*. Perhaps only such men, committed to a love of men and of life beyond vested interests can be trusted with the latent power over others and the power to comprehend and even master the forces in the world. Hence the mature age of the Taoist, the Kabbala initiate, etc.

But this is not to say that the unlimited possibility for experiencing and behaving in the world, presently locked up in each man's being, can never be drawn upon. In point of fact, life seems to conspire to elicit or release the mystic dimension in the most average of persons many times in the course of his growing up. Indeed, a technology of sorts is available for releasing the capacity for transcending the presently conceptualized limits of experience. This technology is to be found in varied places, and should, some day, be reviewed for common denominators.

The teacher who succeeds in abetting the learning process in his pupils is, in a sense, a transcendence-technician. The military leader, the political leader who challenges or invites unexpected performances from his followers is another case in point. The dancer, the singer, the jazz musician who go infinities beyond the usual, the expected, or the predicted in the release of their performances have drawn upon their mystic dimensions.

Psychotherapists who succeed in inviting a patient to transcend the contradiction between anxiety and courage, hallucination and reality, between "symptomatic" behavior and "acceptable" conduct are, presumably, releasing the mystic dimension of experience in the patient.

But these are only a few of the technologies available to us. What about the method "used" by nature, or by God, to elicit transcendence in a person, by getting the person to "act out" rather than experience and verbalize his mystic dimension? This method may be termed the production of impasses in existence; a person proposes a project, encounters insurmountable obstacles, he persists with full commitment to pursue the project, and if he is fully focused, at the moment of despair of giving up the expected and known responses, he produces the inspired, reconciling response which works. Why could he not produce this response before he reached the impasse? Presumably because the capacity for transcendent functioning, for the integration of the mystic with the rational and conceptual, requires special conditions, viz: full focus, total commitment (as *proven* by persistence long after the less committed have stopped trying) followed by a period of despair, a cessation of conscious, reasoned trying, and this (somehow) permits the mystic dimension to penetrate or become integrated with reasoning, conceptual-rational mode. Surely, the Zen master who poses as Koan to his disciple, or the leader who poses an "impossible" challenge to his follower, are but imitating Nature's way of eliciting personal growth through the release of the mystic dimension. The "warm-up" among athletes, musicians, dancers, has much in common with ritual and prayer—it gets a person out of his (conscious) mind, his reasoning, distancing, self-conscious ego, and permits him to address his project with all of his mind, including its transcendent potentials, its mystic pole. The properly warmed-up performer, given a repertoire of technique in his background, is able to address his project with his whole organism, not just his disembodied, cerebral cortex or with a body steered at a distance by a watchful ego. This is like Zen in archery or swordsmanship—perfect action.

It is as if, in the mastery of an art or craft, from initiation to mastery, one goes through a process (on a limited scale) that resembles the stages in the attainment of Buddhahood or the personal transmutation of the alchemist. There is a process of differentiation from a global state involving learning (through rote or imitation) certain parts of a total performance. Persistence in the exercise of the techniques is called for, and the commitment of the disciple is tested by such persistence. Mastery is witnessed by an integration of the parts and the integration comes, presumably, when the person is confronted by a challenge, invitation, or purpose that elicits a full focus—doing the job to say something to somebody, like a jazz saxophonist, just because it needs to be said, not to get rich or powerful or famous. When the integration happens, it is *total*. It is always integration for one purpose, a focusing on one goal, and it is the occasion for the release of power of unexpected magnitude. It is as if most of the time the energy system which *is* man, and which is a sample or an access to universal energy, is dissipated or diffused to do many things at once, or else it is bound by the task of keeping an integration, long outmoded, in force. Stated another way, man is integrated in a way which, for example, wins him acceptance, love, power, respectability. This way or configuration for the integration of his being must be dissolved and then reintegrated if he is to address a new challenge wholeheartedly. Thus, a style of integration which serves one objective may prevent the attainment of another objective. Perhaps this is why the most creative artists, scientists, etc., seem (to a "square") to live chaotic lives. They have renounced the way of life that serves "squareness" and respectability after finding that the way of living precludes a full focus and response in the realm of the projects that give meaning to their existence.

The idea of "playing games" is a way out of the impasse between "being square" and fulfilling potentialities through releasing transcendence. If one is among "squares," integrate one's being, warm oneself up, surround oneself with symbols that elicit a "square" integration. Then, when one is seeking to discover truth, or portray beauty, disintegrate the "square" way, and warm up to the new game, to address its challenges with one mind, fully embodied, integrated-for-the-task. This seems to be one useful way to construe the Zen saying, "Sit when you sit, walk when you walk. Above all, don't wobble!"

In principal it should be possible for persons to accelerate their growth, release potentialities, and "act out" their mystic dimension of experience in every "game" they play. However, not all games, for all persons, can elicit the full focusing that seems to be an important condition for disintegration and reintegration. Probably the realms in which spontaneous fascination happens are the realms in which transcendence will most likely happen. A person must stake his existence on a game in order to play it fully, and not all games place a man's existence in issue. Many games permit, even demand, that a man "stay in his ego," stay in his modal, "square," self-conscious, encapsulated, habit-ridden style of integration. All that happens in those games is a kind of leaching of zest, a stifling of spontaneity, a gradual boredom, increase of stress, and perpetuation of a robot-like mode of functioning. Indeed, if the only way available to a person is that way, he will break down or out, and require therapeutic assistance. A good therapist will guide the man into the realm of preconceptual experience, so that he can re-enter the square world standing on a personal ground from which he can play games with just enough seriousness, and enough freedom to grow.

If a man has been able to experience the mystic dimension fully, to live in it, he will return to the consensual world with the capacity to take liberties with the conventional rubrics. His concepts will likely be more richly inclusive, and less starkly and rigidly segregated one from the other. His phenomenal world, his world of meanings will be more fluid than hitherto.

But one can "act out" the mystic dimension, without "swimming" in it—this is what appears to happen in magnificent performances on which a man stakes his existence, viz: climbing Everest or Anapurna, or running a four-minute mile. One has caught a glimmering of possibilities beyond one's present concept of self, of things, and thenceforward, nothing conceptualized will appear so final, so ultimately and essentially defined. One knows, through experiencing them, of possibilities more numerous "than are dreamt of in one's philosophy."

It is interesting to think of the mystic dimension of experience as a *feeling*, like the feeling of anger, or power, or freedom. One can then speak of projecting, or repressing the feeling. The changed experience of oneself, can be, and often is projected to the external world, and it can be and often is repressed, to preserve the illusion of sameness, constancy in one's phenomenal world. Undoing the repression of the mystic experience brings fear of death, or it may bring joy with the glimpse into the *void* of being or the *plenum* of being, (depending on how full or empty one was before releasing the repression).

The only proper posture for a man is to be off-balance, if not always then at least periodically. Poets have always lived or experienced the world from this vantage point, assuming that the prosaic view of things-for-use is a balanced view. Free-dom of metaphor, indeed metaphor itself teases the audience out of its customary instrumental, ego-dominated way of experiencing the world. Perhaps the metaphor is the idiom of the mystic dimension. ✦

[London, November 1964]

# II-6 Prophets As Psychotherapists, And Psychotherapists As Prophets*

*Sidney Jourard was born in Toronto in 1926, and was educated through his Master's degree at the University of Toronto. He completed his Ph.D. in clinical psychology at the University of Buffalo in 1953, where he received his psychotherapeutic training. He learned how to be a psychotherapist, and to keep growing beyond his training in Atlanta where he commenced a part-time private practice in 1951, and he has been (hopefully) getting rid of rigidities in his work and existence at a faster rate as years go on.*

This symposium is an extraordinary happening. Psychotherapists have sought, since before Freud, to ally themselves with science and to regard psychotherapy as a scientifically grounded skill. Connections with religion were regarded as anathema. Yet, a strong affiliation with religion may be found in many of the great psychotherapists; Freud's connection to the Jewish mystical tradition has been documented by Bakan. Fromm, though not theistic, is an Old Testament scholar whose studies influence his work. Jung, of course, was the son of a clergyman. The religious streak in Whitaker and Warkentin is obvious. Paul Tournier is patently a Christian psychotherapist. Frankl's logotherapy seeks a kind of religious conversion, and we know that Carl Rogers intended a career in the clergy. Hobart Mowrer has been insistent upon a view of psychotherapy as a moral "turning."

*Paper read at the Symposium "Psychotherapy As A Secular Calling," American Psychological Association Annual Meeting, Washington, D.C., September 4, 1971.*

For many years I prided myself on my secular approach to the understanding of human suffering and my intervention therein. But the thinker whose work most influenced me beyond my initial training was Martin Buber, and so in spite of the fact I had no formal instruction in being a Jew, there was and remains an Old Testament flavor to my thinking, writing and ways of being. And, so, after a recent visit to Israel, I began to read the Old Testament for the first time. I am finding it a fascinating, extraordinary document about the struggle of some prophets and leaders of a recalcitrant people to become human beings freed from the idolatry of place, tribe, family; whose worship of their deity is not in words, sacrifice or ritual, but through *living in a way*, a way that is informed by Divine Ecology, Divine Public Health, and Divine Interpersonal Science. When this stiff-necked people fell away from living in the way prescribed by *JWH*, their punishment was swift and terrible. I prefer, however, not to regard defeat in battle, famine and disease and other evidences of the Lord's wrath as evidence of the Lord's wrath; rather, they seem to be outcomes of not paying attention to long-range consequences of one's present ways of treating the weak, the lowly, the strangers in one's midst, the soil, the waters, the animals, and oneself.

The ancient Hebrews were as vulnerable as Portnoy is today to the temptations of Canaanite *shiksas*, who inveigled them into copulatory rituals that were thought to keep the soil fertile—and even if they didn't, it is difficult for vital people to turn down a romp when it is gladly offered. It is important to assure the growth of crops, but not at the cost of neglect of larger questions: "How is life possible? How can I live amicably with people younger, older, of different culture and tradition?" The laws and ordinances proclaimed by Moses, and amplified elsewhere in the Old Testament can be viewed as answers to this question, supposedly announced by *JWH* and which, if followed, would lead to multiplication of one's seed (an index of grace no longer needed) and improvement in the quality of existence. In short, to live in the Way—being like God—*was* worship and redemption, the choice of life over death.

The prophets, beginning with Moses, and through Elijah, Elisha, Jeremiah, Isaiah, Amos, Ezekiel, Hosea and others, sought to bring an entire people back into the way when they preached. Their preachings were not bland and they were not, themselves, seeking to be liked—there was no Dale Carnegie school in those days. When they were not preaching to masses, they were, some of them, in a position analogous to "The President's Analyst," or those of our colleagues who work for Rohrer, Hibler and Replogle—consultants to men of power and decision, so that the latter will not destroy their companies or cause the loss of profits. The prophets were *unpaid* and unsolicited consultants, in many cases, to the kings of Judea and Israel, reminding the latter that they were supposed to rule in godly ways. They were not at all like Machiavelli who was advisor to his Prince, seeking to help him maximize his control over the people. The Old Testament prophets wanted their kings to rule by the example of an upright existence, not through cunning, bribery, mystification and threats.

The prophesies that were presented often grew out of visions. The prophets were, in some ways, ecstatic men, with vision informed by imagination. The biblical records are not complete enough to provide a basis for understanding how an ordinary person became a *navi*. Some cataclysmic crisis, perhaps suffering, experienced by them as an encounter with God, induced them to abandon their former conventional existences, driving them to proclaim the evil, suffering and injustice to which others were blind and indifferent. We can infer that they were not totally in the thrall of their culture and of the prevailing, conformist ways of seeing, construing, valuing and behaving. If God spoke, then they could hear where all others were deaf. They could see what was there. They could see that if kings and people continued to behave in the ways they were behaving—worshipping the work of human hands, mistreating widows, orphans, strangers in their midst, pursuing pleasure through eating forbidden foods and indiscriminate screwing— dire consequences would follow. Since life was insecure in those days, we don't today have to say that God smote the people whom he smote. A human, livable existence in those days called for continuous vigilance, continuous attention to the basic conditions that made life possible in the face of a hostile physical environment and hordes of hostile cultures. The teachings of Moses were explicit descriptions of these conditions.

The prophets, like Ralph Nader, told it like it was. They were like divine agronomists, military advisors, family counselors, ecologists, public health officers and muckraking journalists, pointing to, and reminding and showing others a better way, if not the "Right Way."

Over the years I have been examining and re-examining psychotherapies and psychotherapists from the standpoint of different models and metaphors. The one model most compelling for me over the past ten years is that of exemplar, or role-model of authentic existence. Now the very term authentic existence means more than simply living in truth and choosing one's existence. It also implies increasing enlightenment, so that one can make choices compatible with life, growth and self-actualization. Psychotherapists in increasing numbers have been taking their own lives and growth seriously, seeking to authenticate their professional contacts by themselves being exemplars of the quest for growth, truth and self-fulfillment. And they are seeking, some of them, to share their visions and knowledge with masses of others; to function, in short, as prophets outside the consulting room.

The psychotherapist, according to this view, embodies part of the way of a prophet, that of being an exemplar of the way of life he wishes to invite others to follow for their own good, and, by implication, for the good of the community. And he is a prophet when he points out the truth about destructive behavior. Old Testament prophets were desirous that the polyglot aggregation of Hebrew tribes might overcome their limited and autistic perspectives and become a people, a community called Israel, united under one God, living in exemplary ways as a beacon and example to all mankind. An extraordinarily modest ambition. A modern psychotherapist—insofar as he can see connections between and implications of usual ways for people to be and sickness, social disorganization and stultified growth and madness on large scale—can tell individual patients or seekers *what* he sees. And he can prophesy in market-places, before temples and in the places where people work; and modern prophetic psychotherapists have access to the press and the mass media—TV, movies, etc. to present their diagnoses and prescriptions.

According to Abraham Heschel, a prophet is extraordinarily sensitive to evil; he feels fiercely, he sees injustice and indifference to evil and refuses to excuse or to ignore it. He shrieks of what he sees. He pays attention to what others regard as trivialities, too obvious to note, but which signify a person or a people hell-bent on self-destruction, or destroying the very conditions that make life possible. Prophets are not mealy-mouthed; they do not write the bland pabulum of Norman Vincent Peale. A prophet is, without compromise, committed to the highest good of which man is capable, and he mourns, castigates and incites in order that mediocre men might rise to those heights. Like the *outsiders* of whom Colin Wilson wrote, the prophet sees too much, hears the groans of pain to which others are deaf. Yet the prophets have a compassion for mankind and they seek to invite all men to take responsibility for the fate of man and life in this place and time. The prophets feel the blast from heaven, they inveigh against callousness, indifference and yet take no pleasure in the lot to which they have been called. Prophets are seditious, cranky, threats to the status quo.

This is the way Heschel answers the question, "What manner of man is the prophet?" I see adumbrations here, as I said, with Colin Wilson's *outsiders*—the raw nerve-endings of our times: the Lawrence of Arabias, the Nijinskys, the characters who never could be swallowed up by the hypocrisies and false values of their times, but who, as Wilson points out, were destroyed because they lacked insight and didn't know what was going on. What psychotherapist measures up to the stature of a prophet rather than a mere *outsider*? Which is a true and which is a false prophet? Wilhelm Reich, I feel, was a *prophet manqué*, who had magnificent revelations to share, but he was arrogant in a way that perhaps the prophets were not. I suspect he was ruined by his upbringing in a Germanic culture, which made him wish to be appreciated as a genius. The prophets were not on an "ego trip." Brock Chisholm, after World War II, became a prophet at risk of reputation. He preached against the teaching of myths to children so they would not be vulnerable to incitements to war. Israel Charney, a colleague in psychotherapy whom I have not yet met but whose writing I have sampled, seems to fill some of the job description of a prophet. He is sensitive to the violence of our time, to the viciousness that prevails in marriage, in families; Auschwitz can be foreseen in the German family structure. Ronald Laing and Aaron Esterson, both psychotherapists, are prophets in their writings, pointing out how the family serves as a place within which some members are sacrificed to the mental hospital rather than allow the cosmetic image of a happy family to be besmirched. I presume to prophesy, as I have in print, that cosmetic family structures are responsible for physical disease, including cancer. I suppose I have had a prophetic function, too, in my writing about research and therapy as exploitive and adjustive disciplines, striving to find more humanistic and liberating ways for psychologists to be.

The psychotherapists whom we consider great—I have argued—are great not because of their theories, which are efforts to scientize existential courage and enlightenment—but they are great because their lives were threatened by some aspect of facticity and they learned how to tame, to transcend it, and could teach others how to be free and upright in the face of doting, destructive parents, addiction to heroin, or lack of awareness of others' destructive games. But many of the writing psychotherapists overstate their cases and believe that God has told them *the* reason why everyone suffers, and has confided the best and rightest solution. The plethora of oversold theories and techniques in individual and group therapy, in encounter groups and in Primal screaming, in gestalting, rolfing, yoging, meditating, to me is evidence of arrogance and false prophesy. Look at the prophet, not his methods and words, to see if he knows how to live.

The fact that seems obvious to me about life in the time of the Old Testament prophets is that no one knew how to live in a way that would sustain life for self and others; and no one knew how to live in a way that would foster growth of more than a brutish few of man's infinite possibilities. The statutes, commandments, ordinances that Moses received "from God" may be regarded as the inventions of a highly imaginative and intelligent and compassionate man. Perhaps God spoke through him. Moses fascinates me—how did he (or they) arrive at a statement of ways to live in that time? Perhaps being reared in a civilized culture (Egypt) without being *of* it was a factor. Moses' writings and teachings were the equivalent of the writings of Dr. Spock, Ralph Nader, Rachel Carson, Adelle Davis, Mohandas Gandhi, and other contemporaries (Hobart Mowrer, George Bach) who have tried to help people live in viable ways. Failure to live in a viable way is to court disease, stultification and death. This is as true today as it was in biblical times. The prophets could be viewed as existential teachers who were horrified at the ways people, through lack of leadership from the responsible authorities, were behaving daily, ways that courted disaster and which already were yielding full measures of suffering for some. The prophets could not be indifferent to suffering and injustice and they addressed kings directly, urging them to mend their ways and to do what they were anointed to do.

Today's psychotherapists treat individually and in encountering groups with people who suffer, with people of stultified growth, with people who, simply, are not living right for themselves and possibly not right for others. The therapist is prophetic insofar as he has learned, and authenticated in his very being and presence, viable ways to live—what the ancients may have called righteousness. If they invite others to change their ways and threaten them with dire consequences if they do not, they are being as much prophet as the times admit. The prophets tried to make men realize their freedom to choose and to choose to change from "sin" to righteousness. A psychotherapist who is not as sensitive to self-destructive behavior and who is not committed to learning and living and leading in viable ways, is neither prophet nor therapist.

One of the defining characteristics of the Old Testament prophets was the idea that the one true God, *Jaweh*, spoke through them. This, I believe, is a metaphor signifying that the prophet was able to achieve a perspective on his culture, on the behavior of self and others which enabled him to see what those embedded could not see. The psychotherapist in modern days must be capable of achieving such an outsider's perspective, of attaining what Buber calls "distance," but he must also have the capacity to "enter into relation," in order to have his vision and message heard. In modern terminology, an effective psychotherapist, like an effective prophet, can detach himself from prior ways of being and then return into community with one other, or many others, and share his vision. But I hold the hypothesis that the prophetic psychotherapist and the psychotherapeutic prophets are effective to the extent to which they embody, in their very *being*, the ways to live that are most compatible with life together in this time and place. It is not possible, I argue, for a true prophet to preach one way and live another. This may require that the psychotherapist in his prophetic function (which is not incompatible with healing)may be, for the moment, a very irritating, infuriating person who discloses the truth that hurts, that fosters guilt, anxiety, and intense suffering. But, like the prophets, he does not confront for the joy of inflicting pain, but out of profound concern. If the therapist, like the prophet, is angry, it is because there is something to be angry at. We can view Carl Roger's wrath at certain dehumanizing aspects of graduate and undergraduate education and his promulgation of encountering as "a Way," as a case of a therapist "gone prophet."

Frank Shaw, my late friend whose ideas are not widely enough appreciated, viewed talent in phenomenological-behavioristic terms: talent was a matter of a specialized fascination with something in the world that one could not resist tinkering with in order to make it "right." We might look afresh at prophets and psychotherapists in order to discern whether they might resemble one another in terms of talent thus defined. It is clear that the therapist and the prophet are fascinated by "sin"—pathology-producing behavior—and by suffering: they cannot neglect it in self or in others. It is as if they are receiving sets tuned in permanently on the wave-length most interesting to them. But the fascination is not a passive one. No psychotherapist I know of, and no prophet who is recorded could resist responding to the sufferer (the prophets felt God's suffering), in spite of the fact that many therapists claim that indifference to whether one is helping the other is, paradoxically, the best way to be helpful. Prophet and therapist alike will not rest until they are doing what they deem best to remedy the situation. We have no evidence that therapists who see what a patient is doing wrong and simply say, "Stop doing that, and start living right," have a lower success rate than any other kind of therapist. I can verify that with certain people who have consulted with me, I have behaved as much like a prophet as like a contemporary therapist: "If it makes you sick—and it does, why don't you stop doing it? Start to stop doing it right here in my office, because I find it sickens me."

The wheel has turned full circle. Beginning several decades ago, men of the church turned to psychology and psychiatry to learn how to function better as pastoral counselors. As time went on, increasing numbers of clergymen dropped out of the church and turned toward a more humanistically oriented career in psychology or counseling, because they felt they could not be true to the prophetic motives that perhaps directed them to a religious career. Less prophetic clergymen who stayed in the church made use of many of the techniques of non-human-istic psychology to gain and keep members: the techniques of Madison Avenue and folksy, non-threatening flattery.

Now, it seems to me that growing numbers of working psycho-therapists are moving increasingly toward a prophetic and uto-pian vision of the good society and may become a new kind of churchman. It will be interesting to see where some of us go next. ✦

# *III* *Psychotherapist as Growth Coach: Teacher, Self-Discloser and Transcender of Facticity*

# *III-1*  The Psychotherapist as Psychedelic Man

We have entered the electronic age. People are brought into encounter now who never knew earlier how the other experienced this shared world and time. Confrontation between perspectives that terrify or challenge the participants are now taking place. This also is the age of growing automation. We live on the brink of untold leisure. Work is being done for us by machines that are supervised by other machines that are regulated by master machines. Increasing numbers of us have spare time. Our hands are idle. We keep them out of mischief with insensate busy work. I am reminded here of Parkinson's Law. Idle minds, liberated from obsession with thoughts of getting it made, or having it made, are likewise faced with a challenge or a threat because of automation.

For thousands of years, men faced the challenge of securing their life and their livelihood and didn't ponder the question, "What is my life for?", because if they mulled too long they might starve to death, or be exterminated by an enemy to whose approach they were inattentive. But now and in the future, if we don't ponder this crucial question, and if we don't explore more of our locked-in possibilities, we will not be able to endure our existence.

Until recently, psychotherapists and counselors have truly been a specialized breed of socialization agents. Their job has been to pick up where the family and school and other agencies of socialization have failed to complete the work of shaping up a citizen whose behavior would otherwise be a problem to society. People who didn't fit were designated criminals, sinners or mentally ill. For those who were tagged mentally ill, the whole mythology of illness and its cure was evolved by the medical profession. No psychotherapist is unaffected by this ideology.

Psychologists, clergymen, social workers, and counselors of all kinds were trained to view misfitting people as sufferers from mental disease. They were lead to believe that if they mastered certain theories and techniques for transacting with *them,* the patients, they would then effect a cure, and in this way *we,* the psychotherapists and counselors (solid conforming professional men, with a stake in the *status quo*), serve society. And we can take pride in the fact that we did it well, earning our money with hard scientifically informed work. We were always pledged to protect our patient's well-being, but curiously enough our concepts of wellness were nearly identical with those versions of personality which would fit into the social system that subsidized us, with its established class structure and its resistance to change. Revolutionaries, anarchists and rebels—rebels against the *status quo*, such as hippies, poets, painters, writers—could be easily seen as sufferers from unresolved oedipal conflicts. Psychotherapists did not view each man seriously as a unique source of authentic experience, a perspective that in a more pluralistic and more enlightened society might be confirmed rather than invalidated. We shared the short-sightedness of our established society and called the officially sanctioned view of the world "reality contact"; everything else was "madness" or "autism." From the established point of view (the point of view that many psychotherapists and counselors share) people who want to make love and not war can be seen as impractical, schizoid, or seditious.

No matter what our private sentiments may have been, we were pledged unwittingly to protect the *status quo* by invalidating the experience of those who found it unlivable. We called this invalidation "treatment." In effect we were, and for the most part continue to be, a peculiar breed of commissars, or spies-watchdogs over human experience, pledged to annihilate any experience designated "mad" and to substitute those modes of experience that we arbitrarily call "normal." Like it or not, there is a politics of counseling and psychotherapy, just as there is, in Ronald Laing's words, a "politics of experience." In fact, it is more than analogy to regard psychotherapists and counselors as experts in ideological indoctrination—the ideology being that limited perspective on the world which is called normal, and mediates behavior which preserves the *status quo.* It is instructive to realize that to many hippies, psychotherapists and counselors are regarded as "shrinks"—headshrinkers who put you down by putting a tag on you. We are not seen as sources of help by many of this growing sub-culture.

Man can experience himself and his world in myriad ways. The world, Being, can be likened to a projective test. In itself, it is nothing. Being, as it discloses itself to man's consciousness, can appear as most anything. The sun can be a distant star, or it can be the eye of God, evoking life wherever it looks. To insist that it is one rather than the other is politics. To persuade a man that it is a star and *not* the eye of God is to be a propagandist for somebody's vested interest. We have been confirming what Freud, with incredible courage, found for himself: that our possibilities for experiencing are infinite, and infinitely beyond that tiny splinter of awareness that we acknowledge, call "normal," and disclose to others. In fact, to the extent that we find our own ordinary consciousnesses banal, to the extent that we find our own company boring, we have an answer to a riddle. How was it possible for Freud to spend 12 to 14 hours a day for so many years listening to people disclose their offbeat experiencing to him? How did he avoid swooning from fatigue or boredom? One possible answer is provided by the experience revealed by users of LSD and marijuana. Freud encouraged people to disclose their unselected experience to him and I have little doubt that it turned him on. It "flipped" him.

As I think of Freud, his psychoanalytic practice was like a 40-year psychedelic trip. Or 40 years in a gallery of surrealistic art. Hour after hour, day after day, exposed to dreams, fantasies and memories that shattered his conventional rubrics and expectations about the human experience, it could only expand his awareness of his own being and the possibilities for experiencing the world. That highly prized state, "being normal," must have looked like banality and fraud incarnate—especially to a man who dauntlessly opened Pandora's Box and became privy to the secrets of expanded experiencing which he found in both himself and in his patients. Each disclosure from a patient must have exploded his concepts and expectations of what is possible.

Now, those of us who are therapists and counselors of one kind or another are keeping Pandora's Box open, and in so doing, we have been infected—or perhaps it is better to say, disaffected. We have been infected with the truth that we can experience much more than we permit ourselves, and more than the guardians of the *status quo* would like us to experience. And we may have been disaffected from unthinking compliance to the rigid, unimaginative, established ways of living our lives—ways of relating to our fellows, ways of experiencing and living in our bodies. We are beginning to study man for himself, for possibilities of development and fulfillment which go beyond mere conformity with prevailing norms. In short, the truth is on us. There is no more *them*. There is only *us*: graspers and gropers after meaning in a social structure which aims to shrink our being, yet alive in a world which is no more *them*. There is only *us*: graspers and gropers after meaning in a social structure which aims to shrink our being, yet alive in a world which requires us to grow. If we insist that patients belong in the category of *them*, then I, for one, have become one of *them*. I have come to believe that my task as a psychotherapist is no longer a specialized, technical practice. Rather, it is the task of an explorer of realms of experience and behavior—an explorer of ways to relate to others, and to the social order, which enliven me and keep me fit and frisky and vital and loving and responsive and growing, of inventive ways that evoke new possibilities for achievement, contributions, enjoyment.

My criterion of success in this quest is not solely whether my behavior appears normal to others. Rather my criterion of success in my own personal quest as a man is my *experience*—my experience of dialogue with my fellows, my experience of feeling free and responsible and potent and alive. The criterion of success has shifted from exclusive attention to behavior to experience. I have been aware for too long that in appearing "normal" to others I felt benumbed and dead within, a habit-ridden plaything of social pressures and expectations. And I have known too many people, fellow seekers (I used to call them patients), who are exemplary in their conduct but dead or desperate inside; they could tolerate their "normal" existence only with the aid of booze or tranquilizers or periodic hospitalization for ulcers.

A new specialist, it seems to me, is called for in our times, and I believe those of us who presently are trained to be counselors or psychotherapists may be in the best position, if we earn it, to grow beyond our training into the new role. I see him as a Westernized version of his Eastern counterpart, the *guru,* the wise man, or teacher. You might call him, to use our idioms, an existential guide and explorer. Or we might borrow some of the hippie talk and call him a psychedelic man, a consciousness-expanding expert, a growth counselor, a self-actualization agent-or maybe more succinctly, a lover. Such a person would be a guide to more expanding and more fulfilling ways to experience life as a *person* rather than a mere *functionary.* He would be a world shatterer and rebuilder (the term "world" here means a person's experience of *his* world).

As a world shatterer and rebuilder, he has a robust interest in his own fulfillment. He pursues this interest, in part, by helping others to fulfill themselves. But part of his function is not as an expert so much as an exemplar of a turned-on life, a waked-up life, as a revealer and sharer of how he has found his own way. It is very interesting to go to a convention of counselors, psychotherapists, psychoanalysts, physicians, ministers—people who are concerned with human growth and wellbeing—and look at the people who are "experts." They occasionally are fit, frisky, beautiful people, but more often they are haggard, harried, desperate, bored, well-intentioned seekers—but not finders. And they are relying on technical know-how to help other people find the path to living the life that they are living.

This new guide, or teacher, or *guru*, is himself reborn in the Sufi sense, or possibly in the Christian sense, or he is awakened and liberated in the sense of the Zen masters or the Taoist teachers. He is a Bodhisattva rather than the Buddha himself—awakened, not out of this world, but very much in it. Instead he remains in dialogue with those of his fellow seekers who are themselves seeking to become men, rather than adjusted people or social functionaries of one kind or another. This teacher shows and tells how he himself has been awakened, and he serves as a guide to others. He is an experimental existentialist—literally. He has experimented with *his* existence, not with the *other fellow's* existence. He is seeking to find that way of being in this world, with his fellow man, which generates in him maximum enlightenment, freedom, love, and responsibility. This view of a psychotherapist or counselor as a *guru* or psychedelic man (what I mean by psychedelic here is not an acidhead, but someone whose impact upon others broadens their experience) has implicit in it an entire new theory of suffering, of growth, of practice, of settings for practice, of schools for training—the total paraphernalia of a profession. It calls for an enlightened perspective on society, on one's role within society. It calls for expanded views of human possibility that are authenticated by the discovery of new possibilities within oneself. It calls for a going away and then for a return—renewed. If not 40 days in the desert, maybe 40 hours. It calls for a kind of death and a kind of rebirth. Many of the hippies and dropouts and, for that matter, many of the people in the looney bins around the country have taken the first step: the leaving. If they are to become men or women, they will return to renew and humanize the society that they left.

This is what I see the times calling us in these "helping" professions to become. In a sense we have been members of the helping profession, but we haven't been helping people to become men. We have been helping people to fit a social system which has not necessarily permitted them to grow to full stature. The aim for counselors and psychotherapists is not exclusively to help their fellow seekers to grow more fully. Rather, they themselves must be very actively and robustly involved in their own growth and liberation and awakening from brainwashing that we all received from Mom and Dad and Sunday School and college. (Even college seldom enlightens in this day and age; it indoctrinates.)

How does this enlightened person, this liberated person, who might invite or challenge or guide his fellow seekers to fuller human beings, how does he look, what does he look like? In short, "what is healthy personality?" The characteristics of this guide and exemplar (healthy personality) describes a way for a person to be in his world—a way that yields growth without placing other important values in jeopardy. People commit themselves to a variety of values and they live for them. One who is a healthy personality seeks to fulfill them, and he defends them when they are under threat. A healthy personality is to himself as a dedicated farmer is to his farm. He does everything in its time. The abundance of the crops, the state of his livestock, the condition of his outbuildings, are testimony to the good farmer's alert and responsive care.

The healthy personality likewise shows evidence in his very being and presence of his alert and responsive care for himself. He finds his life meaningful with satisfactions and some accepted suffering. He loves and is loved. He can fulfill responsible social demands made upon him, and there is no doubt as to who he is and what his feelings and convictions are. He doesn't apologize for being himself. He can look out in the world and see it from the point of view of how it presently is, according to social consensus, but he can also see himself, the world, and the people in it from the point of view of possibility. He can regard the world as a place in which he can bring into being some possibilities that exist just now only in his imagination.

Neither the world, other people, nor himself are seen by a healthy personality as a sclerosed, frozen, finished, defined once-and-for-all.

Such a person has free and ready access to a dimension of human being that is much neglected by the square, the hyperconformist, the typical personality. I am referring to something that has been called by various names throughout history. Freud called it the unconscious; others have referred to it as transcendental or mystic experience. This hidden dimension of the self, sought for centuries by men who have longed for personal fulfillment beyond rationalism and conformity, is usually dreaded by the average person. When his unconscious threatens to speak, when direct experiencing of himself or the world invades his consciousness, he becomes overwhelmed with anxiety and may temporarily feel he is losing his mind and sanity. Indeed he is on the point of going out of his ego. His present self-concept and concepts of things and people are shattered by explosions and implosions of raw experience from within and without. The hypothetical healthy personality experiences his being in dimensions presently unfamiliar to him and hence frightening. But if he is moving toward healthy personality he will recognize that his unconscious, his persistent but usually drowned-out-dream, his source of new truth, is the voice of his true self—his possibilities. It is a statement, perhaps, of how he has mistreated himself; or it is an invitation to new possibilities of being for which he has become sufficiently grown and secretly, unconsciously prepared.

*Gurus* have always known that when the unconscious speaks, when fresh transconceptual experience reaches awareness, it is better to pay attention. The breakdowns or checkouts really are the final outcome of not listening to our real selves. The symptoms and suffering are but the voice of the real self—the voice of a human being protesting in language that the person himself could not understand. And so the person persisted in behaving in the usual way, and experiencing in his usual ways, thereby undermining his own integrity.

Healthier personalities listen to their boredom, their anxiety, their dreams and fantasies, and grope for changes in ways of meeting the world that will permit greater realization of potential self.

Healthy personality is manifested as well by a mode of being that we can call authenticity—or more simply, honesty. Less healthy personalities (people who function less than fully, but who may fit nicely in their social niche) suffer recurrent breakdowns or chronic impasses in their relationships, and more fundamentally, they can be found to be liars. They say things they do not mean. Their disclosures have been chosen more for cosmetic value than for truth. The consequence of a lifetime of lying about oneself to others, of saying and doing things for their sound and appearance, is that ultimately the person loses contact with his real self. The authentic being, manifested by healthier personalities, takes the form of unself-conscious disclosure of self in words, decisions and actions. It is a risky way of being, especially in a social setting that punishes all forms of action, experience and disclosure of experience that depart from current stereotypes of the acceptable man. The healthier person will experience many a knock, bruise and criticism for being and disclosing who he is, but he prefers to accept these blows rather than sell his authentic being for short run acceptability.

Indeed, authenticity before others is the same mode of being that permits a man to have access to the underground realm of experiencing—his unconscious. Defensiveness and concealment of self before others unfortunately are the same modes of being that screen off a man's unconscious, his preverbal experience, from himself. The currents of feeling, fantasy, memory, and wish that would get a man criticism from others also produce anxiety in himself, and so he blocks these from the view of self and others in the service of self-defense. In time he succeeds in fooling himself (as much as others) into believing that he is the man he so expertly seems to be. In truth, he is an invisible man: whatever is authentic of him, whatever is most spontaneous and alive, is buried so deep not even he can recognize it. One of the reasons less healthy personalities are so self-conscious, so deliberate in their choice of word and action before others is that they dread revealing something which truly expresses their feelings, something which will get them into trouble. They are, as it were, idolaters of that state of artificial grace known as staying out of trouble. In fact, they have sold their soul for a good, but false name.

Healthier personalities, of course, are not always fully visible to others. Chronic self revelation may itself be idolatrous, and is even suicidal in certain circumstances. Certainly we would expect a healthier personality to have enough common sense and judgment, or even cunning, to preserve himself in a hostile environment, dropping his guard only when he is among trusted and loving friends. In fact, a healthy personality will have been able to enter into and maintain relationships of trust and love with one or more people, people he has let know him and whom he knows and to whom he responds.

Another dimension of healthy personality concerns the realm of values itself. Healthier personalities seek and find meaningful values and challenges in life which provide an element of direction and focus to their existence. Less healthy personalities, estranged as they are from their real selves, usually pursue only cliché goals and values current in their present social milieu. This consequence of growing automation concerns me. If people have not been able to discover values beyond two Cadillacs, two outboard motors, two wives, two of everything, then when they no longer have to work they will literally drink or bore themselves to death. The goals toward which most people are socialized will not challenge or inspire the average person to fuller integration and development.

The upshot is that the average person (not the healthy personality) will feel trapped—or worse, will feel that he is losing his mind. This latter fear is most likely to occur when a person looks at the externals of his present situation and finds that he has accomplished, or has been given, everything to make a man happy. But in honesty, like most middle-class, married people in their 30's, 40's or 50's, who more or less have it made, when they look within (if they are capable of looking within) they may really find that they are indeed miserable, bored and confused about what to do next. He has loved ones, a family, material success, nice house and car, but he finds his work increasingly boring, more like a treadmill, his relationships with others empty, formal and all too predictable. He may entertain fantasies of murdering loved ones, or chucking it all and going to the South Seas, only to repress these ideas with the anxious thought, "I must be insane to harbor such notions." He might scurry into further busy work, or start drinking to excess, or create excitement by treading primrose paths at great risk, or do other searching in the outer world for new meanings. He looks in the wrong place—the right place being within his own experiencing of himself and the world. The healthier personality, less estranged and less afraid of his real self, can look within *and* without; he can create and find new sources of value when old ones are worn out.

The healthy personality lives with and in his body. He is an embodied self. He is not afraid or ashamed to touch his own body or that of other people with whom he is on intimate terms. He is able to freely move his body, which has a look of grace, coordination, relaxation. He dances through life. The less healthy personality, on the other hand, is afraid to live in his body. He despises his body, or is terrified of it. He represses his bodily experiencing and feels his body alternately numb and dead, or as a dangerous stinking cesspool charged with explosive nitroglycerin. He must take care, lest an urge, a feeling, an impulse, a movement, break through the tight control. For him, this would be disastrous. One of the most common evidences of disembodiment is muscular tension that reveals itself as stiffness in body posture, awkwardness in gait; the mouth becomes a thin red line. (I've developed an unscientific but possibly helpful pair of terms for this last condition. I call it "Methodist Mouth" or "Presbyterian Lip." There is no malice intended here toward the respected theologies.) Touch one of these disembodied people on the arm, or place your arm around their shoulder, and they will instantly stiffen, or experience panic, or jump as stabbed. He may experience a mixture of sexual arousal, or guilt, or anxiety. The healthier person has a more fully lived and experienced body. His face is more mobile and expressive; he speaks in a voice that is free, not one that is fighting off an impulse to say something else at the same time that the present speech is being emitted. It is no accident that average people receive psychothera-peutic benefit from instruction in vocalization or freely expressive dance, or from massage and other forms of direct experience of their bodies. The therapist of the future will, without doubt, be obliged to learn to live gracefully with their own bodies, and to learn ways of inviting and leading fellow seekers back into theirs.

An important part of bodily experience is sex, the erotic impulse and feeling. Perhaps our puritanical avoidance of body contact in everyday life is expressive of our mixed attitudes toward sexuality. A healthier personality is able to experience his erotic feelings without fear, and he is able to express them in a relationship with a chosen partner without needless inhibition, as part of the sexual dialogue. The less healthy person usually is so self-conscious that he cannot let sexuality happen in his attempts at loving transaction, and so he tries to force matters. The results may be the broad variety of sexual unhappiness that comes to the attention of a marriage counselor. The beginning of a cure (or better, liberation) from sexual difficulties is made outside the bedroom, inside the self.

The ability of healthier personalities to find and maintain relationships of love and friendships in the world insures that a healthier person will have access to relief from the existential loneliness in which we all live. (I use the term relief, not cure, of existential loneliness.) Loneliness is not a disease from which one can be cured; rather, it is an inescapable fact of human existence. Less healthy personalities, cut off as they are from the fount of their real selves, find themselves terrible company. They cannot long tolerate solitude, and they run willy-nilly into busy work or superficial companionship with others. They do not, however, truly encounter another person, and enter into dialogue with him. Hence, the feeling of loneliness, of not being known and understood. This feeling chronically nags at them, like a boil on the buttock or a stone in the shoe.

A healthier personality, because he is less self-concealing and has readier access to his own possible experience, the experience of possibility, is less afraid of solitude when that is his lot; and when he is with others he can feel secure enough in his own worth that he can let encounter and dialogue happen. During the process of such dialogue the shell that encapsulates him as a separate being ruptures and his inner world expands by receiving the disclosed world of experience of the other. When the dialogue ends he has experienced himself in the new dimensions evoked by the other person and he has learned of the personal world of another. He is enlarged and changed.

Authentic dialogue with another person is more psychedelic than LSD, and has much less likelihood of a bad trip. Dialogue will blow your mind in a wholesome way. Less healthy personalities defend themselves against being affected or changed in their contacts with others. They rub shells, or clink character armor with other people, but don't truly *meet*.

Mine is a kind of utopian view, an extrapolation from what little we know about the possibilities of growing to full manhood and womanhood ourselves. No amount of technical competence that we might learn in the academies and graduate schools and training institutes can be as effective in helping a seeker grow as that of finding our own way and offering this in an encounter with a seeker. This kind of dialogue and experience might make one a man. ✦

[1968]

# *III-2* On Becoming a Psychotherapist

I can't recall ever deciding or wanting to be a "healer" as such. I don't have the passions of a physician, or the passions which I think physicians have. But I have always, as far back as I can recall, been fascinated with other people's experience—their thoughts, feelings, memories, hopes—partly I think because I lived in a part of the world where people didn't talk much about their personal existences. I found myself puzzled and mystified by others, an also by myself; I wanted to see if others were as confused, frightened, overjoyed, angry, excited, at the same sorts of things that I reacted to.

As a youngster in Mount Dennis, the working class suburb of Toronto where I lived the first 20 years of my life, I always felt myself to be an outsider; our family was the only Jewish family in the area. Within the family, I felt myself to be rather "freaky," because—I don't really know why. I masturbated a great deal as a child, and felt vaguely guilty about that, until my cousin told me he discovered it some five years after I had. I used to rifle through all the bureau drawers in the house, and engage in petty theft from my brother and sisters and parents, and wonder why, what perverse streak in me led me to be so ungrateful and criminal.

I had an insatiable curiosity to learn what went on in other people's heads, and so I both talked and listened a lot with chums. By the time I was in my teens, I was already thinking of myself as a writer, after the fashion of Thomas Wolfe. I used to prowl the streets and back alleys of Mt. Dennis after midnight, on a caffeine "high," unable to sleep, unable to become tired. I would imagine the lives going on behind the shaded windows that I would pass in the night; and in bursts of energy, I would often run three or five miles, and still not be able to drain off the explosions of vitality I felt within myself. All this between the ages, say, of 12 to 16. Of course, too, I felt lonely most of my life, now as well as then. Except for one chum, there was no one to whom I could fully confide, and even with that special chum, much was taboo. We were living in Canada, and the Canadian culture did not encourage open self-disclosure between people any more than New England reputedly does, or doesn't.

I suppose it is fair for me to say, then, that there was not any especial desire to heal the sick, or to relieve suffering that characterized me as a child and adolescent. Rather, I was fascinated with human differences, and of course, I had a robust interest in myself, in trying to understand my likes and dislikes, failures of moral resolve, the wildness of my imagination, and wonderment over my chronic feeling of being different, an outsider. The peculiar thing is that, from an external point of view, I was a not uncommon Canadian youngster. I was active at all sports: hockey, skiing, swimming, football, soccer, baseball, track and field, water polo, etc. But I read anything and everything in orgies. And I alternated between wild enthusiasms which obliterated any interest in myself, and long periods of ferocious self-absorption.

It was during the last of the two summers I spent on a farm in 1942 and 1943, to help out the war effort, that I decided I wanted to go to college. Having made that decision, I next had to decide in what area I should study. As I shovelled manure and hoed turnips, I would spin alternatives through my head. I can recall studying the catalogue of the University of Toronto, and not getting much help from it. I knew what I did not want to enter—medicine, dentistry, engineering and law were all popular choices among those of my friends who entered college rather than the Army, but all felt no strong "call" in those directions. My father ran his small clothing business, and I knew I didn't want to follow in his steps. And so, to stall for time, I selected "Social and Philosophical Studies" as my beginning college program. This was the name of the introductory program leading to a "major" (we called it Honours) in numerous fields, e.g., psychology, sociology, anthropology, geography, philosophy, political science. During that freshman year I found myself fascinated with, and challenged by all the courses I was taking but I somehow was most turned on by Mary Northway's lectures in introductory psychology, and by the outside readings I was doing for her course. We did not use a textbook, and we had to read primary sources to supplement her lectures on learning, perception and kindred topics. But once I got into the psychology section of the main university library, as well as the psychology department library, I discovered forbidden fruit—books by Freud, Jung, Hart, Rivers, Knight Dunlap. These dealt with adjustment, mental health, abnormal psychology and the like, and I read everything I got my hands on. I had a virtual orgy of self-diagnosis and self-discovery through the pages of these many books, with not a jot of discipline to make sense out of it all.

When I decided, at the end of my freshman year, that I was going to do Honour Psychology, I had made a decision that quieted my conflicts. But Toronto psychology soon appeared very boring to me, and irrelevant to my main concern, which, by then, was the positive lust to make myself intelligible to myself as a person; I was not remotely interested in sensation and perception, and the intricacies of learning theory. I was looking for myself, or for some perspective on myself. Once, as an undergraduate, I was so confused I felt I just had to talk to someone. At that time, the Canadian version of machismo was very prevalent, and I'd have lost much face to admit weakness before my friends. And my psychology professors didn't seem to invite much in the way of self-revealing disclosure. We had a professor, Farrell Tombs, who had been trained in the (then) new discipline invented by an American, Carl Rogers, called "non-directive therapy." I made an appointment too see him; he was in the industrial psychology program, as I recall.

He appeared friendly, with a bland face, and started reflecting my feelings, but I panicked, ended the session quickly, and fell back to my own resources.

My college life was full and rich and confusing and enlightening; women did not enter my life until I was half through my sophomore year. Canadians started late, perhaps because of the Puritan influence. In my mind, of course, through avid reading of everything under the sun, I was the most suave and experienced lover and fornicator west of Khajuraho. In fact, I was naive, had had only one or two awkward dates in my freshman year, and was in dread of being rejected by a girl if I indicated I wanted to date her, or kiss her, or start something with her. I was shocked to learn in my senior year that one classmate in psychology on whom I had a hopeless and silent crush had had daydreams all through college of "making it" with me. I was, essentially, steered into an affair with a blonde girl who I thought I had picked up at a tea dance one Friday. Later, she told me that she had picked me out some weeks before, and practiced a scheme her mother taught her: you pick the boy, and learn his comings and goings. Simply be where he goes, almost like a part of the scenery. Then, stay away for about a week. Upon reappearing, he will discover he noticed you and missed you, and is glad to see you. At this stage, he will "take the manly initiative" and ask you out.

This is exactly what happened, and though I was relieved and flattered to have a girl friend, a mistress really, I was vaguely troubled by the fact that I seemed to have little to do with our coming together. Perhaps that experience contributed to my present abhorrence of manipulation.

I was heavily invested in literature, journalism and abortive efforts at creative writing as I was in psychology throughout my undergraduate years. My main quest, however, was the effort to make sense of myself and other people who I always found puzzling to me. I think I always had the feeling that something was going on between people that they weren't telling me about, and that I was missing out on. The Freudian overtones, relating back to my family, are obvious.

By the time I was through my senior year in Honour Psychology, I had been involved in debating, running a rebel newspaper, presenting papers at the Historical Society, playing soccer, water polo, participating in long-distance running, competitive swimming; I had spent one summer on a travelling carnival, traversing Canada, another summer hitch-hiking down to California and up to British Columbia, with a one-month sojourn in California, first in Sacramento County Prison for 10 days, then for three weeks in a detention camp for aliens; I had spent another summer at a children's camp, where I met the woman I married three years later; and during these four years I had gratefully yielded my virginity at age 18 to a 14-year-old overdeveloped girl I met on the carnival; followed it that same summer with an experience in New York with a black street-walking hooker; that same summer was fellated during a drunken stupor seated on a park bench in New York, trying to lose my dizziness so I could ascend the steps of the fraternity house where I was bunking; I had been in love and jilted; and I was confused about my next move toward a career. For want of anything better, I chose to go to graduate school at Toronto, to get a Master's degree, and spent the summer at the same children's camp. ✦

# III-3 *The Transcending Therapist\**

A therapist can be viewed as repairman, trainer, doctor, "guru," "zaddik"—each model, or metaphor calls for him to do or be in some ways, and proscribes other ways.\*\*

Here I explore the image of therapist as a *transcending specialist*, one who has become expert at mastering some aspects of the human condition to which men hitherto have adjusted. The master learns to liberate himself from dehumanizing forces, freeing himself thus to live the life he has chosen. He is then in a position to show others how he did it, so they might "do it" too. His technique is to serve as a model, to show off, to make his magnificence transparent. This view of a therapist is not meant to replace other models—indeed it cannot. It is intended, rather, to supplement prevalent images of therapy and to encourage more therapists to explore the therapeutic possibilities of "modeling," of telling it to their patients "like it is" for them.

The hypothesis may be stated as follows: A psychotherapist is not effective because of scientific expertise; he is effective when, as a person, he has become expert at mastering some conditions which have threatened to diminish his existence. Her knows these conditions, he has wrestled with them; they are his beloved enemies, sent to test him. He has learned what it takes in the way of human courage, imagination, re-

---

*\* This paper, an extension of an earlier article in* Voices, *is based on a talk given at the AAP conference in Philadelphia, October, 1970. A tape-recording of the talk may be available through the AAP tape library.*

*\*\* See Sheldon Kopp's splendid new book,* Guru: Metaphors from a Psychotherapist. *Palo Alto: Science and Behavior Books, 1971.*

sourcefulness and cunning to flourish and grow as a person in the face of these circumstances. The effective therapist is, perhaps, only adequate at taming many of the situations he encounters, but he is *magnificent* at coping with one particular kind. He is thus heroic and graceful in his victory. By conquering some *one* force, he has learned a great deal about conquering any and all dehumanizing forces.

If psychologists, as intellectuals, are good for anything, it is at exploring the generalizing possibilities that are embodied in one person's manifest magnificence! Moreover, I think that this is itself one of the common factors which unite the odd assortment of eccentric human beings who make up the membership of the American Academy of Psychotherapists—who see no contradiction between being professional, effective psychotherapists, and becoming as magnificently human and personal as possible. I don't think that either the American Psychological, or the American Psychiatric Association emphasize personal growth toward magnificence as a criterion of membership. Perhaps that is just as well.

Since every human being stands as a metaphor, as a possibility for every other human being—*nihil humani a mihi alienum puto*—then for one man to conquer dehumanizing forces means he can show others how to "do it." The great therapists, like the great teachers, stand as heroes of our and all time, witness to the fact that biological, psychological, sociological demons can be tamed, transcended, or neutralized, in order that a man can be free. It seems to me that this is what the Old Testament is about.

A corollary to my hypothesis is that a psychotherapist cannot himself, lead a person to freer, more enlightened existence that he himself has attained or can imagine for himself and is presently seeking. He leads and influences his patients like the Israeli officers, who do not say, "Charge!" They say, "Follow me!"

I invite you now to look with me at the exemplary magnificence of some psychotherapists whose careers seem to me to be evidence to support my hypothesis.

Sigmund Freud mastered some forces which could have prevented him from becoming the man who invented psychoanalysis. He suffered Portnoy's complaint, as millions of people in the West have: a seductive, doting mother and a father who was both strong and weak, loved and feared. The result of struggling with such conflicting parental demands has been neurosis and diminished self-actualization for many. Freud's courage lay in facing his recollections and fantasies, his sexuality, his anger, and discovering that one's past need not preclude fuller functioning, whether genital, intellectual, or physical, in adult years. I believe he was most effective as a therapist with persons whose suffering grew out of anti-growth forces comparable to those which he tamed. The therapeutic technique he taught others has not been notorious for its effectiveness. Freud showed *in his very person* that it is possible to marry, make love, raise children and defy all kinds of social pressures in one's time and place in spite of having been raised as a middle class minority group member, with parents whose demands and expectations were not always compatible with free flowering of individuality. He might have helped his patients more swiftly if he were not so shy, so reluctant to share his experience with his patients.

Hobart Mowrer certainly was not helped with his incapacitating depressions by more than seven years of orthodox Freudian therapy. He lived into adult life plagued with guilt over some childhood peccadilloes and adult transgressions against his own ethical and moral standards. There are millions of people who must try to live meaningful and rewarding lives though they are possessed by powerful, puritanical consciences. What Mowrer found to be ultimately, and recurrently, therapeutic, was absolute openness and transparency before all those with whom he dealt. For him to lie, even a little, was analogous to a heroin addict in process of the cure, deciding to take "just one little shot." And so Mowrer developed his Integrity Group Psychotherapy. He participates in an ongoing small group to help him stay "on the level" just as a member of Alcoholics Anonymous meets with fellow alcoholics, or the heroin addict stays engaged with his Synanon fellows to help in the struggle with the forces which would diminish him as a human. Mowrer showed that the temptation to lie and cheat, to misrepresent oneself, *can be tamed*, thereby averting profound guilt and depression for those afflicted with similarly tyrannical consciences.

Carl Rogers was reared, one would imagine, in the American version of the Protestant ethic. Such upbringing produces a strict, and rather provincial conscience—one which keeps people "at it" when there is a frontier to conquer, a fortune to be made, duty to be fulfilled. This is the way of the "inner-directed" character so well described by Riesman. This conscience makes for conditional self-regard, it obstructs empathy, and makes it difficult for a person to be "congruent" in his dealings with others. I would propose that Rogers' greatness, and greatest effectiveness lies, not in his invention of the client-centered techniques, nor in opening psychotherapy to scientific research, nor in his theories, but rather *in his conquest of the upbringing that would limit his growth.* He is a model of a way to be, a way which, when adopted, makes for more mutually confirming and authentic relations with others and which averts sickness. When Carl Rogers was most compulsive as a "reflection" therapist, he was still helpful to his clients (where other "reflectors" were not helpful to their clients) because the man, the person shone through.

The founder of Gestalt therapy, Fritz Perls, discovered that there are many factors operative which prevent a person from living fully in the immediate present, with all senses and modes of experiencing fully active, and with the freedom to act spontaneously. He identified these factors and spent his personal life taming them. He was himself, in person and beyond any of his writings, living testimony of man's power to transcend and prevail, or at least the resolve and the effort to those ends. He was able to show many people how "it's done."

At this point I find myself wondering: why do any of us feel the need to scientize (that is, dehumanize) our discoveries; and to try to be helpful in technical ways? I find myself less and less impressed by the theories and techniques of these men of whom I am speaking. What is wrong with any therapist saying, "Here is how I 'do it' and I can show you how it's done if you care to learn."? I suspect such explicit modeling would cut down the time and cost of therapy.

I have a colleague, Hugh C. Davis, whose background is lower middle-class, rural South. He achieved professional status beyond that of his schoolmates and family members, as did many of us. He is expert at helping people of comparable—and, for that matter, of any background—"make it" in middle class society. His image for describing what he is up to as a psychotherapist and as a person is as follows: "I see man clutching to the edge of the world he wants to live in by the first two knuckles of the fingers on his hands. When he weakens, or when someone is stomping on those knuckles, I reach over, give him a hand to get those two knuckle-lengths hanging on. I try to show him how to get another knuckle or two on the edge." He is superb at doing this. If I were in dread of letting go, dropping into the abyss from which there is no return, I would not hesitate, I would go to this colleague instantly!

The alcoholics, drug addicts and obese people who "kicked" their self-destructive addictions to live effective and meaningful lives, are testimony that persons can tame such addictions. The ways of life evolved by the founders of Synanon, Alcoholics Anonymous and Weight Watchers are teachable, and they do tame the urge to engage in self-destructive behavior. I see a similar dynamic at work in Women's Liberation, in the various Black movements, in the American Indian movement and the Gay Liberation Movement—some one person understood and mastered the forces which were controlling and defining people as a master controls his victim. The liberated woman and the self-respecting Black, both attest that the forces which were diminishing the victims could be transcended. "Consciousness (of being defined and diminished)-raising" meetings are very important in this regard.*

I want now to explore some of the implications of this hypothesis for psychotherapeutic practice.

I think it is high time we stopped regarding those people who are unable to get on with life as *sick,* because we may then feel it is essential to cure them. Better to regard them as *sickened,* or better, as unenlightened and misguided persons. In such cases, one can enlighten and guide more appropriately. Clearly the sickened ones have not known how to transcend the forces which sicken people. How elegant if those committed to healing and helping would, themselves, be exemplars of ways to live that maintain vitality and foster growth.

To whom do professional psychotherapists turn for help when they find themselves at some sickening or dispiriting impasse in their lives? Do they seek yet more analysis, or client-centered therapy, or gestalt psychotherapy? *I do not!* Instead, I pull back, withdraw from the ways in which I had been living up to the point of impasse, and through meditation, or conversation with some honest friend, try to get a perspective on my situation. I try to re-invent my situation, and my ways of being in it, in some enlivening ways. This takes time, and so I need to be able to put up with depression, boredom, and some anxiety; I'm glad to get all the forbearance from friends and family that I can get during this time of withdrawal for re-invention. If I turn to psychotherapists, it is not because of their technical orientation, *but because I know them as persons, and I respect their prowess at coping graciously with dilemmas which presently overpower me.*

---

* *"Consciousness-raising" (I learned from "Women's Lib" people) refers to meetings where diminished humans (Blacks, women, homosexuals) discuss with each other how they were diminished as human persons that day. Such sessions help the participants firm up their resolve.*

As I struggled with the realization that others see me as "middle-aged," I turned not to a professional therapist, but to a colleague in my own department, Wilse B. Webb, a graduate research professor, who has handled this possibly devitalizing time of life graciously, even with elegance. If I were suffering because I had to spend my time struggling against an impulse to dissociate and hallucinate, I wouldn't seek the help of someone skilled at controlling anger; I would want to consult with an acknowledged "madman" who has proven his ability to "pass" in the straight world. I would want him to show me how he "did it" and to supervise and challenge me as I try to find my way.* Such a therapist is one who "passes," who is graceful and secure in his "cover," effective because he knows all the forces and factors which threaten to "blow" the cover. This is one of the meanings of human magnificence. Here, then, is an argument, for psychotherapists, and for that matter, counselors and encounter group leaders, to examine themselves and answer the question, " In what ways am I magnificent? What devitalizing and dehumanizing forces do I transcend with the greatest elegance?" If we can answer these questions, then we might be able to help others in a more direct way, once they came to trust us. It is thus an argument, or justification for psychotherapists to share with their patients, not just their technical expertise or their authentic feelings, but also their ways of staying alive and vital and growing when this is relevant in the therapeutic dialogue. Perhaps a new system of classifying specialists is implicit here. Imagine a brochure which listed the names of all AAP members, not by their theoretical orientation, but rather by the kinds of dilemmas, backgrounds, and crises that they had faced and transcended! ✦

---

* This is the kind of "knowing" or expertise that is under study by Garfinkel. Garfinkel, H. Studies in ethnomethodology. Englewood Cliffs, N. J.: Prentice-Hall, 1967.

# III-4 Psychology: Control or Liberation?*

Sartre (1956) described a scene in which a voyeur peeps through the keyhole into a bedroom.[1] Suddenly, he is discovered by another, and becomes, thereby, an object for the other, and for himself. His experience of his freedom oozes away. Whenever a person is caught in the act, when someone hitherto concealed is seen, then the looker turns the one looked at into stone. Psychologists have been inviting the subjects of their research to become as natural objects, like stones. The surprising thing is that the subjects have cooperated. For the life of me, I cannot fathom why, because I do not know of *any* good that has accrued to the subject as a consequence of *being a subject*, that is, an *object*. This is a strong statement for me to make, because I am a psychologist, with 25 years of my adult life dedicated to this discipline. I really do not believe that the humans we have studied, in the ways that we have studied them, have benefitted from our research! I do not believe that the quality of personal life has been improved by the results of 80 years of the scientific investigation of human consciousness and action. In fact, there is more basis for me to believe that the knowledge of man that we have acquired has been used to control and limit him rather than to enlarge his awareness, his dignity, or his freedom.

---

* Presented at the meetings of the British Psychological Society, Nottingham, 1972. Copyright © 1972 by the author.

[1] Research psychologists would do well to read Sartre's sensitive account of the experience of being looked at.

In research, as most psychologists have practiced it, subjects are recruited and asked to make themselves available to the psychologist for observation, interviewing and testing. He records their speech, actions, and reactions with various kinds of equipment. He analyzes his findings, and publicizes them. Typically, the psychologist defines psychology as a scientific discipline which seeks to *understand* the behavior of man and other organisms. Proof of understanding is evident when the psychologist can *predict* the action or reactions under study, by pointing to signs, or by bringing them under some kind of deliberate *control*. Great pains are taken to insure that the observer does not influence the behavior he is studying,[2] so that the persons or animals under study will show themselves "as they really are." Ideally the subjects of study would not know that they were being watched,[3] because the experience of being observed affects action.

It is clear from this description that scientific psychology has been patterned, since its inception by *Wundt*, after the natural sciences. While we now draw distinctions among natural, social and behavioral sciences, in each of these, similar assumptions are held by the respective scientists, for example, that determinism prevails, and that the "laws" which govern the phenomena under study can be discerned if the right questions are asked of the subject-matter in the right way.

Science, so understood, embodies two ambitions which enchanted me as a youngster. One was the wish to read the mind of others. It was fascinating to try to discern what was going on behind my friend's, or some stranger's opaque exterior. Did they like me? Were they going to harm me? If I could see into or through them, i would have fair warning about their

---

[2] Rosenthal *(1966), of course, has produced much evidence that the experimenter is an important source of variance in the outcome of psychological research. Efforts to make allowance for this influence are discussed in* Miller *(1972).*

[3] *For a review of methods to study man without his awareness, see* Webb et al. *(1966). A more detailed overview of methods for "peeping" at man is given in* Westin *(1967).*

intentions, and I could govern myself accordingly. In fact, if I could read minds in this way, it would give me a certain power over others.

Such power over others was the second childhood wish. I imagined what it would be like to be able to get other people, and animals, to do exactly what I wanted them to do. Snake-charmers and hypnotists provided a kind of model of the type of control I sought, in entertaining these fantasies. To this day, I am intrigued and mystified by the ways in which trainers can get animals to perform intricate tricks.

Let us look at psychology, as a natural science, in the light of these childhood quests for omniscience and omnipotence. It seems fair to say that psychologists aim to read their subjects' minds, and to gain increments of power over their experience and action.

In the dawn of history, man was probably victimized by nature; animals, plants, seas and soil all acted with "minds" of their own, indifferent to his needs and wishes. When nature was seen animistically, or deistically, early men could seek some measure of prediction and control by talking to the souls, spirits and gods which moved natural happenings. They would try to propitiate or bribe those animated beings, in order to get them to tell their intentions, and to help a man get power over hostile nature and untrustworthy, unpredictable strangers. Presumably, those men who could best foretell the future and influence the outcome of events were seen by their fellows as having either more powerful gods, or a closer relationship with the gods. In any case, nature was seen as capricious and hostile; man could improve his lot if he could read her mind (predict what was going to happen) and get her to act in ways that would serve his needs and interests. Natural science was developed to tame and demystify hostile Nature.

The modern scientific psychologist faces his subjects, his subject-matter in a posture similar to that of the natural scientist. The other man's action is not always friendly to *someone's* interests. *Someone* can gain if a man's action can be predicted (i.e., if his mind can be read, if his face becomes a transparent mask through which his stream of consciousness can be read), and if he can be induced to act in ways that serve someone's interests. The subjects of research in scientific psychology are deliberately seen as Other, as one of Them, *as a part of nature different from the scientist and those other persons whom the scientist designates as Us.*

Yet we must remember that a psychologist is a human being, living in a time and place, in a society with a class structure, a power structure—and he has economic interests. Typically, he is salaried, and the costs of his research are borne by private or public agencies. We have to assume that these agencies will not willingly countenance research which will undermine their power over people. A pharmaceutical firm is unlikely to spend millions of dollars in the study of placebos, so that drug use in medicine will be diminished. It does not seem farfetched to me to regard the most rigorous, truth-seeking psychologist as a servant, witting or unwitting, of the agencies which pay him and his costs. The agencies that believe it worthwhile financing research into human behavior typically believe that their interests will be furthered if man's behavior becomes less unpredictable. They want men to be transparent to them (while they remain opaque to others), and they want to learn how to make man's action more amenable to control. Men who can be controlled can serve the controller's interest without knowing it—in which case we could say that they are mystified. If a psychologist studies men, and makes their action predictable, and their experience transparent to some elite—but not to the persons whom he has studied, then he is indeed a functionary, even though he may be a passionate seeker after truth. He may share the class interests of some elite, and he may serve those interests by viewing the subjects of his research as Them, creatures not unlike natural phenomena—floods, earthquakes, animals—which must be understood in order that they be tamed.

My hypothesis is, that unless the behavior scientist explores the broader social, political and economic implications of his work, then he is a functionary indeed; worse, if he does not realize it, then he is being mystified by those who employ him.

The psychological testing movement, likewise can be seen in this light, as a quest to read people's minds, and to fathom their talents, strengths and weaknesses, to serve someone's ends, not necessarily the ends of the person being tested. Beginning with *Binet's* contribution, up to and including *Rorschach's*, the ability of one person, the tester, to discover something about the testee is not necessarily good for the latter. I can remember the excitement I felt, as an undergraduate, when I first heard about tests of intelligence, and of personality, by means of which one person could literally make another transparent. But now, the blacks and other so-called culturally deprived people are less than sanguine in their appreciation of what psychometrics are good for. In fact, quite properly, many blacks see the testing movement as one of the many means by which their subordinate status in the education establishment, and hence the professional world, is maintained. And as we come to take a fresh look at psychiatry, for which profession the projective and many "objective" (like the MMPI) tests of personality were developed, we see that psychiatric classification is less an analogue of differential medical diagnosis, and more a subtle way to invalidate a human being.[4] Projective techniques can be seen as violations of the fifth amendment in the USA—sneaky means by which a person might reveal himself to another. "Unobtrusive measures" which have come to be seen as an answer to uncooperative research subjects, or to experimenter bias, likewise are ways to get a person to reveal himself unwittingly, thereby giving information which may not help him (*Webb et al.*, 1966; *Westin,* 1967).

Am I saying any more than that knowledge of man, like knowledge of nature, gives power, and power corrupts? Perhaps not, but saying that is still to say something which we in

[4] Szasz, T.: *Ideology and insanity (Doubleday, Garden City, N.Y. 1970).*

psychology must take into account. Are we seeking the truth about man that sets all men free? Or are the truths we discover (which our subjects let us learn about them—because men are part of Nature, but they are men who can cooperate with, or block our efforts to study them) only making some men more free and powerful, while others become more vulnerable to manipulation?

It seems clear to me that the image of man entertained or assumed by a psychologist researcher or practitioner will affect his research strategies, his theories, and his ways and areas of consulting. If he views man as a natural object, rather than as a being not unlike himself, his science and its applications will be as I have described.

I will now look at the fields of psychotherapy and counseling, as well as at the behavior-modification movement which also serves as an area for the application of truth learned by scientists—in and out of the laboratory—about man.

Once again, economics rears its head. Psychological practitioners, who apply scientific knowledge of man artfully, do not sell their services cheaply. If in private practice, they charge substantial fees to the individuals and agencies which engage their services. Otherwise, they are retained or salaried by government or private agencies, to utilize their know-how in order that the agency might fulfill its aims more fully. For example, psychologists are employed by advertising agencies, business concerns of many kinds, in order that the public being "served" will more readily buy the company's products or in order that workers will produce more, and more cheaply. Sometimes the service sold by the psychologist is knowledge about how masses of people will respond to symbols; sometimes, they train people in the art of seeming sincere, friendly and authentic.

The arts of counseling and psychotherapy, seen from the perspective of a natural science of psychology, become arenas for the practice of *techniques*, ways to influence the experience and hence the action of the client or patient. Psychoanalysts, behavior-modification experts, even client-centered counseling technicians are all encouraged to believe that if they master a repertoire of laboratory-tested or clinic-tested techniques, they will "get the patient to change." Of course, the techniques of behavior modification by environmental control, as in token-economies in mental hospitals, represent a subtle exercise of power. Hypnosis, "shaping," and aversive conditioning all represent ways to alter someone's action. The *person* who employs these techniques can remain invisible behind a professional manner. If he practices his techniques well, he will earn a fine salary from a grateful agency, or many fees from those rich enough to afford his services. Those individuals who are rich enough to afford his services are seldom spokesmen for liberal change in the political and economic system within which they earn the money to pay for their "treatments." Moreover, some of the more radical psychiatrists are beginning to assert that psychiatric intervention, of whatever sort, is a kind of social control aiming to invalidate and perhaps avert dissent.

If the basic and applied behavior science we have developed thus far has primarily been a quest for knowledge which makes men predictable and controllable, then clearly what is called for is a complementary science, one which uses scientific discipline and knowledge to liberate a man from being the victim, not only of the forces of nature, *but also of the concealed efforts of other men to influence him* for weal or woe.

Man's action and experience are indeed affected by mass media, by leaders, by genes, by his past experience, by reinforcement contingencies, by his biology and physiology, and by the social and interpersonal setting within which he lives his life. Any way of discerning how these realms affect experience and action can be of some use to the person himself, and to others. I think that we psychologists have not served that person. Perhaps this is what Humanistic Psychology, or what psychology as a *human* science, can do.[5]

---

[5] *An introduction to psychology, seen as a human rather than natural science, is given in* Giorgi *(1971).*

In 1957, I began to study self-disclosure. This was before I had ever heard of anything called humanistic psychology. I was trained in experimental as well as in clinical psychology, and a program of research has always been part of my view of the practice of my profession. I defined self-disclosure as a subject for scientific study because I began to wonder what we knew, or could find out about the conditions under which people would reveal personal information to others. *Freud* amply pointed out that psychoanalysis entailed overcoming a patient's reluctance to let his analyst know him, and psychotherapeutic practice called for being an encourager and listener to another's intimate disclosure. And so using what I regarded (and still do) as appropriate techniques for research, I began collecting self-report data from thousands of people about their past disclosure to parents, friends and other target persons. I wanted a "scientific" understanding of self-disclosure in order to predict and control this kind of behavior. Certainly, that is what my scientific training in Toronto and Buffalo encouraged me to do and think. Ironically, I soon discovered that *one of the most powerful correlates, if not "determiners" of one person's self-disclosure was self-disclosure from the other person in the dyad.* Several questionnaire studies pointed to this hypothesis and we confirmed it in numerous experimental interviews conducted under laboratory conditions. We found that we could maximize a person's disclosure of personal data by offering such disclosure first, as a kind of invitation, suggestion, or example of what action was appropriate to the situation. My students and I, in conducting these experiments, did not *pretend* to disclose personal subject-matter. We *really did*, and it was sometimes risky and embarrassing; but we functioned in the spirit of adventurous inquiry, and found the outcomes we have mentioned.[6]

I had begun to experiment with my ways of being a psychotherapist, beginning soon after I discovered that my training did not prepare me to be helpful to Southerners with diffi-

[6] *See* Jourard *(1968, 1971a, b). These three volumes summarize my research and the theory that has grown out of research in self-disclosure, to the present.*

culties in living. I had begun as far back as 1952 to break my professional anonymity, by sharing with a client any experience of mine with problems comparable to those he was exploring with me. I found that such authentic sharing—within bounds of relevance and common sense—encouraged my patients to explore and reveal their experience more fully and freely than was hitherto the case for me. It was as if I had bungled into a new kind of technique, but one which entailed some risk, indeed, some inclusion of my patient into the world of Us, rather than seeing him as one of Them—the neurotics, the psychotics, etc. This experience in conducting psychotherapy appeared to support or confirm my survey and laboratory findings in the study of self-disclosure. But my experience as a psychotherapist influenced my view of research more profoundly. I was motivated to be helpful to the person who sought my professional help, and I found, increasingly, that one way to be helpful was to demystify the patient insofar as it was possible. The patient suffered from difficulties in living because he did not know what was going on. People lied to him, and he to them. Some patients were mystified by nature, others by social structures. It was difficult to know oneself, others and the world. Our therapy sessions could be seen as an effort at authentic communication between two persons, so both would know what was going on. I found myself sharing *my* understanding of how people not only mystified one another, but invited others to be diminished creatures. I would show, and role-play the way people attributed imaginary traits to one another, which they would then embody and act out—like *Genet* becoming the thief he was defined to be early in life. Gradually, my understanding of what a psychologist's task might be underwent a change. I came to see that, if hitherto, research and practice grew out of a view of man as a natural phenomenon to be studied by an elite in order that he be better mind-read and controlled, it would be elegant to strive to do psychology for man. This, I came to see, must be what a Humanistic Psychology would be, and be for.

Humanistic Psychology could be defined, I saw, as an effort to disclose man and his situation *to himself*, to make him more aware by any and all means, of what forces were influencing his experience and hence his action. I could see that human subjects would not really disclose themselves, would not really let themselves be known to researchers or anyone else whom they had reason to distrust, and so we commenced a program of research within which the researcher was as much to be interviewed by the subject as vice versa. Though we have made only a token beginning at this, the results confirm that different perspectives on man will emerge when more such research is done.

If various institutions aim to control man's action and experience in order to serve the institution's aims, then a task for a humanistic psychology could be to study the means by which the propaganda, rules, and environment produced conformity, so that a person could better choose to conform or not to conform. I discovered in the process of this inquiry that for one person to lie to another is an effort to control this experience and action, so that he will indeed be mystified, and "determined," so long as he believes the lies. This is exactly equivalent to the situation of man facing a hostile nature which he does not understand. Not to understand is to be vulnerable to prediction and control—victimization, whether by mystifying nature, or by one's lying and self-concealing fellow man. To be understood, and not to understand the one who understands you, is indeed to be vulnerable—to be a transcendence transcended, as *Sartre* (1956) puts it.

I suppose that the project is to give it away—as fast as man is studied by natural-science psychologists (to learn about the determiners of his experience and action), humanistic psychologists (who can be natural-science psychologists too) can make apparent to all the ways in which their freedom is being eroded by hostile nature or hostile people.

Psychological research, from this perspective, becomes an enterprise wherein the subject becomes privy to the aims of the researcher, and wherein he is free to learn about the researcher as the researcher learns about him.

Counseling and psychotherapy, from the standpoint of humanistic psychology, become enterprises wherein patient and therapist, counselor and client share relevant experience so that the latter can become more enlightened, more liberated from his influences that constrain his growth and self-actualization. Indeed, I find myself using the word therapy less and less, seeking some metaphor more aptly descriptive of what goes on in such helping transactions. Terms like teacher, guide, guru, liberator suggest themselves, though all sound fairly pretentious. But in all these cases, one thinks not of a person manipulating another, reading his mind in order to gain power over him; rather one thinks increasingly of a dialogue between I and You. ✦

### References

Giorgi, A.: *Psychology as a human science (Harper, New York 1971).*

Jourard, S.M.: *Disclosing man to himself (Van Nostrand Reinhold, New York 1968).*

Jourard, S.M.: *The transparent self; 2nd ed. (Van Nostrand Reinhold, New York 1971a).*

Jourard, S.M.: *Self-disclosure. An experimental analysis of the transparent self (Wiley-Interscience, New York 1971b).*

Miller, A.G. (ed.): *The social psychology of psychological research (Free Press, New York 1972).*

Rosenthal, R.: *Experimenter effects in behavioral research (Appleton-Century-Crofts, New York 1966).*

Sartre, J.P.: *Being and nothingness, p. 259 (Methuen, London 1956).*

Webb, E.J.; Campbell, D.T.; Schwartz, R.D., and Sechrest, L.: *Unobtrusive measures: non-reactive research in the social sciences (Rand McNally, Chicago 1966).*

Westin, A.F.: *Privacy and freedom (Atheneum, New York 1967).*

# *III-5* Changing Personal Worlds: A Humanistic Perspective

Everything depends on what you believe man is like.[2] If you assume that man is something like a machine, that assumption is, in a way, not an assumption alone. It is sort of an invitation and a prescription to man to be in the world in ways that mimic a machine. Man seems to me to be a very peculiar creature: he can conform himself to all kinds of images, because he doesn't have any rigidly fixed nature or design to determine how he will be in the world, how he will act, and how the world will be for him. Now, if you assume that man is a being like a monkey or a pigeon, then that too is a kind of invitation that a person may accept.

I have been exploring with as much vigor and ingenuity as I know how the implications for living, for doing psychological research and for applied psychology when I assume that man is *human*, and hence more like me than a machine, monkey, or pigeon.[3] One implication of this assumption is that, as I learn something about myself, I will have learned a certain amount about you. When I assume that you are a being something like me, this will influence the way I interact with you when you are my friend, a member of my family, my student, my research subject, or when you're my patient. I'll probably address you truly in the second person, as "you," rather than speak to you in the pretense that you are indeed a "you," a being something like me, while in my imagination I'm really talking to my colleague who truly is "you" to me. He and I are talking about the "him" which is "you": you exist for us in the third person from this perspective.

Now I will explore the theme of changing personality, which might also be called changing behavior, or changing experience. Actually, I prefer the title "Changing Personal Worlds: A Humanistic Perspective."

First, we'll concern ourselves with the theme of personality. From my point of view, the term "personality" simply means *one's way of being a person.* To be a person refers to a way of experiencing the world and a way of acting upon the world.[4] You can turn that around, and say that to be a person is a way for the world to be experienced and acted upon. If you have two persons present, you have two ways for the world to be experienced, and two ways for it to be acted upon. When I say "experienced," I'm using the term experiencing in the phenomenological sense; that is, I am referring to the different modes of experiencing, which include perception, remembering, thinking, imagining, fantasy and dreaming. These are all ways for the world to be experienced by persons. Each one of us embodies a way for the world to be perceived, thought about, remembered, imagined, and so on.[5] But your experience is a determiner of your action. As you change your ways of experiencing the world you'll also be changing, to some extent, your ways of acting in the world.

The theme that I am addressing, then, is how does personality change occur? How might somebody foster it, or facilitate it, or make it happen, or help it happen, when we talk about man, not as a "him" or an "it" in the third person, but as a "you," as someone who exists for me in the second person, and for himself in the first person. Personality change, when viewed from the perspective or a humanistic perspective on man, entails some disengagement of a person from his present ways of experiencing and acting in the world, followed by an opening of his field of experience to new dimensions of experience that were always possible but were not yet realized, followed then by a reentry into one's situation in order to make it more livable. This is a view of personal change that has gradually been emerging from my own thinking and my own research.[6]

Let me address the theme of *trying* to facilitate or invite change in another person. This is what a professional counselor and psychotherapist does.[7]

A psychotherapist can be seen as a repairman, as a trainer, as a doctor, as a guru, as a zaddik—each model or metaphor calls for him to do or be in some ways and proscribes some other ways. I refer you in this connection to Kopp's recent book.[8] Here I want to explore the image of a psychotherapist as a specialist at transcending, one who has displayed expertise at transcending some aspect of facticity to which men have hitherto adjusted. The master learns to liberate himself from dehumanizing forces, freeing himself thus to lead a life that he has chosen. He is then in a position to show others how he did it so that they might do it too. His technique, if he has any, is to serve as a model, to show off, to make himself transparent. This view of the therapist is not meant to replace other models, simply because it cannot. But I intend it, rather, to supplement prevailing images of therapy and to invite more psychotherapists to explore the therapeutic possibilities of modeling, of being a model.

Let me just make a digression at this point. We're talking about trying to foster or invite personal change, change in a person's way of being in the world. This presumably is what psychotherapists are supposed to be skilled at doing. There are two ways to approach this. If one experiences the other individual as "him," in the third person, then one's approach to personal change almost necessarily calls for techniques of manipulation, influence, hypnosis, shaping, doing something. From a broader perspective you can say that this is the exercise of power *over* another, when one experiences the other in the third person. When one is inviting change by example, then the other individual exists in the second person, as "you." Other metaphors make sense; one is seducing, one is showing off, one is inviting, one is challenging.

Let's just pursue this. Modeling, (showing off) can be seen as a case of *the attribution of power and strength* to somebody.

To attribute one's own capacity to cope to another person is what is implicit in the act of modeling, in letting another person see how you've done it. I'll develop this question in several ways here. We can just ask this question, "to whom do you attribute the power to change your situation: to another person? to yourself? to God?" This question is decisive. If we think of modeling as a special case of attributing power to others: power to cope, power to transcend, it brings therapy into the possibilities of research by techniques that already have been developed in social psychology by people like Fritz Heider[9] and Ronald Laing.[10] One has to become interested in the whole logic and theory of attribution. How do I experience you? What power or capacity to cope or to grow do I attribute to you? Do I see you as a creature inhabited by forces over which you have no control, so that you need my power to help you control it? Or do I experience you as someone with the capacity to cope with damn near anything? If a person becomes a patient, it's because he has clung to a way of experiencing himself, others and the world, and he has clung to ways of acting in the world *which no longer are life-giving*.

When a person is suffering, it is almost *prima facie* evidence that his ways of being are no longer viable. They are no longer effective in sustaining well-being and growth, and it is time for him to change some aspect of his world.

Let us explore just what it is that we think needs to be changed. If one addresses a person with the resolve to alter his behavior, to extinguish or shape it, (this terminology comes from a behavioristic approach to the study of man) this can alter that person's experience of power. But the question is, *whose* power is a person experiencing when he has altered his behavior at the instigation of some expert at behavior change? He may have his view confirmed, that *the other person's* theories and powers are very powerful indeed, but it may not enhance his own sense of his own powers, or his felt capacity to change his world and his situation at his own initiative. As for myself, I resolutely refuse to see another person as one who is condemned to weakness or as one whose existence and growth is dependent on drugs, doctors, or on charting his response. I insist on seeing the other person *as a person* who has the capacity, when his life has reached a stalemate, and he is no longer living in viable ways—*I see him as one with the capacity to transcend that*, to cope with that, to withdraw, get a better picture of what is going on, to charge right back into the situation and change it in some non-destructive way so that life is more possible. And I see the great psychotherapists (or psychotherapists whom I see great) as specialists in coping with some dimension of facticity that most people yield to or accommodate themselves to. The great therapists stand as living proof that that which has subjected most other men is to them a challenge that they have tamed or transcended. By so doing, they are living exemplars of the possibility that you and I and anybody else can do it.

Everything can be a metaphor for anything else. For instance, you can see me as a tiger or a monkey. Or a woman can be seen as an iceberg or an inferno. Metaphor and simile and analogy are all tokens of a vital imagination and these release man from the hypnotic spells of perception and memory. Every metaphor is an invitation or a challenge to transmute what is perceived or remembered into the metaphor. As soon as one envisions a different self and a different world and begins to make them actual, then the present self and world become a kind of metaphor, a pale simile for the world to come.

A therapist can be seen as a metaphor for the patient. His way is a possibility for the patient if he shows how he did it, how he tamed some facticity, how he emancipated himself, healed himself, perfected himself. From this perspective, the patient is his therapist *manqué*.

The most obvious implication of this view is that it really doesn't matter in what theoretical school a therapist has been trained, nor do his techniques matter. What seems crucial to me is that he be a continually growing person, that he be continuously engaged in the struggle between his freedom and the facticity amidst which all of us live. The effective therapist is, perhaps, adequate at taming most of the facticity he encounters but he is magnificent at coping with some one dimension of it so that he is heroic and graceful in his victory. Such a person is proof that a mere human can do it, almost as if to say, "If I can do it, so can you" or "If he can do it, so can I and you."

My flying instructor—I take flying lessons—is a boring man outside of the airplane. He speaks in a monotone, his personal life and his political philosophy, as I know them, are unimaginative and stereotyped. To me, however, he is a hero, the master of flight, a tamer of gravity, a birdman. He holds a certain charisma for me. He's willing to show me how he does it and I'm learning and oddly enough he shows me how it's done by imitating a teaching machine. As we sit in the airplane, he gives me "frames." He offers frames from a program instruction booklet that change you from a groundling to a pilot. I don't, however, consult with my flight instructor for help in how to live my marriage, my professional life, or my life in the community in ways that would preserve my eccentricity and magnificence.

I invite you, now, to look with me at some psychotherapists whose careers seem to me to be evidence to support the hypothesis that I've been presenting, that the great psychotherapists are exemplars at taming and transcending some aspects of the factical world that subjugate most of us.

The hypothesis seems obvious to me. To assert that some other factor such as training, tricks or techniques are the only effective agents in psychotherapy, teaching or influence seems to me to be stupidity, bad faith, or a futile quest for the means by which little men can pretend to be larger men in order to influence others out of proportion to their merit. I might add, be careful whose techniques you use, because you may not be person enough to use them properly. A corollary to this hypothesis is that a psychotherapist cannot himself lead a person to a freer and more enlightened existence than he himself has attained or can imagine for himself and is presently seeking.

According to this view, he leads and influences his patients like the Israeli officers who do not say, "charge," they say "follow me."

Now let me turn to what I call the "exemplary magnificence of some psychotherapists." We'll start with Freud. We could actually start with Moses but Freud is a good place to begin.

Freud mastered some forces which could have prevented him from becoming the man who invented psychoanalysis. He suffered "Portnoy's Complaint," as millions of people in the west have—a seductive, doting mother and a father who was both strong and weak, loved and feared. The result of struggling with such conflicting parental demands has been neurosis and diminished growth for many. Freud's courage lay in facing his recollections and fantasies, his sexuality, his anger and discovering that one's past need not preclude fuller functioning, whether it was genital, intellectual or physical functioning, in adult years.

I believe he was most effective as a therapist with persons whose suffering grew out of anti-growth forces comparable to those which he himself had tamed. The therapeutic technique he taught others has not been notorious for its effectiveness. Freud showed in his very person that it's possible to marry, make love, raise children and defy all kinds of social pressures in one's time and place in spite of having been raised as middle class, minority group member with parents whose demands and expectations were not always compatible with the free flowering of individuality. I suspect he might have helped his patients more swiftly—he sometimes kept patients seven years or more—if he were not so shy and so reluctant to share his experience with his patients.[11] It's interesting that Freud apparently was never so effective with older people as Jung was, people who had already struggled through their childhood hangups but were finding life meaningless in their forties and fifties, not because of unresolved Oedipal problems but because life, as an adult, had reached the end of its tether. It was time to let go of those forms in order to go forward.

Now I'll discuss the magnificence of Hobart Mowrer. Mowrer was not helped with his incapacitating depressions by more than seven years of orthodox Freudian therapy. He lived into adult life plagued with guilt over some childhood peccadillos and adult transgressions against his own ethical and moral standards. Hobart Mowrer doesn't mind my presenting this information because he has already put it in the public domain. There are millions of people who have to try to live a meaningful and rewarding life though they are possessed, notice what I say, they are possessed, they don't possess, they are possessed by a powerful, puritanical conscience. What Mowrer found to be ultimately and recurrently therapeutic was absolute openness and transparency before all those with whom he dealt. For him to lie, even a little, was analogous to a heroin addict who in the process of trying to get rid of the habit decided to take just one little wee shot. And so Mowrer developed his integrity group psychotherapy. He participates continuously in an ongoing small group to help him stay on terms of authenticity with himself and others. Mowrer showed that the temptation to lie and to cheat, to misrepresent one's self can be tamed, thereby averting profound guilt and depression for those who are afflicted with a similarly puritanical conscience.

Now let me mention Carl Whittaker and R.D. Laing. I suspect that Ronald Laing and Carl Whittaker enjoy the kind of experience that many of their colleagues call schizophrenic. They can maneuver effectively in the conventional world despite or because of the fact that they are capable of such transcendental experience. If the average person is terrified by the experience of the dissolution of his world and his identity, then he must repress his capacity for enlarged experiencing, thereby limiting his capacities for growth and for functioning. (Whittaker is Professor of Psychiatry at Wisconsin, Ronald Laing is probably one of the best known writers on themes relating to living life and a very competent, practicing psychotherapist.) Both these men show that it's possible to be effective in personal and professional life and to live with one's possibilities for madness, which they see as an opportunity for either the destruction of one's world and letting it stay or the beginnings of an enlarged world in which one can live more fully.

Let me mention Alfred Adler and Eric Berne. I believe that we can look at Adler as a person who in his lifetime suffered from other people's efforts to make him feel inferior, to put him down. Many people yield to other's suggestions that they are worthless and they live only half-lives because of such yielding; and everybody has been victimized to one extent or another by someone who can say, "Oh, you're looking very well *today*." Adler recognized the games that were being played with him, and the self-defeating counter-games he was playing, and so he became a *Magister Ludi*, a master of the game. He was able then to help others who grappled with the same dilemmas. He strongly influenced Eric Berne in the process. Now, because of the writings of Adler and Eric Berne, millions are shown how people try subtly to gain control over one another's existence and how one can gracefully get on with life in spite of such games or, better, without them.

Now let me mention the founders of various self-help, non-professional groups. The alcoholics and drug addicts and obese people who "kick" their self-destructive addictions in order to live more effective and meaningful lives are giving testimony that addictions can be tamed. The way of life which the founders of Synanon, Alcoholics Anonymous and Weight Watchers developed is teachable or demonstrable. The way of life that they embody does tame the urge to engage in self-destructive behavior. I see a similar dynamic at work in Women's Liberation and in the various Black movements. Some one person understood and mastered the forces which were controlling people as a master controls his victim. The liberated woman and the self-respecting Black both attest that the forces which were diminishing the victims could be transcended.

Fritz Perls, the founder of Gestalt therapy, discovered that there were many factors operative that could prevent a person from living fully in the immediate present with all senses and moods of experiencing fully active and with the freedom to act spontaneously. He identified these factors and spent his personal life taming them. He was himself, in person and beyond any of his writings, living testimony to man's determination, as well as his power, to struggle to transcend and prevail over forces that would diminish his sense of vitality. And he was able to show many people how it's done.

Victor Frankl impresses me, not so much by his therapeutic theories, but by the very fact of his survival as a magnificent human being, in spite of the Nazi effort to incinerate him. Frankl was able, daily, to find *raisons d'etre*—reasons for living—when all about him in the death camp others were giving up, or permitting themselves to be killed by Nazis, or by weakness.

Now I would like to look at some behavioristic psychologists—Skinner, Ogden Lindsley, Professor Wolpe, Eysenck and my colleague, Pennypacker. They too are all exemplars of a certain kind of magnificence which I take to be the discovery of techniques for teaching others how to analyze large behavioral units into manageable bits, the better to control it. It's unclear to me yet how effective these men are at attributing power to patients. I think they believe power resides in the idea of behavior modification, or the various conditioning theories and techniques. What I found most fascinating about the whole field of behaviorism or behavior science is that its appeal is to those who are most fascinated with the problem of management and control of somebody's behavior.

Now I'm most familiar with the efforts of my colleagues at Florida where we have a very flourishing division of behavior management within our department. My colleague, Pennypacker, has hundreds of people "managing" reading-behavior. He trains one group of students as "managers" and they have questions on three-by-five cards: students read chunks of a book, and then chart the number of correct answers they get in five-minute episodes. They all get straight A's because they can answer questions efficiently. It's still not clear yet what this kind of monitored studying does to the capacity of the student to tackle large challenges.

I have to share with you an amusing anecdote. Pennypacker and I are very good friends and colleagues and have been for the past ten years; we each were compulsive smokers. He and I both were smoking two ounces or more of pipe tobacco a day every day, inhaling every puff. We were totally addicted. About two years ago I decided to quit. But as an addict, I had withdrawal symptoms. I became terrified. I asked myself, "How can I quit? I know what, I'll do what Hank Pennypacker does. I'll count something. I'll count puffs, chart it, and establish a base rate."

I then said, "The hell with it, that's for children and animals, and I'm neither. I will trust in my own theories." I was interested in yoga, and I developed this technique for stopping my smoking out of a Hathe Yoga exercise. I kept my pipe in my hand at all times; every time I got an urge to smoke, I would take a slow yoga breath.[12] If the urge persisted, I would do another one. The first day I had to do about fifty cycles of that but then the second day it was cut to twenty-five, and the third day about a dozen, the fourth day about half-a-dozen and the fifth day two or three. That was it, there was no more. I have not smoked for two years now, and I have had no urge to resume.

Pennypacker believes in his own techniques and he keeps careful count. He has a wrist counter, and he's on to cigars now and he's trying to bring his urges and the cigar under stimulus control. It's hilarious. He has one of those little buzzers, a one hour buzzer. You can set it for an hour or half-an-hour. At executive committee meetings we'll be talking away about the policy of the department and all of a sudden buz-z-z. Pennypacker will whip out a cigar, but my colleagues all start drooling like Pavlov's dogs because you never know what's being conditioned with that.

I want to explore, briefly, some of the implications of this hypothesis for psychotherapeutic practice. What I'm saying, incidentally, extends to some of the so-called humanistic growth promoting techniques that you read about or involve yourself in—encounter groups, yoga, the various sensitivity training techniques—they all share something in common with the thesis that I'm presenting here: a refusal to yield to the path of least resistance which is one way of saying "being determined." They share a struggle, in other words, to disengage from that which was controlling you in order to discover new possibilities of one's self and of the world in order then to dive back in, as Odysseus returned to Ithaca, to make it fit for a grown man to live in. I think it's elegant that I'm here in Ithaca because the Odyssey myth looms large in my life.

I think it's high time we stopped regarding people who aren't able to get on with life as sick because we may then feel it's essential to cure them. Better to regard them as sickened or better, as unenlightened and subdued or misguided. In such cases, one can enlighten, encourage and guide more appropriately. Clearly the sickened ones have not known how to transcend the forces which sicken people.

How elegant if those committed to healing and helping would themselves be exemplars of the ways to live that maintain vitality and foster growth. Now to whom do professional psychotherapists turn for help when they find themselves in some sickening or dispiriting impasse in their lives? Do they seek yet more analysis or client-centered therapy or behavior modification or Gestalt psychotherapy? I don't. Instead, I pull back, I withdraw from the ways in which I'd been living up to that point and through meditation or conversation with an honest friend or travels to get away from the scene, try to get a perspective on my situation. I try to reinvent my situation and my ways of being in it some enlightening ways. This takes time, so I need to be able to put up with depression and boredom and some anxieties. I'm glad to get all the forbearance from friends and family that I can get during this time of withdrawal in order to reinvent myself. I don't want to be healed. I just want to be left alone or talked to as a human being. If I turn to psychotherapists it's not because of their technical orientation but because I know them as persons, and I respect their prowess at coping graciously with dilemmas which presently overpower me.

I struggled with the realization that others see me as middle-aged. I've got bifocal lenses, I have gray hair, I'm in my forties, and my children are nearly grown. I arrived at a kind of impasse that Jung has described with considerable vividness. I and a lot of my colleagues and friends find ourselves in this particular bind, and as America becomes increasingly affluent, people will arrive at this bind at younger and younger ages—in fact, they already are. Then the question is, how then do you cope in life-giving ways with an impasse of this sort? I turned not to psychotherapists but to one of my colleagues who happens to be a sleep researcher. He has handled this possibly devitalizing time of life very graciously and even with elegance. It was in conversation with him that I coined the statement of an immortal truth which might catch on: "Middle age is definitely not for children." But just as one does not send a student who wishes to learn dancing to a voice teacher, I think it's ridiculous to send someone who can't control his urge to drink to someone who's expert at overcoming his dead parents' influence on the way he lives his adult life.

If I were suffering because I had to spend my time struggling against an impulse to dissociate and hallucinate, I wouldn't seek the help of someone skilled in controlling anger: I would want to consult with an acknowledged madman who has proven his ability to pass in the straight world. I want him to show me how he did it and to supervise and challenge me as I try to find my way.

Here then is an argument for psychotherapists, and for that matter, counselors and encounter group leaders and teachers to examine themselves and answer the question, "In what ways am I magnificent, what aspects of facticity do I transcend with the greatest elegance?" If we can answer these questions then we might be able to help others in a more direct way once they came to trust us; and they would if we were trustworthy. This is an invitation to psychotherapists to share with their patients not just technical expertise—which is what one applies in the third person as one talks about it in the second person to one's true peers—but also their ways of staying alive and vital and growing when all about them others are devitalized. Sharing this when it becomes relevant is the dialogue that I call psychotherapy.

Perhaps a new system of classifying specialists is implicit here. Imagine a brochure which listed the names of all the therapists, not by their theoretical orientation but by the kinds of dilemmas, backgrounds and crises that they had faced and transcended. This actually does have some far-reaching implications. You know how they have computerized dating and mating. You fill out a card; you like chess, you like horseback riding and this music and that literature and you shuffle the cards together and the computer drops out the names of five or ten possible people. Well, I don't see why it wouldn't be possible in a neighborhood or a community to identify the people who are just superb at transcending some dimension of facticity so that when someone is overwhelmed or near suicidal from it, you call Aunt Molly, or the bartender or Uncle Willy who is good at it, and he comes over, just as in Alcoholics Anonymous when someone is ready to take a drink he calls a buddy and they sweat it out together. One could identify those people who had tamed the facticity that is subjugating somebody else and they might then avert the necessity of a great deal of professional care.

Let me conclude by saying that there is a sense in which I regard efforts to foster change in another by environmental control or by shaping techniques or by any means that are not part of an authentic dialogue as in some ways pernicious and mystifying, probably not good for the well-being and growth of the persons to whom these efforts are addressed; and probably not very ennobling for the people who practice them.

## DR. JOURARD - QUESTIONS

<u>Question</u>: You mentioned that part of your effort is to invite people to avoid the path of least resistance. Since that tends to involve suffering, I was wondering if you could expand a little bit on the value of suffering that must be recognized?

<u>Answer</u>: I've been reading the Old Testament for the first time in my life and finding it fascinating. I have become enthralled with the difference between worship of the true God, which to me means, "living in a lifegiving way," as opposed to idolatry. Idolatry is, in a last analysis, living in devitalizing or killing ways. Suffering, it seems to me, is an indication among other things that you're not living right. But there are also times when in order to get from here to there—it's worth getting there—that there's hardly any way of avoiding suffering.

Now, there's some balance that calls for wisdom: to seek out suffering is a peculiar sort of idolatry or it's a very old way to live one's life. To avoid suffering in a compulsive way, and to do everything in one's power not to experience effort and pain is in itself a kind of idolatry. Let's say it is painful to experience anxiety, and it really is. An anxiety onslaught is devastating. But to struggle as a so-called neurotic does, to live an anxiety-less existence, he pays a tremendous price for it. He gives up damn near anything in order not to experience anxiety. The ability to hang in and to gird one's loins and grit one's teeth and endure pain and suffering in order to get at something worthwhile seems to me, among other things, to have the capacity to build strength.

<u>Question</u>: You were saying that we should categorize therapists according to what dilemmas they've overcome. What does a person who is thinking of going into therapy do? Should the person say, as a therapist, that I have been through something like this? (Sure) Would the therapist really turn around to a person and say, "No, I have not experienced something like that, I don't want to take the responsibility of helping you through this thing because I haven't been through it myself." They sort

of have this thing, you know, this overpowering god-like image at times that they can help a person.

Answer: I think honesty is what is essential on the part of the therapist. I've never experienced what it's like to menstruate; someone may have menstrual cramps and that may interfere with their life or something of the sort. But I've had diarrhea and belly cramps. That's a trivial example. I think I have been consulted by people who have had devastating tragedy in their life and it's incapacitated them and I have not experienced tragedy of such intensity, of such havoc-producing dimensions. I wouldn't pretend to, but I would let them know how much I had experienced and that I would struggle to try to understand them and to help them endure it and to grope, try to be helpful in groping with them for ways to live in spite of the tragedy. There are many professional people, however, who insist on a mask of professional anonymity. That's all right, too, because there are many people who attribute power almost in a magical way to the professional anonymity of the expert. Their experience of power residing in the therapist would be diminished if they discovered that he ate, drank, made love, went to the toilet and so on.

Question: But you are saying that there are generalizing qualities to the ability that you have found to handle the problem in your own life, which you can generalize to other kinds of dilemmas which you haven't faced which someone else has?

Answer: There may be generalizing power such that if you coped with one kind of dilemma, that gives you the capacity to hang in there, to use your imagination, courage and resourcefulness to cope better with others. I believe that to be true. I believe it to be true to such an extent that I believe that efforts to make everything easy and effortless and in small manageable steps is training for flabbiness. I see this as interfering with the development of strong men and women.

Question: If I'm hung-up with one experience which you never experienced before and I wanted to come to you as a therapist depending on how different my hang-up is from any of those you've experienced, then you've got a judgment about whether you could relate to me or not relate to me?

Answer: Let's take the very term "hang-up." You see that implies that my world and my way of being in it are fine and splendid except for some one attitude, a way of experiencing or way of acting in a situation that gets in my way. If that is indeed the case, then I would think that the most appropriate way of coping with that obstruction to a more fully lived life is to seek out someone who is very good at breaking habits, someone in the behavior modification or conditioning tradition. There are many instances where some attitude or habit persists long past the point of serving any adaptive function; it is often difficult to get rid of such habits. If I couldn't break it myself, I wouldn't hesitate to ask someone to help me break it. But the peculiar thing there is that I cannot help but feel that there's a self-fulfilling prophesy there. I know very well that my habits, like smoking, can be broken in an instant. If you've got faith, it can be done. Pennypacker has no faith in breathing. He would say that it's through reciprocal inhibition, the inhibition of one habit by acquiring another. But you don't see me taking deep Yoga breaths all the time.

Question: I was very glad to hear you include the Black Nationalists in the category of psychotherapist and I was thinking particularly of Elijah Mohammed and Malcolm X, and I can see very clearly that they would not be effective psychotherapists for, let's say, middle class white college students who have struggled with different problems. My question is, is the effectiveness of that movement and those people in changing people's lives simply a function of the fact that the men who were prominent, who have been prominent in it, have struggled with the same problems as the people who they are trying to help or does it have something to do with the positive solutions which they're offering which tend to be rather highly structured and precise, especially if you take Elijah Mohammed? Do you see what I'm driving at? Is the effectiveness of the psychotherapist just a function of the problems with which he has struggled or does it have something to do with the solutions or the ideology which he offers?

Answer: That's a difficult question. Let's start off first by saying, I don't know. But then I'll talk for a minute, like a college professor. We can make the assumption that people want to live as groovy a life as it's possible for them to live with as much satisfaction and meaning and challenge and value in it. And when someone is being subdued or diminished by circumstances he may believe that that's what life is all about: to live a subdued, subjugated existence. Until he sees somebody with whom he can identify, somebody who's "like us," who has made it, who's gotten out, who's gotten on top. Once he sees that, he can no longer pretend that he is fated to remain where he was. If I were a dictator and I had managed to convince people that this is the way life is, and there is little we can do to escape, and then someone escaped, I would want to destroy him as swiftly as I could because others would see him and say, "If he can do it, I can do it." Now the man who transcended it may not be able to show in any but a superstitious way how he went about doing it, but at least he's living proof that it can be done.

Question: How do you know when the madman that you're consulting for your madness isn't back into a mad streak right then? What guarantee do you have that now he's out of his madness?

Answer: I think there is a very basic factor of human trust and trustworthiness that develops out of dialogue between a person and the one he is consulting. And while people are vulnerable to being misled, in time they discover when they are not being helped by someone whom they were consulting for help. And if Ronald Laing's or Carl Whittaker's patients found that their capacity for living was radically destroyed by consulting them, they would probably stop consulting. I was a patient of Carl Whittaker for a while; I trust him, and I don't think my capacity to cope with existence was diminished for having seen him. And I don't know what that proves. Your question, I think, is a searching one.

Question: If you helped that man who had helped himself would you go down with him when he is reverting?

Answer: I certainly wouldn't go down with Laing or Whittaker.

Question: Because of the issue of authority, I was wondering if somehow you could have people that were actually magnificent heroes and yet wouldn't come down in such a way so that when the person gets some change occurring he can attribute it to himself?

Answer: I make this assumption for myself, that the other person has much more power than he ever dreamed he has. When he consults with me, he is arguing, "You are strong, I am weak." And I'll say, "You don't seem weak to me. You've got the strength of a horse." "No, I am sick," he might reply. "You don't seem sick to me. You seem bewildered or confused or befuddled or timid." He attributes characteristics to himself that I disagree with and I attribute characteristics to him that he disagrees with. And we have a kind of argument going. If he wins the argument, he loses a great deal indeed, because he is saying over and over again, "I cannot, I cannot." And I'm saying essentially, "You can, you can. I have done it. He has done it. We are human. You are human. You probably may be able to do it." And so on.

Question: But suppose afterwards, now he wins this argument with this magnificent figure and he comes across feeling, "Gosh, I really can do something." But suppose then, you know, a couple of months later he thinks, "Gee, that guy was clever." He didn't tell me about the sort of subtlety of what may really be manipulative in the sense that he may attribute it to a kind of game where you let him win this argument so that he would feel that he had this kind of personal control. But then he becomes aware of it a few months later, and what's he left with? (I don't know.) Isn't it better to come straight on with it like a behavior therapy kind of technique where you're saying, "Well, this is the game of life, these are the rules, this is what the change is going to be attributed to, and so forth." Then you'll not be left with this appendage where a person simply doesn't know at the end what produced the change or if *you* really produced the change and not himself?

Answer: I don't know. I think I can say this, that if someone is seeking the help of one who is competent and who has faith in behavioristic techniques and principles and that's the package that is being presented and sold, I have no quarrel with it. But for that person to pretend to be doing something other than what he's doing, I have some quarrel with that. I do think there is a way of looking at the human scene in the light of attribution; we'll call it attribution theory for want of a better name. How do we regard ourselves? How do other people regard us? To what extent does the other person's view of me affect my view of myself? If you want me to be diminished, then all the time I'm in your presence and if I spend a lot of time in your presence, you need never say a single word but I probably will feel diminished. And if you want me dead, in due time I may find my zest for living diminished. If you want me impotent, I suspect... I'll tell you an anecdote. I worked in a setting with a bunch of professional women once and I noticed that for months at work I never once felt remotely erotic. Some of these women, you know, had conventionally attractive appearances and I discovered as I came to know them better, that these were people who had some difficulties with men and could best deal with a man who was desexualized. And so there was a marked absence of all the little flutters, and wiggles, and twitches that remind a person of the difference between the sexes. It was not something that was actively being done; it was simply an incarnated expression of the wish that the other person be desexualized. I'll state as a hypothesis, that the view of the other person's possibilities that I truly hold and act upon is a very important factor in the transaction between him and me, whether I state it in words or whether it is a continuous nonverbal expression of this view that "you can do it, you can do it, you can do it."

Question: I wonder if it's your intention to leave the audience with the idea that you can only help somebody with a problem if you've experienced it yourself? I think lots of times, in terms of one's experience of psychotherapeutic relationships with another person, no one does know what to do unless one lives through a situation with another person; and in this sense what grows is a laboratory of adaptive behaviors which you can help the other person model or develop for themselves.

Answer: No, it is not my intention to leave this audience with the impression that one can only help another person with problems that one has conquered oneself. I believe that it is true that the more experience that one has had oneself, and through watching other people struggle and learning from them and maybe intervening helpfully with them, the more one does develop a repertoire of common sense knowledge—I'm not sure I would say expertise, although that may be involved. I introduced this paper on modeling by saying it's not meant to replace, but to invite therapists and others to discover just what is their magnificence and to share it. It may enlarge their capacity to be helpful. Incidentally, I am that committed as a therapist and teacher, that if I'm truly engaged with somebody and that which is standing in the way of wherever we think he's going to go is going to call for shaping or standing on one's head or doing Yoga, then by God that's what we'll do.

Question: A fault is that a patient comes to you and says, "I'm having a problem coping with this." You're saying to them, "Well, just follow me, watch my example. Yes, you can do it." I can think that my own response has to continue to be, "That's terribly threatening because here's a guy who can do it and I can't do it; I don't need to be reminded of the fact that it can be done, but I can't do it." If I really believe I can't do it, then I'll believe the therapist doesn't understand me.

Answer: You were saying, suppose the seeker was intimidated by the chap who already has coped. Well, all right, if you've consulted with me and you're intimidated, let's talk about that. You see, there's a lot more to being helpful than modeling. There's discussion, there's argument, there's clarification. I spend a lot of time getting a person to stop kidding himself. I have an 18-year-old girl consulting with me. She has a 36-year-old lover who's married with three children, who lives on the West Coast. It's the romantic affair of a lifetime. He spends $1,500 a month telephoning her, to control her life. And she's complaining about the control. And she also has a 35-year-old man in love with her back home and she can't quite understand how these men get so involved with her. "You can't understand? What are you talking about? You're having the time of your life. The only other men available to you are 19-year-old pimple-faced lads." She began to say, "Well, yes."

Question: I don't know how applicable all you're saying is to young people, but I work with early adolescent kids, and I've seen a lot of evidence of developmental theories of moral growth and learning; and it seems to me that at certain stages of people's lives they aren't ready to follow models. That is, there needs to be some other kinds of motivating factors, some other kinds of inter-personal interactions which far overwhelm the effect the model will have. Wouldn't that leave the model looking terrible?

Answer: Let me put it this way, we really don't have a hell of a lot of choice in a model whom we follow. We are to follow available models who are right there from literature or from fiction or in our own imagination. The fact that I may not be a very good model to some teenager for something or other doesn't preclude the possibility of my being helpful to him in some way other than being a model. I repeat: I was presenting a hypothesis about how some therapists who are regarded as great, why they appear great to me. And I believe that there is some generalizable validity there, but it's not to say that the only way that one person can help another is by being an exemplar. But I'll state it the other way around. It's doubtful to me, if someone can for long inspire the confidence and trust of people as a source of help in living their lives, when he himself is totally inept and maladapted and lousy at coping with his life.

Question: Necessary but maybe not sufficient.

<u>Answer</u>: All right, necessary but not sufficient.

<u>Question</u>: Suppose you felt physically attracted to this type you mentioned who are twittery coy-type women and not particularly physically attracted to, shall we say, a stronger woman, would you disclose this feeling you had to her and, if you felt it beneficial would have sexual relations with her?

<u>Answer</u>: To the last, no. No. It isn't worth the trouble and I'm not sure that it would be beneficial. But I would disclose the feelings that I was experiencing if it came up in the context of our ongoing dialogue. As with this little 18-year-old, 19-year-old girl, I'd say, "I feel attracted to you, too. I can see how you would be devastating for middle-aged men." But I'll be damned if I would follow along that path. The question that you're raising is, "Do I think that a professional psychotherapist can perform love therapy?" It's not licensed yet; and I'm fairly straight.

<u>Question</u>: I'd like to comment on your statement describing great psychotherapists; and you mentioned Freud. Some of the research that has recently been done by the feminist movement is that his way of analysis was actually a violence against the mentality of women. I think it's rather dangerous to put him in that kind of light, if you knew what had happened when he saw women. The other comment I would like to make about psychotherapists is that we could interpret it as advocacy of a person's wish to express himself in a different way and to help that person actualize it regardless of the therapist's own feelings, opinions, leanings, repulsions. As for example, I think another violence that's practiced today is the whole area of working with people who are homosexuals, in view of the taboos. And there are not enough people to help people who want to express themselves this way and want to feel good and whole and acceptable and marvelous.

<u>Answer</u>: You're making, I think, a very important point: to wit, what is the view of the good society, let's say, that a given therapist embodies, because that cannot help but affect what he regards as acceptable and unacceptable ways of being men

and women, black and white, young and old. And I think the "radical" therapists as well as Ronald Laing and Fritz Perls are utopians of varying degrees of clarity of vision, either anarchists or socialists, but certainly opposed to rigid definitions of social roles that may well be destructive to the person living them. I mean, in point of fact, if I were to claim a kind of magnificence for myself in this area, it's in stubborn refusal to limit myself to other people's definitions of what my age, sex, occupational, familial, and other kinds of roles ought to be. That's the response I'd like to make to you. ✦

(1973)

### References

[2] *It seems to be the case that we seek to understand the unknown by comparing it with aspects of the known world which it resembles. Psychologists since Wundt have compared aspects of man with chemical compounds, animals, machines, hydraulic systems, etc. I am proposing that we explore the resemblance between a person's experience of himself, which he knows directly, and other aspects of the world. In short, I am exploring a new kind of anthropomorphism.*

[3] *Several months after this talk was given, I obtained a copy of a recent book in which an anthropomorphic model of man is explored as a basis for explaining man's social behavior. See Harre, R. and Secord, P.F.,* The Explanation of Social Behavior, *Oxford, Basil Blackwell, 1972. This sophisticated essay in the philosophy of science made me see more clearly that the use of myself as a conceptual model guided my conception of psychology as I wrote it, especially in my book* Disclosing Man to Himself *(Van Nostrand Reinhold, 1968).*

[4] *This definition is adapted from that provided in Laing, R.D.,* The Politics of Experience, *New York, Ballantine Books, 1967.*

[5] *Cf. Jourard, S.M.,* Disclosing Man to Himself, *especially pp.174-177.*

[6] *Jourard, S.M., Ibid., pp.111-120; 152-172.*

[7] *Parts of the following remarks are from a forthcoming paper of mine; see Jourard, S.M., The transcending psychotherapist.* Voices: The Art and Science of Psychotherapy, *1972 (in press).*

[8] *Kopp, S.,* Guru: Metaphors from a Psychotherapist. *Palo Alto: Science and Behavior Books, 1971.*

[9] *Heider, F.,* The Psychology of Interpersonal Relations, *New York: Wiley, 1958.*

[10] *Laing, R.D., op. cit.*

[11] *There is something pernicious, to me, about viewing people with difficulties in living as sick and weak. This seems to be a case of the attributions of weakness to a person, who then experiences himself as weak and helpless.*

[12] *I would inhale slowly, to the count of 8, hold the breath for 8 counts, release it to the count of 8, and await the next inhalation for the count of 8. This constituted one breathing cycle.*

# *IV* The Disaster Areas

# IV-1 *Marriage is for Life**

I feel rather honored to have been invited here, and I am rather dismayed and delighted in a way to see how many people there are fighting the good fight. And it is, indeed, a good fight. I'll throw in my 10 cents worth or whatever denomination you might want to put after it.

The title of my talk has nothing to do with chronological time. When I chose a title "Marriage is for Life" I meant that marriage is to enhance life, and it is not so much an answer as it is a search. I want to direct my remarks to that search, the search for life itself.

## Ideal (and False) Images of Marriage

The image of the good marriage is perhaps one of its most destructive features. The ideal marriage is a snare, a trap, an image the worship of which destroys life. The ideal marriage is like the ideal body or any other ideal, useful only if it engenders the divine discontent which leads to questing and authenticity. Whose image of a way to live together will guide a relationship? This is a question relevant for a president and his electorate, a doctor and his patient, a parent and child, a researcher and his subject, or a husband and wife. Shall it be an exercise in the concealment and display of power or a commitment to dialogue? Failure of dialogue is the crisis of our time, whether it be between nation and nation, us and them, or you and I.

---

* Taken from the tape recording of plenary address at the annual meeting of the American Association of Marriage and Family Counselors and the National Council on Family Relations, October 26, 1974, St. Louis, Missouri.

I had thought of putting together a book of my several writings on marriage, education, psychology, politics, and business and entitle it "Disaster Areas," for that indeed is what they are. The state of marriage and family life in this country can easily be called a disaster. I think it stems in part from unrealistic expectations and in larger part because of a culturally induced arrest of growth in adults. Perfectly good marriages are ended because something has gone wrong. Actually, I would say they are ended right at the point where they could begin.

There are two fallacies perpetuated which keep the disasters happening. One is the myth of the right partner. The other is the myth of the right way to act so as to ensure peace, joy, and happiness. People believe, or are led to believe, that if they just find the right partner, the right answer to the riddle of their existence will be found. Once having found the right person and the way of relating that is satisfying at this time, the partners try to do everything to prevent change. That's tantamount to trying to stop the tide. Change, indeed, happens, but it happens underground, is concealed, and then it's introduced and experienced as a catastrophe. Instead of welcoming it, the partners find it devastating. Each may then seek to find someone who will not change, so that they never need face the need to change themselves.

## Marriage as Dialogue

Marriage at its best, according to the image that is making more sense to me, is a relationship within which change is generated by the very way of relating—dialogue, so that growth as well as identity and a sense of rootedness are engendered. Change is not so much a threat as it is the fruit of a good marriage, according to this image. Marriage is for growth, for life. It's a place to call home, but like all homes one must leave it in its present form and then return, and then leave it, and then return, like Odysseus, leaving Ithaca and returning.

Kierkegaard refused to marry and thereby defied the nineteenth century. I have refused to divorce, and I defy the twentieth. When one marriage in three is dissolved, or maybe it's 2.6, to remain wedded to the same spouse is virtually to live an alternate life style. If so few marriages endure, then something is non-viable about that way of being married. I have tried in the 26 years of my marriage to be married in the ways designated by tradition, by the mass media, by my friends, by textbooks on marriage, by my wife's image of a good marriage, and none of these ways were for life. None were life-giving, but were rather images, or better, idols. To worship idols is idolatry, a sin. To worship means to live for, to sacrifice what is of ultimate value. To worship an image of marriage is like any other idolatry, the expenditure of one's own life, time, and vitality to enhance the image. That such marriage is disastrous is self-evident. When it endures it becomes a major cause of psychological distress and physical illness in our land.

Conventional medicine, psychiatry, and psychotherapy, and for that matter, marriage counseling and family counseling, frequently function very much like combat surgery. The illness and suffering which reach the healers stem from the stress and "dispiritation" engendered from inauthentic family relationships. Laing and Esterson documented the way a family image can be preserved at the cost of one member being scapegoated as a schizophrenic (Laing and Esterson, 1965). The wards for cancer, heart disease, gunshot and knife injuries, suicide attempts, and other stress ailments provide evidence that non-dialogic family life engenders unrelenting and destructive stress. To be married is not an unmixed blessing. If marriage is hell, and family life is a major cause of disease, which indeed it is, why stay in it, or get in it?

Is the family dead, as David Cooper observed (Cooper, 1971)? If it's dying, should we then kill it, put it out of its misery?

What do people do who have tried marriage and then gotten out of it? The overwhelming majority remarry, and try to live the second, third, or seventh marriage in a way that is more life-giving for the self and others than the first. Frequently, these marriages "fail," as did the first, and I put "fail" in quotes, because I don't think marriages fail; I think people fail marriages.

Wherever I go in this country I get uncomfortable. I think it's more so in California than elsewhere, and it's not with smog or even the inhabitants of Orange County, but with the people one encounters everywhere. I am a trained and rather experienced psychotherapist, tuned in to the non-verbal expressions of despair, loneliness, anguish, and need. So many of the adults I encounter casually or in depth are suffering a rupture of their last lawful or common-law marriage, and are desperately looking for a new one or despairingly avoiding all but superficial relationships in order to avoid risk. The silent shrieks of pain deafen me. To be married is for many boredom or hell. To be unmarried, legally or unlegally, as many experience it is hell and despair. Is there an alternative?

Everything depends on the model or metaphor which defines the marriage one will live, seek, grow in, or die from. There are lethal images of marriage and family life, and there are life-giving models. I take it that enduring, growing relationships are essential for truly human life and for personal fulfillment and growth. I take it that happiness, pleasure, or growth if sought as ends in and of themselves will not happen. They are by-products of a fully-lived life. A life lived in continuing dialogue with some few others will encourage, even force growth.

I take it as true that there is no way to go through life without some pain, suffering, loneliness, and fear. We can help one another minimize the shadow side of life; none can avoid it completely. To seek to avoid pain at all costs is to make an idol out of pleasure or painlessness. To avoid solitude at all costs is to make an idol out of chronic companionship. To avoid anxiety and depression at all costs is to make an idol out of safety and elation. To have to achieve orgasm with somebody in particular is to make an idol of that person or of the genital experience. To sacrifice everything for the breathless experience of being in love is to make an idol of breathlessness.

Many people live in such idolatrous fashion. They marry for those ends and divorce when the other side of reality creeps or bursts into the magic circle, only to seek another playmate or protector in relation to whom the idol may once again be worshipped and the sacrifice of life continue afresh.

Marriage as dialogue through life is for me a viable image, one that engenders life and growth as the conversation unfolds. Dialogue for me, as for Martin Buber (Buber, 1937), is the appropriate way for human beings to be or to strive to be with each other, not imposition, power plays, and manipulation. Family life is an appropriate place for dialogue to be learned and practiced. And through dialogue it's a place to grow in competence, self-sufficiency, and self-esteem.

To me the great failure in marriage as in American education is that neither institution as lived and practiced fosters enlargement of self-respect, respect for others, or growing competence in the skills that make life livable. Deception, manipulation, bribery, and threats are as American as apple pie and mother. These skills are learned in relation with Mum, Dad, the teacher, or the teaching machine.

There is, as near as I now know, no assured way to practice marriage as dialogue except by living it. As soon as a relationship becomes habitual, dialogue has ended. Predictable, habitual ways for people to act with one another are simply non-verbal ways to say the same things to one another day after day, year after year. Habit is the great anesthetic, the annihilator of consciousness.

Non-dialogic ways of being married are either exercised in a chronic struggle for power and control or they are harbors to escape those aspects of life that would engender growth. Some people stay married so they will have someone to control. Some people stay married so they will have an ear to talk into. Some people stay married so they can suffer or make their partner suffer. Most curiously, some get divorced when their partner will no longer be controlled, will no longer listen, or will no longer consent to suffer. The other's changes may be, indeed, a sign of the other person's personal growth. The one who gets a divorce may find yet another partner with whom control can be practiced or who will listen to undisciplined chatter with apparent interest or who will accept pain.

All this is by way of saying that I think in America and in the countries that follow the example set by the American way of life, we expect more out of marriage than it could ever deliver and we expect the wrong things. God, in Her infinite wisdom, so designed us that we are of two kinds and we find one another irresistible at various stages in our lives, so much so that we decide to live together. So far, so good. It's joyous to find another person attractive who finds you attractive, then to make love, even to have children.

Then the honeymoon ends and the marriage begins. It is at this point that I think most divorce happens. We are hung up on honeymoons. My honeymoon was a disaster. I knew next to nothing about tenderness and solicitude, sex, women's sexuality, my bride's sexuality. I was incapable of dialogue. I wanted to be seen in a certain way. I needed my wife to be a certain way, and obliging girl that she was, she obliged. She seemed to be the kind of person she thought I thought she was, the kind of person she felt I would like. We carried out this double masquerade for about three years. It took me that long to cheat. By seven years I was an accomplished dissembler in the realm of my sex life, not my love life, where I was a truthteller in all realms except that.

With our first separation I had a modest collection of female scalps, so to speak, to my credit and my wife, to her credit, after the shock of disclosure wore off discovered the dubious joys of semi-guilty infidelity. Through some fluke, though, within a month of a decree of divorce, we decided to resume our by now somewhat scarred relationship, rather wiser and more honest with one another about who we were. This openness for those not practiced in it was pure hell. It was painful, I assure you. It was painful for me to learn that my wife had a mind, a perspective, and feelings of her own different from mine. She was not the girl I married; in fact, she never was. I married my fantasy, and so did she. She had some coping to do, discovering that I was not the saint I had once seemed. She learned I was, and still am to some extent, a scarcely bridled privateer, a pirate, and adventurer, barely domesticated to her or American conceptions of married males.

How do two or more eccentric and energetic people live together? With humor or not at all. I did not become selectively gelded upon marriage. The more I reflect upon it, the more I like myself, having had the courage to pursue those ways of keeping vital and alive as nondestructively as I did. I could have done worse. I could have sought a divorce or have been divorced by my wife. If the first three years were the honeymoon—actually only about one year was the honeymoon—boredom and pretense at joy in our sameness is a better description of our next two years. My cheating was the beginning of a marriage with some authentic companionship, some lying and getting on with the career, and the experience of living with several very young children. This marriage or this way of being married lasted until seven years when I experienced the death of my father, the completion of my first book, and the dreaded disclosure of my rather complicated affairs with several other women. Here was a real opportunity to be taught a lesson or to learn a lesson. I didn't divorce, however, nor did my wife divorce me, because we retained some recollection of affection between us, we had some children to care for, and a vast amount of anger and mutual reacquaintance to go through. It is, I assure you again, a painful experience extended through time to make yourself known to the person with whom you live and to learn aspects of her experience, attitudes, hopes, fears, and so on which shatter your image of her.

But my marriage and family life were not all my life. I had friends, other interests, and I pursued these, as did she. My life did not begin when I met her nor end when we were out of contact with one another.

My third marriage to her began with hope and resolve, as we struggled to find some enjoyment in living and to care for our children. I suspect we were growing in experience, self-sufficiency, and self-esteem. I hesitate to use certain words, but I'll say them. The point I was going to make is that marriage and family life is a wonderful place to learn shit, fecal detritus, because if you don't know shit, you have not lived. But if that's all you know, you have not lived.

I don't know how many marriages I have had by now, but I am married at the present time to a different woman of the same name in ways that are suited to our present stage of growth as human beings. I am not breathlessly in love with my wife, nor is she with me. Now, she read this and there are some asterisks in her handwriting. It says, "Maybe not breathlessly, but I do love you now with more intensity and depth and true caring than I ever have in my life."

When we spend a great deal of time in one another's proximity, we can both know irritations, even rages of astonishing intensity. It is difficult for two strong and passionate and willful people to share space and time without humor and respect for the other, even though she is wrong, as from my point of view she is. It would be so much easier for me to divorce her and to live with, even marry, some younger woman who has firmer breasts, a smaller waist, who is as sexy as a civet, who worships me and wants to have an intense and meaningful relationship with me, who would attend to my every word, and think I was the Messiah or at least worthy of the Nobel Prize. Many of my colleagues have done that. I could never see—except when I was most exasperated with my wife and fed up with being a father—why these friends of mine, otherwise sensible, wished to play the same record over again. I find someone whose perspective is smaller than mine, or who wants me to be their father, or who is but an echo of my own perspective, rather boring. Flattering, but boring. And I don't want to father anybody because I've been a father. I find a grown person of the opposite sex incites me much less to rape or riot than a young girl but more interesting by and large, at least to listen to.

It takes a long time to give up manipulative and mystifying ways of relating to others in order to trust oneself in dialogue. My training and experience as a psychotherapist has influenced my conception and experience of marriage, or perhaps it's the other way around. My colleagues in the American Academy of Psychotherapists are indeed a rather eccentric lot with many backgrounds and theoretical orientations. All were trained in some way of acting with a patient which was believed to influence, heal, or otherwise impose magical power upon the sufferer. All learned through experience that whatever else they did, they helped people grow by entering into dialogue with them, by being fully present, struggling through impasses, and growing through those struggles. Impasses were not to be avoided, they were to be sought out and celebrated, as painful as they were. They helped their patients grow by staying in relationship with them. The growth that is crucial in this conception of therapy is increased awareness of one's own worth as a person and a realization that one is vastly stronger than anyone had ever imagined. This sense of worth and of strength protects one from entering into and staying in a way of relating to another that is devitalizing and sickening.

A book on marriage which I have read—and I have read many including the O'Neill's (O'Neill & O'Neill, 1972)—which addresses this mystery of growth with some of the respect that it deserves is a small volume written by Israel Charny called *Marital Love and Hate* (Charny, 1972). Compared to his vision, many of the other books fail to acknowledge, I think, the depths of misery and destructiveness which are the other side of personal growth. Charny sees the family not strictly as haven or a place for fun and games, although it can be that, or as a place for sexual delights, but as a place where that most savage of all creatures, man, can learn to share time and space nonviolently and nondestructively. Armed by his vision, as well as by my own, I can see that many so-called successful marriages and happy families are that way because someone is repressing his perspective or is colluding with others in the destruction of his own perspective.

According to this view, marriage is not for happiness, I have concluded after 26½ years. It's a many-splendored thing, a place to learn how to live with human beings who differ from oneself in age, sex, values, and perspectives. It's a place to learn how to hate and to control hate. It's a place to learn laughter and love and dialogue. I'm not entirely persuaded that marriage and family counseling is a profession with any particular contribution to make to the quality of life. There is so far as I now know no way for people to live alone or with others that God endorsed as *the way* that She intended. (Laughter) Why is that funny? Certainly She intended that we cohabit to conceive and then to rear children, but the exact way we should live with one another was never specified. We have to grope and search, according to this view. As near as I can see, such groping for viable, non-destructive ways proceeds best within a context of dialogue.

Dialogue takes courage and commitment to honesty. When people find they can no longer live with their partner, it is not divorce or separation that is indicated. This is in some ways like suicide. The person who tries to kill himself is being unduly literal. By his act he is saying that he no longer wishes to live in the way he has been, and he is also saying that he can imagine no other way to live. He doesn't necessarily wish to stop living, just to stop living in that way. His failure is a failure of imagination as much as it is a failure of nerve.

Divorce too frequently means that one partner or the other refuses to continue living married in that way. The divorcee then finds someone with whom some other dimension of himself can be expressed. This looks like change or growth. I have wondered whether hitherto unexpressed dimensions of self could not have emerged in relation to the spouse because with the new partner an impasse will arrive and there will be the necessity to struggle with it.

If there is growth in serial marriage—and there is—one wonders why there could not be growth in the first. I know of many marriages in which one partner or the other refused to acknowledge or value the change in the other. The unchanged one ordered the changed one to revert to the way he or she was earlier, on pain of divorce.

The failure of marriage is the failure of our culture to provide models and reasonable expectations about human relationships. Because we lie so much about our relationships, especially to our children, and because the breadth and depth of authentic experience is not presented in movies, comics, books, or TV, nobody knows what is expectable or what is healthy or lifegiving or potentially lifegiving in marriage. People think that if they get angry or bore one another or fail to respond sexually that the marriage is finished, that they are out of love. Perhaps the overestimation of romantic love is one of the more pernicious patterns in our society.

When spouses deceive one another for the first time that is the time the potentially life and growth-promoting aspects of marriage can begin. When the couple finds themselves in rage, that is the time not for divorce but for celebration. Whimsically, I thought that the first betrayal of marriage should come on the honeymoon, so that it can be gotten over and the dialogue resumed.

Marriage is not an answer, but a search, a process, a search for life, just as dialogue is a search for truth. Yesterday's marriage or way of being married is today's trap. The way out of the trap is to resume the dialogue, not to end it, unless someone is pledged not to grow and change. One of my colleagues is being divorced after 22 or 23 years of marriage. He is a Southern fellow, his wife an extremely pious member of the Methodist Church, a "lousy lay" he assures everyone, and he explored another young woman. And the way he put it, "You know, when I went to bed with her she liked it." He carried on, "It was great and I discovered there was another way, but then my wife found out about it and she made me confess to our children and then made me give her up" and so on. And, sadly, he is divorcing her, or she is divorcing him, they are divorcing each other, because she wants to remain exactly as she was when she was 14 or 15. He's growing and searching. Yesterday's way of being married is today's trap. The way out of the trap is to resume the dialogue, not to end it.

If marriage counseling is not training and experience in dialogue, then it falls short in my opinion of its help-giving potential. How does one function as a marriage and family counselor? In the same way two porcupines mate—with difficulty and great care. I know of no techniques for counseling individuals, or couples, or entire family units. There is something about the experience of having struggled to retain one's self-respect and joie de vivre in the face of marital disaster, one's own marital disasters, that helps one to listen with empathy and humor to others' difficulties. I think that inventiveness and a profound faith in every individual's capacity to overcome all disasters and to find their own strength is helpful. I am always astonished at how couples convince themselves that they cannot live more than five minutes if their partner changes in one way or if they are incommunicado from their partner for five minutes. That is astonishing when you think about it, two reasonably adequate human beings live together and then if one of them changes in one jot or tittle, the other person is either to commit murder, suicide, or divorce. Or if they split for a day, or a week, or a month to recenter themselves, the one who did not choose to be apart for a while will very frequently do everything in their power to punish the one who is seeking to recenter herself or himself.

In various earlier papers I have explored the importance of modeling, of being an exemplar of viable ways to live, or of the possibility of overcoming difficulties in living. Theory and technique are valuable in counseling, as they are in any other enterprise, but they can be the refuge of scoundrels and fools, like patriotism. If he or she is not a spokesman for and an exemplar of dialogue, integrity, and a relentless commitment to a search for viable ways to live and grow, then he or she will be found out. There is no way to impersonate integrity for very long. As in all realms where human beings deal with one another, there is no place in family counseling for dissembling and technical manipulation by the professional person. Marriage and family counseling to enhance or to terminate marriages proceeds best, perhaps only, through dialogue.

## Dialogue with Audience

Question: Explain what you mean by dialogue.

Response: The image of dialogue that I speak from is dialogue as expounded by the philosopher Martin Buber in rather poetic terms. As a conversation between I and Thou is the way he put it. But to put it in prose, dialogue is to speak your truth in response to the other person's truth, with no effort in a concealed way to lie or to con or to manipulate the other person to be in some way what he is not. It's speaking your truth and then waiting to hear the other person's truth, which you can never predict or control. As soon as you try to predict or control it, dialogue is ended. Out of it, incidentally, comes growth. Without it there may be change but it's not necessarily the change you would call growth.

Question: Is this view of marriage as dialogue an appropriate view of human relationships outside the marriage, but in relationships within the community, and so on?

Response: I would say, absolutely, that it is the failure of the desire for and the trust in dialogue that engenders the way of life of power manipulation, the desire to influence friends and to control people. Business and politics are the refuge of liars and cheats. (Comment from Audience). Absolutely right. The comment was, "Dialogue works only if both are committed to it and understand something of its rules." And this raises the question—and it's more than a question, it's a challenge—where do you learn dialogue? When you've never experienced it or encountered it within your own family, where let's say your mother and your father for cosmetic reasons lie to you about themselves or about their own relationship, where your teachers in school lied to you in one way or another by withholding personal perspectives in order to be functionaries and spokesmen for those who wrote the curriculum—where do you learn dialogue? I'm still learning, but I've thought of changing my professional title from Professor of Psychology to Professor of Dialogue to express a commitment to learn dialogue and to teach dialogue. But the way that you teach it is by living it. It's one of those ironies where you can't talk about it, you live it. And the only way to learn it is by example, by invitation. And I think that the real challenge for the so-called helping professions is not to become more sophisticated in the design of research to prove that they are more or less effective than somebody else. And the real challenge is not to develop even more sophisticated theories of influence and technique and theory. The real challenge is to learn oneself how to achieve greater competence and capacity for dialogue with a wider range of humanity, people who differ from you. Growth in dialogue is growth in two ways: growth in the capacity to enter into and sustain a relationship of dialogue with someone radically different from you, increasingly different from you; and/or the ability to commence a dialogic conversation with another person and follow it where it will lead without resorting to lying or evasion. That kind of growth is extremely rare.

Question: (Inaudible)

Response: First part of the question: Such integration is done with difficulty. That's glib. I think it's absurd to separate the two. Not to be concerned with your own growth and integrity is to be out of touch with something very important. To be concerned only with your own growth and integrity is to be short-sighted. They are coterminous, for want of a better word.

Question: Do you believe in justifiable divorce?

Response: Absolutely. Please, do not construe what I have said as being the path for everybody, because that's not my intention nor my belief. Human beings being human beings, we have many ways to find our own way of life. We have our own styles and places for growth and I have no reason to doubt that for those individuals who have chosen to further their quest for life and meaning and growth by moving out of one relationship into another that there are nondestructive and life-giving and growth-promoting ways of doing this. There are some good books that have been written by people who, loaded with their scars, can actually say as a friend of mine said on being divorced, that it really is not as bad a state of being as my enemies could wish nor as blissful as my unhappily married friends would hope. Dialogue is not just words. You see, actions are words, and a friendship, a marriage, a parent-child relationship is a dialogue; words and a dialogue in actions, my turn to bow, your turn to curtsy. We're saying something about ourselves by our actions and what we are saying. What I do is in some way an expression or a continuation of my dialogue with the persons I am involved with. Dialogue is in words and it is in those actions that are words too. Actions speak louder than words lots of times.

Question: Is dialogue to be limited and its contribution to growth limited only to one's personal relationships, intimate personal relationships? Can one not engage in dialogue and grow through one's work, through one's reading, one's contacts with nature?

Response: I have to say "Yes." What we're talking about, really, both in dialogue and in being in nature is, again I'll quote Buber, Buber made some such comment as this, that the essence of human life involves distance and relation. To put something at a distance is to let it be itself and in letting the other be itself/himself/herself, one is being oneself and letting that which is reveal itself, so that you're not imposing your preconceptions on the tree, the car, the book, the other person. The response is on the other side, and for me my relationships with people involve distance and relation. One cannot stay chronically in relation. If you can't back off, it's devastating, but if you can't enter into relation, it's devastating. It's never either/or, it's both.

Question: (Inaudible)

Response: The comment is that this conception of dialogue seems utopian. To some extent I agree because I think it takes growth, courage, and commitment to enter into and stay into dialogue, and it's difficult and I think it's a manifestation of growth. You start out unable or unwilling to enter the rigors of dialogue or to stay in them very long, and depending on the degree of enlightenment, really enlarged awareness, that you will achieve will depend whether or not you grow in the capacity to enter into and stay in dialogue or whether you will choose to live a life of seeming semblance and power manipulation games. It's a matter, I think, of experience, the practicality of it.

Question: (Inaudible)

Response: This is the challenge for which I have no advice whatsoever. Except by offering oneself as an invitation to dialogue and as an exemplar of someone who speaks truth with as much tact and humor and compassion as you can, but who speaks truth and who will sense when the other person appears to be speaking less than the truth and then answering tactfully, "I wonder if there are not some other aspects of your experience that you are not admitting," and inviting, really inviting without trying to make it painless, effortless, or whatever? I think we underestimate people's capacity to live with depression, pain, anxiety, and so on.

Question: (Inaudible)

Response: I am one. (Laughter) To have been reared in a culture that predefined roles, that where everyone was told how men are, how women are and for that matter, in a white-dominated society, how blacks are. For a white cracker to this day and age to encounter a black who is not like Uncle Tom—he needs help. Because he was never equipped by training, experience, or example, let's say to deal with a woman who wasn't just an itty-bitty thing. If you're a "good ole boy" women are "lil ole things." And for the "lil ole thing" to prove to have a mind of her own is mindblowing and very threatening. How to address this problem? Again, I know of no solutions. With humor, I think. I don't mean to laugh it out of existence; I mean, it's part of the human comedy. We've got to learn how to change our views and our expectations about what other people can be like and what their capacities are, and it very frequently means giving up some prerogatives and privileges, which is done painfully and reluctantly. And, I think, increased awareness is very helpful, but I don't know any way of easing the pain unless it's to stay drunk all the time. It's desirable to ease the pain. The question is, are there some rules and guidelines? Well, "Yes" is a better answer. One rule is to try truly to listen to what the other person is saying with their words and their nonwords, truly to listen because truly to listen is to explore your concepts of what the other person is like. So, to learn through practice, to suspend preconceptions, and truly to listen to what another person is saying with their words and gestures. And the other rule is to struggle painfully to find the courage and the words to speak the truth of your reaction. There's no recipe there, man!

Question: (Inaudible)

Response: Let's see if I can grasp the sense of the question. I'll restate it and see if I have a part of what you're saying. "Is there a place in relationship, is there a time and place to be non-dialogic, but instead to be manipulative or commanding?"

Question: Can dialogue be destructive?

Response: Yes, the whole function of dialogue is to destroy false images of one another. The very nature of dialogue is to destroy illusion. Now that's frequently painful and there's a time and a place, I suppose, that comes with wisdom and experience to choose one's time to destroy illusions. Because sometimes you can destroy someone's illusions and maybe they can't cope with that right now. They might be able to cope with it the day after tomorrow, however. No, dialogue is destructive of illusion and that's what it's for.

Question: (Inaudible)

Response: Fundamentally, when I'm working as a psychotherapist in trying to develop a relationship of dialogue with the other person and within the framework of that relationship I don't have in advance any preset agenda that I'm going to make sure that we get some Gestalt exercises in and some bioenergetic exercises. For me the ongoing conversation is the process, and if in that context it's meaningful as my next response to put my arm around a person, I have no reason not to, unless common sense tells me that's not appropriate. That doesn't elaborate much, but that's as much as I can tell you. ✦

### *References*

Buber, M. I and thou. *Edinburgh: T & T Clark, 1937.*

Charny, I. Marital love and hate. *New York: The Macmillan Co., 1972.*

Cooper, D. Death of the family. *New York: Random House, 1971.*

Laing, R.D. & Esterson, A. Sanity, madness, and the family. *London: Tavistock Publications, 1965; New York: Basic Books, 1965.*

O'Neill, N. & O'Neill, G. Open marriage: A new life style for couples. *New York: J.B. Lippincott, 1972.*

# *IV-2* Failure of Dialogue

The crisis of our time is not a shortage of food, space and energy; it is the failure of dialogue. The learned incapacity to hear and understand what another human being is saying, and the choice to respond in dishonesty, is at the heart of our dilemma on the shrinking planet we call home.

There is no place to learn dialogue. From infancy, each child is exposed to those who wish to shape, influence, persuade, bribe, command, or threaten him. No one invited *him* to speak *his* truth, to listen and hear, and to speak truth in return. Everywhere there is imposition of *one* perspective upon the others.

Education, if it is anything *is* dialogue. It is an invitation from someone, living or dead, to listen to speech which enlarges the perspective, the experience of realities, the grasp of truths of the listener. If education is not dialogue, then is it not education.

What *is* dialogue, that it so seldom happens? It is, first of all, catching someone's attention so he or she *listens* to what is being said, giving evidence *that* he hears and understands. This implies a growing capacity to imagine, or "model" the reality of what is being said, the reality of the speaker's world. Then, dialogue calls for the listener to speak truth in relevant response to that very person—the wish is to understand and make the self understood, so each participant shares in the world of the other's truth. There is no wish to impose a view on the part of either participant.

In education, as in all realms, everything depends upon *who* the educators believe their pupils to be and how they *can* be and who they believe *themselves* to be and to be becoming. Have they ever experienced dialogue, and their own growth? Or are they locked in non-dialogic relations and arrested growth? If teachers truly believe their pupils to be human beings, capable of dialogue, then that will be the medium of their relationships. If they are regarded as animals, then they will be trained; if computers, then programmed. If schools are for training, then where does dialogue happen? Not the family, not the marketplace nor the political arena.

Images of man are no academic matter—my image and yours are what we profoundly and passionately are convinced, beyond *all* argument, man *is*. Images of man are like images or non-images of god—wars are fought in their name. How do you change an image of self, of others, when they are self-perpetuating, self-fulfilling? How do I change my image of you, when you do not recognize yourself as the person I am talking to? How do you change your image of me?

One who never has known dialogue—only deception, duplicity and cunning—believes that a person who is open, and invited him to be open, is *crazy*! In behaviorism, the view is passionately, religiously held that man is a beast to be trained. Without this training and restraint, reversion to bestiality is expected—and it happens. A humanistic view passionately, religiously sees man as capable of growth in capacity for *dialogue*. Without such involvement and invitation, reversion to barbarism, illiteracy, and the degradation of language and speech may be expected, and happens. Talk is used to *overpower*, not to reveal.

Images of self and others harden in times of stress. For example: "I was just beginning to see Blacks as human, when one stole my hub-caps and re-rednecked me." Or, "I was just beginning to see women as persons, when one of them flattered and seduced me, and re-male-chauvinist-pigged me."

There is a bankruptcy of images of possibilities for the person, society, and the world, and we are the reserves called upon like forgotten money in the bank.

Humanistic Psychology might better be called a humanistic approach to the study of man, and other living creatures. "Humanistic" refers to the use of models or paradigms for the comprehension of man which come from the *study of man himself*, rather than from the study of animals or machines; moreover, the study of man which provides the source of the models should include, not just man's action, but also his experience. Humanistic Psychology aims to answer the question, *who is man*, in ways that each man can recognize himself as being included in the answer. Historically, psychology so investigated man, that few of us could find ourselves in the treatises which supposedly described us. We could better recognize ourselves in great works of fiction, and in the accounts by anthropologists who, in studying other societies, took pains to become trusted, participant observers. They learned to speak to, and listen to the natives, and to make sense out of the natives' action by relating it to their experience.

Education is concerned with calling forth those human potentialities deemed valuable, and essential for life. Education is not identical with training, although training is part of education. Training is the art of helping someone learn how to *act*. Education is concerned with a way of being in the world with other living beings—dialogue—not only with contemporaries, but those who have come before, and those who will follow. Education is for dialogue, and it is through dialogue, or not at all. Education is enlargement of the capacity for dialogue and the enlargement of awareness.

Humanistic Education can easily become as faddish as behavior modification. It evokes images of sensitivity training, self-expression, free schools, etc. I prefer to regard humanistic education as a concern on the part of educators—and we all function as educators—to call forth different possibilities in growing persons of all ages—not exclusively children—than hitherto have been evoked. For example, Nixon called forth mindless obedience in Haldeman and Ehrlichman. I wouldn't call their docility or their leader's mendacity "valuable."

Humanistic Education is a protest against persons and institutions which reliably evoke and reinforce greed; dishonesty; provincial perspectives; loss of humor; inability to enter into dialogue with others; rigid and false conceptions of what is real, valuable and important; alienation from one's own body; inability to protest; lack of imagination in all realms save methods of exploiting others; desires to control other humans and other forms of life; destruction of the environment; and failure to master one's own native language, and that of other people. The success of our educational institutions, and the people who embody them—parents, school teachers; those who produce movies, TV shows—in locking people into these limited and least vivifying possibilities is astonishing. Perhaps 98 percent of all graduates of all institutions of training pass these behavioral objectives with high honors. How did the 2 percent get by? Where did the system fail? Where did they fail with me?

If Humanistic Education is not actively engaged in summoning our own, and our children's integrity; compassion; humor; empathy; concern to make the world fit for all forms of life to thrive in, amicably; love of truth, beauty and justice—through dialogue and through example—then it is pernicious.

Education as a response to a call, cannot begin until a child first learns to understand and speak his native tongue. So long as a person is expanding his understanding of speech, and his facility at expression, his education is continuing.

Our institutions for education do not educate in this sense, in the sense of *enlarging* capacity for dialogue. Indeed, I think that our school systems, from "K through Ph.D.," unwittingly and unintentionally train dialogue "specialists"—persons able to understand the reality of what is being experienced, and the language in which it is being said, verbal and nonverbal, only from persons in their own family, neighborhood, or whoever is included in the category of *Us.* And such dialogue is possible only on a narrow range of superficial topics. "*They* are different from *us*, and we can't understand them." If everyone, at any time, could be assess for the *range* of persons with whom he is able to enter into dialogue, speaking and listening with honest, imagination, and integrity, and for the depth and variety of themes on which dialogue can occur, then we would find that everyone is a dialogic specialist in a world and time that call for increasing one's growth toward "general practice" in dialogue. For example, this one specializes in dialogue with 20 year old girls form Palatka, Florida, about pop music, that one with 45 year old Protestant male members of Rotary, about communists.

In its social function, education is a dialogue between a younger person and his elders about life itself—how can one survive, and, beyond survival itself, how can one make life possible and livable for oneself and the other living beings now, and in the future. The younger person is encouraged to listen to, and to read (a kind of listening), not just his elders and people of competence in his school, village or country. He is encouraged to encounter and listen to and question everyone who has ever recorded anything deemed to be of value, truth or wisdom. Training prepares one to survive or dominate in this locale. Education is an invitation to enlarge one's horizons, to learn more about present and past realities, future possibilities—to wish to converse with people (or read them) outside the village. Trained people don't read, or seek to encounter new people. They do not wish to meet persons with a vision and model of man and the world larger than their own. Plato, Nietzsche, or Einstein cannot catch nor hold their attention.

Learning, about which so much has been written, remains a mysterious process. The various theories of learning are grounded in images or models of man which are hardly recognizable as human. They are theories of training. We need theories of understanding. More than anything else, man is a speaker and a listener. He is not solely in the world as an organism confronted by discriminative stimuli, responding in ways that are reinforced. Rather, he is in a world which presents him with meanings, a world which "speaks," a world which he listens to, and "reads."

Man replies to the meanings of his world with his speech. Speech is not behavior, it is part of a person's dialogue with his world. Human behavior, however, is speech. It means something. People speak to one another with words, and with acts. We read one another's action just as we hear one another's speech. We can lie, and we can tell truth with our acts and with our words. Learning, and education is learning to understand what *is said*.

Education is not solely the process of training workers, craftsmen and professionals, although it includes such training. The purpose of education is to transmute biological creatures into human beings, into *persons* whose stay on earth is life-giving for themselves, and not destructive to the lives of other persons, other creatures and the people of other lands, now, and in the generations that follow. Education is to help persons of distorted, uneven, provincial development become more whole, to become persons of understanding.

Unfortunately, schools, as we know them, are not places for dialogue as I have been defining it. They are places for the indoctrination of certain skills, and ideologies, and they are patterned after factories. The children are sent in as raw material at one end; there is some early culling of raw material deemed unsuited for conventional processing. The training or processing operations are carried out on schedule. Quality control, of a sort, is carried out by inspectors. Wages of the processors, wrongly called teachers, are partly contingent upon output, with an effort currently being made to enforce even greater accountability. Kazantzakis felt himself accountable to El Greco—I, perhaps to Buber. In traditional schools, the accountability measure which is yielded is something called "scores" on various "tests." The good processor is one whose pupils answer the largest number of questions right. This process is being nearly computerized, with programmed instruction, learning packages, etc. being sold to more and more public school systems.

The graduates of our schools for training emerge with little love of learning, limited capacity for dialogue, with banalized imaginations, and with a very deficient mastery of the English language. It is not just that they do not speak French, Spanish, or German as a second language. For our school and college graduates, correct English is a second language; their first is the *argot* of peers, parents, and television screens.

The other person's words are the windows to his world, through which I see what it is like to be him. When he speaks to me in truth, he becomes a transparent self, and releases in me an imaginative experience of his existence. If he cannot speak, if I do not listen, or if I cannot understand, then we must remain suspicious strangers to one another, uncognizant of our authentic similarities and differences.

Education in this country has failed to teach people how to speak and understand any language other than the one indigenous to their village. We are a nation, therefore, of provincials.

"Education," in using the methods of Madison Avenue to "teach," debases language, uses it to limit and control vision, as well as action. Sesame Street teaches children to watch TV, programmed instruction teaches pupils how to read in order to answer 10 questions in a minute—the semblance of an educated person. It has been said (by me) that all it would take to transform the average American into a transparent self is one good bowel movement.

We are in the world as speaking creatures. Our world is a world of meanings. The people of the world speak to us, and we learn to understand what they mean. From our mothers, we first learn the names of things, and people, and what they are *said* to do to us, for us, against us. We don't live in an environment, we live in a world that has been packaged and labelled for us by those who encountered it before us. Each kind of person, animal, tree, flower, body of water has been named, and the functional equivalent of an analysis of contents, and instructions for use is appended to it. It is our mother's world. To really listen, we must learn to still the chronic "chatter of the mind," our mother's voice, which always confirms and reconfirms what the world is, and what we are.

If our mothers have insistent voices, then what the world says it can and can't be, will and won't do to us drowns out what other speakers and labellers are trying to say to us. we cannot hear what others say or have said the world is like and can be, or what we are like and can be, so long as the voice of our mothers, or fathers, or peers back in Mt. Dennis, Ontario, is all we hear and so long as we know no other language.

Indeed, this first language, and the world that it describes, the meanings with which it inscribes the world, is indoctrinated into us; we are trained in it, as we are with all of our initial skills. Education begins with a *second* language which is the vehicle for encountering and experiencing another world, another way for the world to be perceived, evaluated, and hence acted in. The second language may be an enlargement of the first language, as when the argot and brogue of Alachua County, Florida, is extended to the English of Shakespeare. Every language and every new word, enlarges a person's world. More important is the fact that someone—the author of a book, or a person with larger perspectives than people in the village, catches the pupil's attention, so that the mother's voice temporarily is drowned out, and other ways for the world to be described, used, and experienced, and other ways for oneself to be and to become are heard, to counter the definition of one's fate, limits and essence pronounced by one's mother. It is difficult, but not impossible, to drown out the chronic meanings, and chronic speech of those who first defined me and my world. This is what Don Juan meant when he helped "stop the world" for Castaneda.

While education is not *only* listening, listening is a necessary part of it. Reading, by the way, is listening; and looking, tasting, feeling and smelling are all varieties of hearing what the world is, and what it is like.

It is no small thing really to listen, because we listen, not just with our ears, but with our entire being—our imagination, our memory, our feelings, our liver, bowels, genitals, our blood and immunity mechanisms. Really to listen means to stop the random chatter with which we silently occupy ourselves. What we hear said to us can be a matter of life and death.

Our speaker is reporting something to us that he has witnessed, and which he believes to be the case—something in the world, something about himself and how he feels, or something he sees and believes about you. Truly to listen to him is to imagine the reality of what has been described. The vividness and intensity of the imagining is a function of the art with which the other speaks or writes, and *the freedom of the listener to play with his imaginative possibilities*.

He, or they, won't listen—why talk to them? Not to listen is to invalidate the perspective of the speaker. When teachers or governors won't listen, they invite the acts that speak louder than words.

The ability to imagine the reality of what is being said, of what is meant, is not only a matter of the brain, or the right hemisphere of the brain; it entails the entire body. If I am told I have terminal cancer, and I believe the reality of what has been discussed; and if I believe, or imagine and then believe, that my blood, or organs are powerless to overcome whatever I imagine cancer to be, then I imagine myself dead, and then die. My immunity mechanisms become involved in my imaginings. If I have strength attributed to me and my body, then the vividness with which I imagine and then believe in the reality of my strength is enacted, not just in my actions, but in the functioning of my supposedly autonomically controlled organ systems. Imagining and believing are matters of the blood and bowels as well as of the head. We can be convinced of our ability to live, and we can be talked to death.

When we are young we live in an enchanted world evoked by a story teller with words of magic. Gradually, the storied world is annihilated by the public trainers, who impose upon young, gentle persons, an image of self and world called reality—the reality of the trainer.

One cannot hear with one's total body—one's body is an ear—*if there are parts of the body one does not own.* Then, there is a deafness of the body. If a person has been so trained that he has been obliged to repress entire dimensions of his experience of his body, then truly, his body will be an insensitive or deaf ear. And, since we speak as well as hear with our total embodiment, then a rigid and tense body will radically limit our vocabulary. Education must involve awakening the potential sensitivity of one's body, our energy, and our freedom to move, to "speak" with our bodies.

The right hemisphere of the brain presumably "models" reality as we believe or imagine—image—it to be. Words charge our minds, our models of the world, and ourselves and bodies, if we really listen to them, if they have new meanings. Hearing old words confirms our present model. In childhood, the right and left hemispheres are not yet separated.

When we trust someone enough to listen to them, we de-rigidify our model of the world. Familiar talk concretizes, or "sets" our model of what the world is like, while new language, if we hear it, remodels our image of the world as a sculptor shapes clay into new images. The greatness of Freud, of Sullivan, of Rogers, is the greatness of a great listener! They hung in and really listened to, heard and understood people whom their colleagues would not listen to.

Truly to listen is to invite and allow the speaker to play with one's capacities for imagining the reality which is being discussed. The speaker sees, hears, thinks, feels, remembers, imagines the world an himself in some ways, and talks about it. I hear him, and I attempt to make my imaginary model of reality correspond with his sensory reality.

To *understand*, to comprehend what has been said, calls for experience which is shared with that of the speaker, otherwise the words fall on deaf ears, or, better, empty imagination. Metaphors and similes which show or point to *parallels* between what the speaker has experienced, and what the listener knows, are the very stuff of understanding. We comprehend the novel and the different by capturing it in the meshes of our model of reality.

Education—learning yet another person's language which is spoken in the world—calls for exposure to the sensory experience which the words and signs describe, and which it is hoped, they will evoke in the auditor-reader. To be educated is to learn the language in which the world is written, and which it speaks, is to learn what the world "means."

We understand the meaning of words and signs when the reality that is thus described is similar to something we already have experienced, and, presumably, understand. Poets stretch our present world of meaning by cutting across "sorts" or classes. Their images fail to be understood if the listener has not had certain kinds of experience. A golden smile is meaningless to a blind man. Hunger keen as a razor is meaningless to a fat man who has never shaven, or to a rich man who has forgotten his humble beginnings.

Vision gives us the surface of things, relentlessly, even when we take a thing apart—we see its inner surface, never its depth. The sound of the world tells us something of what is unseen and invisible. Speech tells us of the invisible—man's experience. To read the world is to know what it means—to imagine the reality beyond, or inside that which is visible. To listen and to read entail the imagination the way mere looking does not.

If education calls for the willingness and ability to listen imaginatively, to imagine the reality of what is being said, it equally requires someone who has something important and magnificent to say and show. Only those are teachers, in this sense, who are exemplars or speakers about magnificent possibilities for man and world. Even if they are not, they can at least introduce the pupils to their *heroes*, masters, and teachers, whose visions they are still engaged in trying to actualize. One would hope, however, that *their* heroes are not Hugh Hefner, Attila the Hun, or the head of the Mafia.

If there are few living exemplars of something magnificent about, or none, then it behooves an instructor to locate teachers for the trainees whom he wishes to educate. He can introduce his charges (who are to become pupils of the exemplars who catch their attention and inspire them to emulation) *to the best that has been and the best that is.* There still is no better definition of education than Cardinal Newman's statement that it is introducing the student to the best that has ever existed.

To be addressed by the best gives one an implicit and explicit world-view, in terms of which one can adjudge what is going on, and what is being said and done in one's village. Not to encounter the best is to be limited in language and perspective, to be entranced by what reality is said to be and can possibly be here in Alachua County, Florida.

We are living in an age when the alteration and expansion of consciousness are being sought as well as studied. It is widely believed that the higher and altered consciousness can be reached through, variously marijuana, LSD, psilocybin; through transcendental meditation, through mantras, chants, arica exercises, rolfing, and a host of other disciplines, old and new. What seems to be overlooked is that man's consciousness of himself and of his fellows and of his world has been altered for millennia through the spoken and written word. Poetry, metaphor and simile in all their forms, good literature have all changed man's view of himself, the world, his fellows. The written and spoken word embody the world-view of someone that is larger and different than that of the audience. This model/image/right-hemisphere/experience of the world can indeed be affected in other ways, but the word does intoxicate, if it is a word of truth. Lies, of course, are poison.

Each *new* word understood is an expansion and alteration of awareness. Each new perspective, disclosed by another person, and imaginatively *heard* is an enlargement of aware-ness. Each authentic encounter with another, initiating the un-folding of dialogue is a continuing enlargement, and sometimes explosion of one's own perspective so cataclysmic to a small provincial world, or experience of the world, as to leave the psychedelic drugs to seem, in their effects, like Coca-Cola.

Great literature and great speech, then, are altered con-sciousness of self and the world. The larger the vocabulary, the higher and more differentiated the consciousness of the world. So does competence with other languages. Whorf, Sapir, and others have shown how language affects perception. To learn French, or Eskimo, or Spanish, or motorcycle mechanics is to carve up the world in different ways, so that now this, now that aspect of a tree, a person, oneself, a machine, is named and perceived, now that. Not to learn another language is to be condemned to the secular, or profane world circumscribed by one's vocabulary, grammar, and syntax.

Indeed, poetry, metaphor, art, religious ritual, are all invita-tions to alter one's way of experiencing the world from the third person, the he-she-it of manipulation, use and control, to the sec-ond person, to you or thou, the second-person singular. Poets re-animate the world, and give back a voice to flowers, winds, sea, sky, and beasts. They help us to say Thou to the world.

Metaphor, the language of the arts and humanities, is the corpus callosum of consciousness—it expresses the fully evolved consciousness of someone living in a time and place, telling it like it is *for him*. It is precisely those with a nonortho-dox vision who are able to address and alter one's sense of reality intuitively, directly, without argument and copious ver-biage. The capacity for critical thought and "reality testing" is essential for viable existence; but frequently such reality test-ing merely confirms one view of reality and denies reality to the nonorthodox. Dictators try, of course, to stifle critical rea-son and conventional reality testing, so that their tyranny and mendacity with either pass unnoticed, or be given another euphemistic mane: lies are called "inoperative statements." Death camps are places for "special treatment."

But dictators also try to stifle the poets and writers who utter truth metaphorically. The politics of reality defines the language of the official reality, which, in turn, shapes the experience and action of those who conform to the status quo. The language one learns—one's mother tongue—induces a model and experience of reality which one's mother transmits along with her milk. Her light illumines her reality, which becomes your reality. ✦

# *IV-3* Some Lethal Aspects of the Male Role*

Men die sooner than women, and so health scientists and public health officials have become justly concerned about the sex difference in death age. Biology provides no convincing evidence to prove that female organisms are intrinsically more durable than males, or that tissues or cells taken from males are less viable than those taken from females. A promising place to look for an explanation of the perplexing sex-differential in mortality is in the transactions between men and their environments, especially their interpersonal environments. In principle, there must be ways of behaving among people which prolong a man's life and insure his fuller functioning, and ways of behaving which speed a man's progress toward death. The present paper is devoted to an overview of some aspects of being a man in American society which may be related to man's acknowledged faster rate of dying.

The male role, as personally and socially defined, requires man to appear tough, objective, striving, achieving, unsentimental, and emotionally unexpressive. But seeming is not being. If a man is tender (behind his *persona*), if he weeps, if he shows weakness, he will likely be viewed as unmanly by others, and he will probably regard himself as inferior to other men.

Now, from all that we can fathom about the subjective side of man, as this has been revealed in autobiography, novels, plays, and psychotherapists' case histories, it seems true that

---

* *From* The Transparent Self *by Sidney Jourard. Complete bibliographic nota-tions from* The Transparent Self *can be found in Appendix Chapter V-2.

men are as capable as women at responding to the play of life's events with a broad range of feelings. Man's potential thoughts, feelings, wishes and fantasies know no bounds, save those set by his biological structure and his personal history. But the male role, and the male's self-structure will not allow man to acknowledge or to express the entire breadth and depth of his inner experience, to himself or to others. Man seems obliged, rather, to hide much of his real self—the ongoing flow of his spontaneous inner experience—from himself and from others.

## Manliness and Low Self-Disclosure

Research in patterns of self-disclosure has shown that men typically reveal less personal information about themselves to others than women (Jourard 1961a; Jourard and Lasakow, 1958; Jourard and Landsman, 1960; Jourard and Richman, 1963). Since men, doubtless, have as much "self," i.e., inner experience, as women, it follows that men have more "secrets" from the interpersonal world than women. It follows further that men, seeming to dread being known by others, must be more continually tense (neuromuscular tension) than women. It is as if "being manly" implies the necessity to wear neuromuscular "armor," the character armor which Reich (1948) wrote about with such lucidity. Moreover, if a man has "secrets," "something to hide," it must follow that other people will be a threat to him; they might pry into his secrets, or he may, in an unguarded moment, reveal his true self in its nakedness, thereby exposing his areas of weakness and vulnerability. Naturally, when a person is in hostile territory, he must be continually alert, hypertonic, opaque, and restless. All this implies that trying to seem manly is a kind of "work," and work imposes stress and consumes energy. Manliness, then, seems to carry with it a chronic burden of stress and energy-expenditure which could be a factor related to man's relatively shorter life-span.

If self-disclosure is an empirical index of "openness," of "real-self being," and if openness and real-self being are factors in health and wellness, then the research in self-disclosure seems to point to one of the potentially lethal aspects of the male role. Men keep their selves to themselves, and impose thereby an added burden of stress beyond that imposed by the exigencies of everyday life. The experience of psychosomatic physicians who undertake psychotherapy with male patients suffering peptic ulcers, essential hypertension and kindred disorders seems to support this contention. Psychotherapy is the art of promoting self-disclosure and authentic being in patients who withhold their real selves from expression, and clinical experience shows that when psychotherapy has been effective with psychosomatic patients, the latter change their role-definitions, their self-structures, and their behavior in the direction of greater spontaneity and openness, with salutary consequences to their bodies. The time is not far off when it will be possible to demonstrate with adequately controlled experiments the nature and degree of correlation between levels and amounts of self-disclosure, and proneness to illness and/ or early death age.

## Manliness: The Lack of Insight and Empathy

There is another implication of the fact that men are lower self-disclosures than women, an implication that relates to self-insight. Men, trained by their upbringing to assume the "instrumental role," tend more to relate to other people on an *I-It* basis than women (Buber, 1937).* They are more adept than

---

* *There is an interesting implication of these observations for the training of male psychotherapists. It seems true that effective psychotherapists of whatever theoretical school are adept at establishing a warm, bilaterally communicative relationship with their patients, one characterized by a refraining from manipulation on the part of the therapist. The effective therapists do not "take over" the patient's problems, or "solve them" for the patient. Rather, they seem to "be and let be" (Rogers, 1958). This mode of being is quite alien to the modal male. Indeed, it can be discerned among beginning therapists that there is often considerable dread of such passivity, because it constitutes a threat to masculine identity. Beginning therapists seem to be most fascinated by "manly," active techniques such as hypnosis, reflection, interpretation, etc.—the kinds of things which will be difficult for them to master, but which will make them feel they are doing something to the patient which will get him well. These techniques, however, leave the self of the therapist hidden behind the mask of his professional role, and have limited effectiveness.*

women at relating impersonally to others, seeing them as the embodiment of their roles rather than as persons enacting roles. Women (often to the despair of business-like men) seem to find it difficult to keep their interpersonal relationships *impersonal*; they sense and respond to the feelings of the *other* person even in a supposedly official transaction, and they respond to their *own* feelings toward the other person, seeming to forget the original purpose of the impersonal transaction.

Now, one outcome that is known to follow from effective psychotherapy (which, it will be recalled, entails much self-disclosure from the patient to the therapist) is that the patient becomes increasingly sensitized to the nuances of his own feelings (and those of the therapist) as they ebb and flow in the relationship. The patient becomes more adept at labeling his feelings (Dollard and Miller, 1950, pp. 281-304), diagnosing his own needs, and understanding his own reactions. Co-incident with this increase in insight is an increase in empathy with others, an increase in his ability to "imagine the real" (Buber, 1957). Studies of leadership show that the leaders of the most effective groups maintain an optimum "distance" from their followers, avoiding the distraction thereby of overly intimate personal knowledge of the followers' immediate feelings and needs (Fiedler, 1957). But not all of a man's everyday life entails the instrumental leadership role. For example, a man may "lead" his family, but he is not a father twenty-four hours a day. Personal life calls both for insight and for empathy. If practice at spontaneous self-disclosure promotes insight and empathy, then perhaps we have here one of the mechanisms by which women become more adept at these aspects of their so-called "expressive" role. Women, trained toward motherhood and a comforting function, both engage in and receive more self-disclosure than men (Jourard and Richman, 1963).

Let us now focus upon insight, in the sense that we have used the term here. If men are trained, as it were to ignore their own feelings, in order more adequately to pursue the instrumental aspects of manliness, it follows that they will be less sensitive to what one might call "all-is-not-well signals," as these arise in themselves. It is probably a fact that in every case of outright physical or mental illness, earlier signs occurred which, if noted and acted upon, would have averted the eventual break-down. Vague discomfort, boredom, anxiety, depression prob-ably arose as consequences of the afflicted person's way of life, but because these signals were "weak," or else deliber-ately or automatically ignored, the illness-conducive way of life persisted until breakdown finally forced a respite, a withdrawal from the illness-producing role. The hypothesis may be pro-posed that women, more sensitized to their inner experience, will notice their "all-is-not-well signals" sooner and more often than men, and change their mode of existence to one more conducive to wellness, e.g., consult a doctor sooner, or seek bed-rest more often than men. Men, by contrast, fail to notice these "all-is-not-well signals" of weaker intensity, and do not stop work, nor take to their beds until the destructive conse-quences of their manly way of life have progressed to the point of a "stroke," or a total collapse. It is as if women "amplify" such inner distress signals even when they are dim, while men, as it were, "tune them out" until they become so strong they can no longer be ignored.

Accordingly, manly men, unaccustomed to self-disclosure, and characterized by lesser insight and lesser empathy than women, do violence to their own unique needs, and persist in modes of behavior which to be sure, are effective at changing the world, but no less effective in modifying their "essence" from the healthy to the moribund range.

A curious exception to these patterns has been noted among college males. Mechanic and Volkart (1961, p. 52) have proposed the term "illness behavior" to describe "the way in which symptoms are perceived, evaluated, and acted upon by a person who recognizes some pain, discomfort, or other sign of organic malfunction." Visiting a physician at a university in-firmary following perception of some malaise thus qualifies as a type of "illness behavior." Some as yet unpublished research at the University of Florida Student Infirmary has shown that male students consulted the Infirmary one and one half times more frequently than comparable female students during the year under study. A breakdown according to religious denomination showed, moreover, that of the "high users" of the Infirmary, Jewish male students were represented with nearly double the frequency of males affiliated with Methodist, Baptist, Catholic, and other religious groups. A completely independent study (Jourard, 1961b) of self-disclosure patterns among members of different religious denominations on the University of Florida campus showed that Jewish males were significantly higher disclosers than were comparable Methodist, Baptist, and Catholic males, none of the latter three groups differing significantly from one another. These findings imply that college males in general, and Jewish college males in particular, may depart from more stereotyped patterns of masculinity which prevail in the general population for the age range between 18 and 23.

## Manliness and Incompetence at Loving

Loving, including self-love, entails knowledge of the unique needs and characteristics of the loved person (Fromm, 1956). To know another person calls for empathy *in situ*, the capacity to "imagine the real," and the ability to "let be," that is, to permit and promote the disclosure of being. The receipt of disclosure from another person obviously must enhance one's factual knowledge about him, and also it must improve one's degree of empathy with him. But data obtained in the systematic study of self-disclosure have shown, not only that men disclose less to others than women, but also that of all the disclosure that does go on among people, *women are the recipients of more disclosure than men* (Jourard and Richman, 1963). This fact helps one better to understand why men's concepts of the subjective side of other people—of other men as well as of women and children—are often naive, crude, or downright inaccurate. Men are often alleged, in fiction, to be mystified by the motives for the behavior of others, motives which a woman observer can understand instantly, and apparently intuitively. If this conjecture is true, it should follow that men, in spite of good intentions to promote the happiness and growth of others by loving actions, will often "miss the target." That is, they will want to make the other person happy, but their guesses about the actions requisite to the promotion of this goal will be inappropriate, and their actions will appear awkward or crude.

The obverse of this situation is likewise true. If a man is reluctant to make himself known to another person, even to his spouse—because it is not manly thus to be psychologically naked—then it follows that *men will be difficult to love.* That is, it will be difficult for a woman or another man to know the immediate present state of the man's self, and his needs will thereby go unmet. Some men are so skilled at dissembling, at "seeming," that even their wives will not know when they are lonely, bored, anxious, in pain, thwarted, hungering for affection, etc. And the men, blocked by pride, dare not disclose their despair or need.

The situation extends to the realm of self-love. If true love of self implies behavior which will truly meet one's own needs and promote one's own growth, then men who lack profound insight or clear contact with their real selves will be failures at self-loving. Since they do not know what they feel, want and need (through long practice at repression) men's "essences" will show the results of self-neglect, or harsh treatment of the self by the self.

It is a fact that suicide, mental illness, and death occur sooner and more often among "men whom nobody knows" (that is, among unmarried men, among "lone wolves") than among men who are loved as individual, known persons, by other individual, known persons. Perhaps loving and being loved enables a man to take his life seriously; it makes his life take on value, not only to himself, but also to his loved ones, thereby adding to its value for him. Moreover, if a man is open to his loved one, it permits two people—he and his loved one—to examine, react to, diagnose, evaluate, and do something constructive about *his* inner experience and his present condition when these fall into the undesirable range. When a man's self is hidden from everybody else, even from a physician, it seems also to become much hidden even from himself, and it permits entropy—disease and death—to gnaw into his substance without his clear knowledge. Men who are unknown and/or inadequately loved often fall ill, or even die as if suddenly and without warning, and it is a shock and a surprise to everyone who hears about it. One wonders why people express surprise when they themselves fall ill, or when someone else falls ill or dies, apparently suddenly. If one had direct access to the person's real self, one would have had many earlier signals that the present way of life was generating illness. Perhaps, then, the above-noted "inaccessibility" (Rickers-Ovsiankina, 1956) of man, in addition to hampering his insight and empathy, also handicaps him at self-loving, at loving others and at being loved. If love is a factor that promotes life, then handicap at love, a male characteristic, seems to be another lethal aspect of the male role.

## The Male Role and Dispiritation

Frankl (1955) has argued that unless a man can see meaning and value in his continuing existence, his morale will deteriorate, his immunity will decrease, and he will sicken more readily, or even commit suicide. Schmale (1958) noted that the majority of a sample of patients admitted to a general hospital suffered some depressing disruption in object relations prior to the onset of their symptoms. Extrapolating from many observations and opinions of this sort, the present writer proposed a theory of inspiration-dispiration. Broadly paraphrased, this theory holds that, when a man finds hope, meaning, purpose, and value in his existence, he may be said to be "inspired," and isomorphic brain events weld the organism into its optimal, anti-entropic mode of organization. "Dispiriting" events, perceptions, beliefs, or modes of life tend to weaken this optimum mode of organization (which at once sustains wellness and mediates the fullest, most effective functioning and behavior), and illness is most likely to flourish then. It is as if the body, when a man is dispirited, suddenly becomes an immensely fertile "garden" in which viruses and germs proliferate like jungle vegetation. In inspirited states, viruses and germs find a man's body a very uncongenial milieu for unbridled growth and multiplication.

Now, from what has been said in previous sections, it seems clear that the male role provides many opportunities for dispiritation to arise. The best example is provided by the data on aging. It is a well-documented observation that men in our society, following retirement, will frequently disintegrate and die not long after they assume their new life of leisure. It would appear that masculine identity and self-esteem—factors in inspiritation for men—are predicated on a narrow base. If men can see themselves as manly, and life as worth-while, only so long as they are engaged in gainful employ, or are sexually potent, or have enviable social status, then clearly these are tenuous bases upon which to ground one's existence. It would seem that women can continue to find meaning, and *raisons d'être* long after men feel useless and unneeded.

Thus, if man's sense of masculine identity, as presently culturally defined, is a condition for continued existence, and if this is easily undermined by the vicissitudes of aging or the vicissitudes of a changing social system, then, indeed, the male role has an added lethal component. The present writer has known men who became dispirited following some financial or career upset, and who fell victims to some infectious disease, or "heart failure" shortly thereafter. Their wives, though affected by the husbands' reverses or death, managed to find new grounds and meaning for continued existence, and got on with living.

### Discussion and Summary

It has been pointed out that men, lower disclosers of self than women, are less insightful and empathic, less competent at loving, and more subject to dispiritation than women. The implication of these aspects of manliness for health and longevity was explored. As a concluding note, it seems warranted to step back, and look briefly at the problem of roles from a broader perspective.

Social systems need to delimit people's behavior in order to keep the systems functioning. No social system can use all of every man's self and yet keep the social system functioning well. This is what roles are for—sex roles as well as occupational, age, and familial roles. The role-definitions help men and women to learn just which actions they must perform, and which they must suppress in order to keep the social system functioning properly. But it should not then be thought that just because society cannot use all that a man is, that the man should then strive to root out all self that is neither useful, moral, nor in vogue.

If health, full-functioning, happiness and creativity are valued goals for mankind, then laymen and behavioral scientists alike must seek ways of redefining the male role, to help it become less restrictive and repressive, more expressive of the "compleat" man, and more conducive to life. ✦

### References

Buber, M. I and Thou, *New York, Scribners, 1937.*

Buber, M. Elements of the interhuman. *William Alanson White Memorial Lectures.* Psychiatry, *1957, 20, 95-129.*

Dollard, J., and Miller, N.E. Personality and Psychotherapy. *New York, McGraw-Hill, 1950.*

Fiedler, F.E. *A note of leadership theory: The effect of social barriers between leaders and followers.* Sociometry, *1957, 20, 87-94.*

Frankl, V.E. The Doctor and the Soul, An Introduction to Logotherapy. *New York, Knopf, 1955.*

Fromm, E. The Art of Loving. *New York, Harper, 1956.*

Jourard, S.M. Age and self-disclosure. Merrill-Palmer Quart. Beh. Dev., *1961 (a), 7, 191-197.*

Jourard, S.M. Religious denomination and self-disclosure. Psychol. Rep., *1961 (b), 8, 446.*

Jourard, S.M., and Landsman, M.J. Cognition, cathexis and the "dyadic effect" in men's self-disclosing behavior. Merrill-Palmer Quart. Behav. Dev., *1960, 6, 178-186.*

Jourard, S.M., and Lasakow, P. *Some factors in self-disclosure.* J. abn. soc. Pyschol., *1958, 56, 91-98.*

Jourard, S.M., and Richman, P. *Disclosure output and input in college students.* Merrill-Palmer Quart. Beh. Dev., *1963, 9, 141-148.*

Mechanic, D., and Volkhart, E.H. *Stress, illness behavior and the sick role.* Amer. Sociol. Rev., *1961, 26, 51-58.*

Reich, W. Character Analysis. *New York, Orgone Press, 1948.*

Rickers-Ovsiankina, Maria. *Social accessibility in three age groups.* Psychol. Reports, *1956, 2, 283-294.*

Rogers, C.R. *The characteristics of a helping relationship.* Pers. Guid. J., *1958, 37, 6-16.*

Schmale, A.H. *Relation of separation and depression to disease.* Psychosom. Med., *1958, 20, 259-277.*

# *IV-4* *The Body Taboo*

To what extent will people let others see and touch their bodies? Little systematic research has been done into this; yet I suspect there is a connection between "body experience" (what someone perceives, believes, imagines, feels and fantasies about his body) and physical and mental health. Perhaps puritanical taboos about the body extend even into the attitudes of inquiring psychologists: the topic is not fit or important enough to study. Some research I have carried out attempts to make good the lack.

My approach was simple enough. I began my inquiries with some self-examination. "Whom have I let see me naked? Whom do I permit to touch me? Where do I allow them to touch me? How do I feel about this kind of intimacy? Are there some parts of my body I am embarrassed to touch myself, much less let someone else touch?" After I answered these questions, I was surprised, and (as an investigator) delighted to find that my attitudes and experience were very complex indeed.

I then asked students, patients, colleagues and friends to tell me their attitudes to body contact and their experience of it. I found fantastic variability. Some people reported that if anyone laid a hand on them, uninvited, they would become furious. Others stated that they liked nothing so much as to parade in the nude, and to receive a body massage at every opportunity.

There are also sharp cultural differences in the frequency with which inhabitants of different countries let their bodies contact others. In Mexico and Puerto Rico, for example, many people walk arm in arm—men with men, women with women—

without anyone doubting their heterosexual integrity. People in conversation come close to one another, tap one another on the chest or arm to emphasise points. But Anglo-Saxon Americans, Canadians and British are more reserved and distant. They are uncomfortable if people "get too close."

I designed a simple self-report questionnaire, not unlike a butcher's beef chart. It consisted of an outline drawing of the human figure, with 22 zones marked off and numbered. For example, the top of the head was No. 1, the hands were No. 15, the buttocks were No. 22. I prepared a little booklet with four of these drawings, one for mother, one for father, and one each for closest friend of the same sex, and closest friend of the opposite sex. I gave these booklets to several hundred college students in my class at the University of Florida, asking them to check which parts of their bodies had been seen, unclad, by each of the "target persons"; which parts had been touched for any reason whatever; and, which parts of these other persons' bodies they had seen and touched. I encouraged the students to be absolutely frank in their responses and said they could leave their names off the replies to ensure anonymity.

The findings rather surprised me. The "visual accessibility" scores were not very interesting, because almost all the students had seen and been seen by the other people in brief bathing costumes. But the touch data were a different matter. Both men and women students touched ( and were touched by) their parents and same-sex friends on only a few areas of the body—the hands, arms and shoulders mostly. When the closest opposite-sex friend was considered, the data were striking. It was almost as if the floodgates were opened. There was a virtual deluge of physical contact, all over the body. But there was much variability in these findings. Not all the students enjoyed a steady relationship with someone of the opposite sex, and these poor devils reported that they were virtually untouched, and out of touch.

This research points up something important—that there isn't a great deal of body contact going on in these young students' lives, outside the strictly sexual context. It's almost as if all possible meanings of a touch are eliminated except the caress with sexually arousing intent. Not that there is anything wrong with the latter; but it does imply that unless a young American (or British?) adult is engaged in sexual lovemaking, he is unlikely to experience his body as it feels when someone is touching, poking, massaging, hugging or holding it. The exception, of course, is provided by physical-contact sports. These give devotees the opportunity to feel embodied in a personally and socially acceptable way. But not everyone takes part in these.

What other forms of acceptable body contact are available to the average person in our contactless society? Physical massage can be purchased for a fee in most cities in the United States and Britain—but this is impersonal and professional. The physically ill may, if their nurse is not too busy sorting laundry, medications and papers, receive a skillful, depersonalised backrub, given either as prescribed TLC (tender loving care), or to prevent muscle stiffness and to relieve tension. Men's and women's hairdressers may provide a certain amount of touching and rubbing of the head without arousing anxieties or embarrassment in their clients. In the United States, many barbers use electrical vibrators strapped to their hand, to depersonalise the contact of hand on scalp. In American motels, beds are often equipped with "magic fingers"—a patented vibrator which, for a 25-cent coin, will shake a person into relaxation without benefit of human intervention. It seems as if the machine has taken over another function of man—the loving and soothing caress.

Thus, because of cultural norms in Anglo-Saxon countries, people are deprived of the most basic way to experience their bodies—through the human touch. Unless they have a sexual relationship going with someone, people in our countries are not likely to be touched after the years of childhood. I suspect that the dog patter, cat stroker and child hugger is seeking the contact that conspicuously and poignantly lacking in his adult life.

Why the touch taboo?

I think it is part of the more general alienation process that characterises our depersonalising social system. I think it is related to the same source that underlies the dread of authentic self-disclosure. When people are committed to upward mobility, in competition with their fellows, everyone masquerades, and keeps his real self concealed from the other who is a potential enemy. You keep others at a distance and mystified by withholding disclosure, and by not letting them get close enough to touch, not letting them know how you feel.

In such a society, our bodies tend to disappear. Not from the other's gaze, or even from our own glance into the mirror. Rather, they vanish from our *experience.* We lose the capacity to experience our bodies as vital, enlivened and as the centres of our being. I think that the restricted experience of being touched is consistent with R.D. Laing's diagnosis of modern man as "unembodied." My own experience as a product of rather puritanical Canadian schooling, and adult life in the United States, has given me personal experience of the disembodiment middle class upbringing produces in these countries. My research and my experience as a psychotherapist both lead me to confirm Laing. I have come to believe that we give up the capacity to experience our body as enlivened, in return for the "benefits" of our increasingly automated and mechanised way of life.

We all begin life as sentient bodies, and then encounter the massive onslaught of repressive forces that aim at annihilating, or at least diminishing, the experience of pleasure and pain, sensuality, fatigue and energy, fullness and emptiness. The purpose of socialising is not only to control behaviour, but also to regulate experience. The capacity to experience one's body disappears—a victim of parents' and schools' efforts to transmute infants and children into respectable adults.

Children who touch their own bodies, as in exploratory masturbation, are punished, and threatened with predictions of insanity and depravity. Children who touch other things (children encounter the world by means of touch) are slapped, and told "mustn't touch." They are taught to keep their bodies at a distance from things and people: look, but don't touch.

Parents' and teachers' efforts to distract growing children from awareness of sexuality also succeed in distracting children from more general sensitivity to their bodies. By the time children reach adulthood, they have managed to set themselves at such a distance from their bodies, that their feet and hands, bellies and genitals, backs and backsides, are experienced as belonging "out there," away from the centre of self.

The diminuendo quality of the average person's experience of his body appears to be necessary, if he is to be able to subject himself to the increasingly automated and regulated styles of life offered him. A day which begins with the rush through breakfast, the hurry to go to work, and the mechanical, meaningless, fragmentary quality of work itself—anybody, anybody, would shriek in protest if he allowed himself to *feel* the violence to which he is subjecting himself. The "normal" state of being—numbness—seems essential for people to continue living in, and preserving social and economic status quos.

The devastated appearance of most adults' bodies when they reach their thirties and forties attests to the violence they have passively accepted. The ways of living life that earn money and respectability are the very ways that destroy the awareness and the liveliness of the bodies that we *are.*

When I lived in London, I used to pass the time on my daily trips to Piccadilly Circus tube station (beginning at Southgate) looking at people's bodies. One phenomenon that impressed me was the "vanishing lip." I would see a whole family seated side by side: the infants and the young children with soft, suckling lips. The adolescents already were getting the tight, disembodied look. The parents manifested what I called "the thin red line"—the lips had vanished, as if re-absorbed, replaced by a tight crack. So noticeable were the missing lips that, on a visit to Paris, I found myself standing in a Metro car, with a plump woman in her fifties to one side, a moustached policeman on the other. Both had such full lips, I felt like turning to right and left to kiss them.

A visit to a public beach, in the United Sates or Britain, is a sobering experience. The adults look hideous or pathetic. Mounds of billowing, pasty flesh, or tight bundles of piano wire.

I have a strong suspicion that a great deal of physical sickness arises because we have not noticed the early, all-is-not-well signals generated by the way of life that is not good for our bodies. If body experience is repressed, then the way of life is continued until stress and pain cross a very high threshold. Someone more tuned in to his body might have noticed the beginnings of malaise and changed what he was doing to (and with) his body, in order to regain a sense of vitality and well-being. Indeed, much of the tranquilising and sedating medicine that is devoured aims at further annihilating body experience, so that destructive life styles can be continued, and the social system maintained.

Dancers and athletes necessarily have a keener sense of the condition of their bodies. They simply cannot perform when they are not warmed up, when they are cramped from inactivity, or depressed by an unsatisfying way of life. They can sense when muscles are stiff, when energy is at low ebb, when they have eaten too much or too little. Likewise, Hatha Yoga devotees regain the alive, centred, organic sense of their bodies that they began life with. The *asanas* (special postures) undo the muscular armouring that is generated by the usual way of life, and bring the body into a dynamic readiness and repose that is not available to the average person.

Smokers of marijuana and users of LSD regularly report that, when the drug begins to take effect, their mostly unused senses become enlivened. They hear sounds ordinarily ignored; smell odours that always have been present; and they feel their bodies with heightened awareness. Such psychedelic drugs seem to detach a person from his chronic projects, in pursuit of which he screens out irrelevant experience. Certainly, a keen awareness of our bodies would interfere with most of our daily or long-term aspirations. When the pull of our projects is suspended, as happens with the consciousness-expanding drugs, our awareness is inundated, as it were, with sense data that hitherto have been chronically screened out. It is as if all the channels on a television set were simultaneously turned on. The amplified consciousness of the body that occurs under "pot" or "acid" terrifies some over-repressed users, but is sought as a goal by others. The hippies—the new generation of non-violent revolutionaries—seek heightened experience of their bodies through drugs, or sensuous contact, as their form of social protest.

Increasing numbers of psychotherapists are becoming interested in techniques for awakening a benumbed body consciousness. In the United States, teachers of body awareness, like Bernard Gunther at the Esalen Institute in Big Sur Hot Springs, conduct classes aimed at undoing the repression of body experience. Alexander Lowen, a pupil of Wilhelm Reich, conducts classes and workshops in New York in which the students are run through exercises that undo cramped muscles, and awaken the possibilities of feeling in otherwise anaesthetic body zones.

In my own psychotherapeutic work, I have encouraged and guided patients into such Hatha Yoga postures that I have mastered myself, and in which I have found much benefit. And I have encouraged patients to learn the art of body massage, and to teach it to others so that this way of awakening body experience, and diminishing social distance, can be introduced into their lives.

I think that much could be done to make life more livable, and bodies more beautiful and healthy, through such reembodying procedures. Neglect of one's body through ignorance; avoidance of physical contact with others; loss of experience of one's body through repression; and misuse of the body in the obsessive pursuit of security or respectability—all these diminish life. As Bernard Gunther puts it (with tongue only partly in his cheek), "If everyone massaged somebody for an hour every day, there would be no war." Certainly, if people sought to regain the experience of their bodies through massage, meditation, exercises, yoga, and other means; and if they explored ways to keep their sense of their bodies alive, there would be much less illness. Finally, in a society which fosters the alienation of person from person, I can think of no more direct way to get in touch than by touching. ✦

[1967]

# *IV-5* The Human Challenge of Automation

In the next moment of history, machine regulated machines will wrest our livelihoods for us. When that moment arrives, we may well not know what to do with ourselves and our time. Man is the only being for whom life poses the existential question most starkly: "What shall I do and be?" So long as he answered, "Live!" for millennia the question was settled; because securing the means for living always commanded the greater part of every man's time and energy. The biblical injunction to observe the Sabbath was epochal because it enjoined man to pause, so he might realize there are other things to do besides work to stay alive, amass power, and indulge senses. But what will happen when every day could be a Sabbath, when work is obsolete, and the prospect of leisure, that abyss of freedom, confronts us? This is freedom at its most dizzying. It is at once a horrifying and challenging future; horrifying because few are ready for leisure and freedom, and challenging because of the promise imminent of a bold leap into as yet unfathomed possibilities of being.

The horror is warranted. Society condemns our "senior citizens" to a residual life sentence of "leisure" as soon as they are sixty-five years old. This liberation from work operates as a rapid death sentence for many. And for still more, release from the experience of feeling useful brings on either the living death of boredom, or the rapid encroachment of gibbering senility in hitherto vigorous men. A friend of mine, a survivor of Hitler's death-camps, visited St. Petersburg one time. The old people he saw shuffling or sitting about the streets reminded him of the "Musselmen" of Auschwitz. They were fatter, to be sure; but the aimless and lifeless expressions of their faces were the same. Next to our prisons and mental hospitals, the retirement centers for those awaiting death are surely American equivalents of concentration camps.

About twenty five hundred years ago, the Greeks lived in a nearly automated society—their work-producing "machines" were slaves and women—and the men produced a flowering of consciousness such as has not existed since. Liberated as they were from the menial chores of producing and distributing goods, men were free to think, imagine, and explore, to perfect themselves in their world. For the Greeks, "original sin" was *lack* of knowledge, not eating from the tree of knowledge. We still have not, today, exhausted all the beginnings they laid down.

Right now, our technology advances inexorably toward near-total automation, and we have responded, not by flights of creative imagination, not by the liberation of our spirits to soar to new heights of possibility, as was true in ancient Greece. We have instead responded by becoming increasingly like our slaves, the machines. We have mechanized more and more our relationships with each other; these become role-bound, boring, far departures from the "swing" of true dialogue. We manipulate ourselves in order to present attractive packages to others. We allow ourselves to be manipulated by advertisers, politicians, salesmen, moviemakers. We routinize our daily round of existence so we will the better fit into timetables for transport from suburb to place of busy-work. We eat, not to nourish and perfect our bodies, but to keep up with Jones, to consume the overproduction of our farms, or to palliate nagging feelings of loneliness. We don't embrace one another in love, despite the liberation permitted by "the Pill"—rather, we fornicate in order to feel, or to feel alive, or to reassure ourselves that we are sexy. We even have our lovemaking scheduled—suburbia on Sunday morning is a place of orgy, after the children are sent off to Sunday school. Our houses are designed for some being other than the human, so little place is there in them for privacy. Every aspect of our lives aims at turning us off, numbing us, so that we will keep our once-born, programmed status in the social system, and not rock boats.

Modern science, in all its specializations, aims at understanding Nature in order to manipulate and control her. This may be fine, for botany, zoology, climatology, physics and chemistry. But the same definition of science, with the same aims, has been extended to the human sciences—especially psychology, but also pedagogy, sociology, political science, economics, and psychiatry. Now no man will consent to be understood, in order to be manipulated and controlled by someone, unless he is mystified and stupefied, so that he doesn't know what is going on. Yet men are being manipulated and controlled daily, and seem unaware that it is going on. Somebody or some institution is playing games with human consciousness, seeking to control it, so that behavior will thereby be controlled, and fit into systems. When man is thus controlled, he has changed in ontological status from person to thing. I submit that this transmutation of man into thing has been going on for a few centuries of western history, but it is continuing today at an accelerated pace.

I'll even indulge a taste for prophecy, and predict that in the next few years, in America, we'll witness a struggle between those who would keep man's consciousness and action to limits that fit a status quo, and those who see in automation the signal for inventing new worlds, for the flowering once again, of human potentialities comparable to the fantastic creativity of ancient Greece. The struggle, as a matter of fact, may be bloody. I hope the champions of human growth in diversity win. I am on that side.

What light might psychology shed on this matter? And what role might schools and universities play in increasing the odds that we will enter a magnificent age of enlightenment rather than an age where each man is even more stringently shaped to roles and statuses that make him useful to the State, but not potentiating of himself in this personal life?

## Social Control of Action and Experience

First, a perspective on social systems. These come into being because man cannot live alone. Originally, they are instituted because they seem efficient ways to divide labor, and maximize freedom from want and danger. But then, a struggle for control over goods, wealth and power takes place and some few gain control over the many, by gaining control over wealth and hence the means of socialization. Marx was correct, I believe, in viewing the major institutions of society as means for maintaining the status quo.

The aim of socialization practices, beginning in the rearing of infants, but extending to formal schooling, is so to train people that they will habitually experience and behave in the ways they *must* behave; or so they will be afraid to behave in any way other than those ways which maintain the status quo. Mass media, religion, the law, custom, public opinion, even the healing professions all collude to keep people behaving, and what is even more insidious, experiencing the world in the ways that keep the present social structure intact. Man's highest purpose and duty in America, so it would seem, is to *consume*, so factories won't close down. Advertising insures he will: more money is spent on that means of "shaping" than is spent on education.

If anyone misses being so brainwashed, he is invalidated—encountered with threats and actualities of imprisonment, ostracism, poverty, or hospitalization—unless he is very enlightened, or very cunning.

This is the way societies maintain themselves. This is the way they resist change, whether it be change in national purpose, change in means of production, or changes in class structure.

But when change in the productive base takes place, as is occurring with expanding automation, these ways have become irrelevant and obsolete. A "world"* has truly come to an end, though few realize it.

*The term "world" (in quotes) refers to the world as experienced by men or by a particular man.

## The "Capsule" We Live In

The world goes on—reality is like a projective test. Man can construe it in myriad ways. The world discloses itself ceaselessly to human consciousnesses, which refract it, and attach meaning to this disclosure in ways that vary from time to time and place to place. A given world view gains dominance in each society. This is a way to structure the world, to attach value and meaning to it. "Worlds" are structured by projects, or goals and values. Change these and "worlds" collapse, to be replaced by new ones. All this is elementary existential phenomenology.

The "world" most of us in America share is a world that once was haunted by European memories of poverty and material scarcity. The aim was to get rich, and we actually have the productive means available whereby everyone can be rich, at least in a material sense. As automation powered with nuclear sources of energy proceeds, we can in principle feed, clothe and shelter the world, even a world with a more fully exploded population that the one Malthusian prophets of doom say we now have. Our past and current patterns of childrearing, our aims and methods of schooling, even our ways of playing in leisure hours all gain their relevance and intelligibility from the fact of scarcity—scarcity that long since has ceased to exist. In a way, as we socialize and train to a nonexistent reality, we can say that our very socialization and training is mad. It is akin to training people in the art of stalking, capturing and cooking dinosaurs. The values, skills, ways of relating to others that make up the curriculum of a dinosaur-hunting school somehow lose relevance when there are no dinosaurs to be caught and cooked.

But "worlds" die hard. Each of us lives in a world that I can best liken to an envelope, capsule, or bubble with semi-permeable walls. These walls screen off much of what is, and admit to our consciousness only as much of being as is relevant to our projects. The world beyond the capsule is filled, according to folklore and popular imagination, with bogeymen, cockroaches, slime, and everything hideous. Shatter the membrane, and let this world in, and people become terrified. Rather than face the prospect of posing new projects and values, in order to construct new "worlds," people patch the rents in the walls of their present "world." Seeing becomes a way of being blind, blind to other possibilities that the world embodies.

In America, young people, mature women, and Negroes all are in process of awakening—some with delight, but more with anger, and rage at the dirty joke that has been played upon them. They are breaking out of their capsules. The world is not necessarily what men have told them it is. It has not been ordained by God (if he lives) that Negroes should be stupid, employed in menial tasks, and housed in bedbug infested slums. Nor did God necessarily demand that women should die of boredom and overeating in automated households. And young people—below the age of 18—are wondering if God wants them to put on gray flannel suits to become professional consumers, or to go to Vietnam.

Young people especially, as I encounter them in the halls of training and learning, are beginning to demand inspiration and enlightenment, not stupefaction at the feet of their instructors. They are beginning to look at instructors as *entire men*, not solely as repositories of alienated skill or knowledge, and they are wondering if they want to become like these men. Increasing numbers of young men and women are dropping out. They are finding that the schools and colleges, instead of enlightening them as to how things are now, or turning them on to challenging new projects and possibilities are training them for a slot in professions or corporate enterprise, which support a way of life and experience they find meaningless. And so they turn to marijuana, LSD, and morning-glory seeds for enlightenment, and a kind of travel.

## Being Outside the Capsule

There is this to be said for psychedelic drugs—they afford a glimpse to the seeker of the possible world beyond our usual, stripped and debased image of it. They open Pandora's box. Since we are in it, they let us see outside. They awaken a person's consciousness to possibilities of perceiving, imagining, feeling and remembering that usually lie encrusted under habit, the results of conventional upbringing. Once a person has taken such a "trip," he is never the same.

The drugs seem to work by suspending the "pull" of conventional values and projects upon a person. This is why their widespread use is seen as subversive. This temporary letting go, or detachment yields a ersatz *satori*, or the experience of enlightenment—but with western efficiency. What might have taken an eastern mystic something like 20 years of discipline, asceticism and meditation is achieved in something like 20 minutes, at a cost of 20¢ or $20—truly cheap grace!

But when the drug-traveler returns to home base, he is seldom prepared for what awaits him. The walls of his usual world have been eroded, even rent in places, and more being than he can cope with may be "let in." This may frighten him, if he is unprepared for it. More insidiously, his grip on past projects has been weakened. This may not be such a bad thing, if the projects (like getting rich, or popular, or powerful) are not of his own choosing, but have been inculcated into him. But he usually has no projects, equally compelling, to take the place of those he has lost. And so, he may drift about in a world that explodes with myriad possibilities, none of which feel more important to him than any other. Nothing is worth doing. God (the values of parents) is dead—he was killed with LSD—and boys are left with a man's job; to invest the world with new values and projects when their value-investing apparatus has been rendered anemic by drugs.* And there are no exemplary men around to give witness to the possibility of a challenging, rewarding and meaningful existence guided by projects other than those of becoming a dumping ground for productive output that can't be consumed fast enough.

---

* Herein lies a challenge for psychological research: What are the conditions and the means by which the experience of value arises in a person? What do we know about the parameters of the attribution of value?

Psychedelic drugs seem to me to be one of many forms of current protest against the stupefying effect that our socialization has upon man. Man can dissect nature in order the better to control it. He can build machines to work for him. He extends his sense organs and muscles with machinery—but then loses his capacity to see, hear, smell, and move. All these things are done for him, in the name of efficiency, by the very machines he has created.

Not only are the various media—extensions of man, as McLuhan calls them—leaching man of his power; but in order that man might not notice the loss of his wholeness and his creative possibilities, he is stupefied more deliberately. Radio, television, movies, books all help keep man in a stupor. If a person begins to sicken, and suffer boredom, pain, or anxiety—those signs that all is not well in the way he is living his life—the medical profession then steps in with some pharmaceutical product that enables the person to continue living the meaningless life, but without feeling the pain and suffering.

In short, we effect those praxes upon our own consciousness which constrict our world. We repress, distort, close off entire sensory channels, banalize our imaginations, and end up helpless to live in a social and material world we made ourselves, and helpless to change it. We only endure it with the help of booze and tranquilizers.

The use of psychedelic drugs is part of the whole scene. The possibility of an expanded and creative consciousness of the world and ourselves inheres in all of us. But we become alienated from this possibility, in consequence of the way we have been reared. And so we invest drugs and substances with "the power," and the only way we can get this alienated power back is by ingesting 100 micrograms of acid. It's like the joke unenlightened physicians play upon us. They know, or suspect that healing inheres in the organism. Yet they pretend that, without doses of penicillin and assorted wonder drugs, everyone would die shortly after the onset of a sore throat. It's a wonderful way to sell drugs, but probably a debased form of the noble profession of healing (in which medicine holds no true monopoly).

## Schools: For Teaching or Training?

The institutions of education are becoming increasingly automated. "Teaching machines" are being incorporated into more schools, as a desperate response to overcrowding and an insufficiency of instructors. Indeed, desperate instructors try to program themselves—their lectures and demonstrations— so that students will be able to blacken the correct spaces on an IBM sheet at the end of a term.

Can you imagine the horror of five or ten thousand people all reading a book in the same way? This is invaluable, if training into pre-set molds and roles is the aim; if individuality, originality and creativity are to be trained out, and uniformity in experience and action is desirable. Indeed, designers of teaching machines could get rich by programming the Bible for a *guaranteed* Methodist, Baptist, Catholic, or Jewish way of reading, and interpreting Scripture.

But this is not education and it is not desirable. Automation will release human energy from the necessity to spend it making goods essential to life. But it will not thereby make life more livable, challenging, and rich in experience. This latter aim calls for *education*—the liberation of human consciousness in its various modes (especially imagination) from the bonds imposed by training. The salvation of man, with the hope he will invent better forms of economic, social, political and interpersonal existence, is education, not training. And education requires teachers, people who awaken and enliven consciousness, not constrain it, like trainers do. Teachers are hard to find. They are as scarce as white whales. Teachers illuminate what is; they are existential explorers, groping for new meanings as they challenge old ones. They are not solely repositories of a skill or corpus of information.

The most powerful psychedelic agent known to man is not lysergic acid, as is so commonly believed. Two more powerful are travel to another land, there to be involved. The other is the awakened consciousness of another human being. Both psychedelic agents may be subversive. This is why travel to some lands is prohibited. And this is why Socrates was given the hemlock and Jesus the cross. Here I'd like to focus upon the self-disclosure of awakened men—teachers. According to this view, a teacher is a man who has been awakened from the illusion that there is only one sane, right and legal way to experience the world and behave in it. He has become "turned on" such that his imagination is vivid. He can perceive the world as others see it, and more: liberated from convention as he is, he sees what others are blind to. The walls of his capsule have been shattered, and rebuilt so that more world is included in his consciousness. He feels, thinks, imagines, and remembers more fully than the average man. He can, perhaps, dance, feel his body, move it and live in it, a Zorba-esque man among nebbishes. Or perhaps he has only a glimmering of other possibilities to which he will be led through his dedication to the beauty that inheres in Latin grammar, or amoebae swimming in slime on a microscope slide (all paths to glory are good).

If such a man, a teacher, discloses the wonder of life as it is for him to pupils, some will indeed "flip." They will be turned on. Their old "world" will explode, or better, implode, when more being is admitted, under the guidance of the teacher.

If this teacher is himself committed to responsibility for some corner of the world—not for money and fame, but for authentic concern and love—then his pupils may be ready to take over when he dies, or extend his vision and responsibility while he still lives.

Where do we find such teachers? How can we disseminate their expanded consciousness of some aspect of the world? It is for the lack of such teachers that young people go to pot or acid. Teachers of this kind are needed more, today, than another cadre of astronauts, or more riot police, psychiatrists, narcotics agents or school counselors.

We are the equals of the Nazis, the communists and the Chinese, at training, mystifying, and stupefying masses of people. We have the possibility, through TV and other media, of getting even better at it. But we also have the possibility of turning on and awakening more people to expanded perspectives on the world, new challenges, possible ways to experience the world and our own embodied being, than has ever been possible before. I don't believe that there is an insoluble educational crisis before us. *I believe rather that we need to sort out our values, to see if we are as serious about educating our population as we have been about training them for the status quo.* If, beginning with the president's office in Washington, a serious dedication to human awakening was awakened, with appropriate budget appended, a fantastic revolution would have thereby been commenced. But such seriousness of dedication would meet incredible opposition from representatives of the status quo—unimaginative and timid men willing to kill in order to avoid the necessity of changing world views. Can you imagine what would happen to advertising, for example—and the firms that use advertising—that art of changing people from men into greedy consumers—if people were awakened? Could you imagine what firms would go bankrupt because an enlightened public would not buy what they produce? Can you imagine which leaders would be voted out of office by an enlightened public? No, we are not, as a nation, serious about education. In fact, we equate training with education, and mistakenly assume that we are giving the people public education when we are really giving them public training.

**The Hidden Teachers**

There is a scarcity of teachers in the land. Colleges of education do not regularly produce teachers. They produce technicians paid to implement a prescribed syllabus, by prescribed means. This is not bad, because education is a *transcending* project, and there must be something to transcend. But the "turned-on" men—they exist as a kind of underground in every institution that is called educational. The problem is *to induce them to come out of hiding*, for that is what they mainly do. Teachers with an offbeat perspective on the world are punished for their very genius. Teachers who awaken pupils so that they ask embarrassing questions, and challenge existing forms, are frequently fired. And so the youngsters "blow pot" and take "acid" as respite from trainers whom they often feel have "sold out." Or they go through the motions prescribed by the syllabus, get their grades, and escalate themselves as thoroughly programmed men into their place in the professions and business. Indeed, some may actually believe that they are educated, and spout canned attitudes and platitudes as if they were eternal truths, and live lives in the suburbs that are patterned by *Ladies' Home Journal* articles, as if those ways of living were the only thinkable ones. Isn't it curious, that we experiment with nuclear energy, ways to organize a factory, ways to train people, but we do not experiment with ways to live family life, or ways to spend our time.

Universities don't have Departments of Experimental Existence, or Departments of Possible Worlds, or Departments of Human Possibility. Instead, we have subject-matter and instructors thereof, which maintain existential status quos.

I anticipate that, when finally automation reaches full flower, almost every aspect of our daily lives will lose relevance, so oriented is it now to the present ways of producing goods and maintaining the present social and economic structure. Yet, when consuming more goods, getting richer, or getting ahead in the corporation cease to be viable goals, what will be the point of much of our child-training practices—which inspire children to be greedy and bottomless consumers, competitive, false, role dominated, and upwardly mobile? And what will we do with our time? Watch TV? We'll have to learn to enter into dialogue with one another—but there's nobody there.

## Living Outside the Capsule

Some of the beatniks and "hippies" who have "opted out" are existential explorers and pioneers. They are risking their time, and considerable money, to see if life is livable outside the usual institutional forms, without the usual hardware of domestic life. Respectable people make it tough on hippies. Indeed, many hippies may be nebbishes. But some I know are serious "opt-outs," serious seekers after ways to live that are more authentic, more meaningful than the prescribed forms of life. *They* may turn out to be our teachers, or teachers of our teachers, when automation expands leisure. Since hippies have no respectability or status to put in jeopardy, many of them are more honest than "squares," at least in love and friendship. Since they work when they feel like it, and play when they feel like it—and moreover, they have someone to play with—many of them are healthier than squares. Indeed, they could be said to be the first enlightened ones to realize our economic-productive system is already quite automated so that one can leave regular employment without starving, and without the economy collapsing. And they are truly experimenting with ways to spend their time, ways for men and women to live together, ways to raise children, etc. They may produce some bungles in such experimentation, but what experiment doesn't, and what kind of experimentation is more important? Be kind to the hippies you see. They have commenced an odyssey of a sort, and you may want them to come home and teach you what they have learned, when you face the emptiness of no productive work (machines do it) and time on your hands. If they are not too bitter over the send-off we gave them, they might teach us how to live life meaningfully and joyfully without recourse to tranquilizers and psychiatry.

**Conclusion**

The world has shrunk, and there no longer is a category of Them. There is only Us—gropers for challenge, growth, fulfillment and meaning in our lives. Some older, some younger; some enlightened, others, mystified and befuddled. Some rich, some poor. Some of us will have to help the rest of the world get as rich as us. Our dilemma is unparalleled in human history. If we are not to die of boredom, or of invasion by the envious, we have two tasks—first, to help the rest of the world solve its material problems, and then to explore how to live, learn and find meaning when there's no work to be done. If colleges and universities are to fulfill their function of education and enlightenment as effectively as they train people into unquestioning conformity, they must encourage teachers to stand forth, and declare themselves in any ways that time, money, versatility, and electronic hardware have made possible. Let teachers disclose, not just the techniques for chemical analysis, or the rules for declining verbs—but also what all this means, how it challenges them in the meaningful pursuit of their lives. Let education approximate to dialogue, and not shaping. Let a college be a community of fellow seekers, not a place where we, the faculty, train *them*, the students. Let the students have contact with heroes with a small "h"—men who are truly seeking enlightenment and wholeness, finding challenges and new values when old ones have worn out. Training will never become obsolete, and we can always find trainers. The social system at large is well protected with safeguards to insure that any change in the fabric of society will be orderly, and not violent or arbitrary. If this is true, and I believe it is, then schools from kindergarten up through university can be places where explorers and trainers cohabit and coexist, where there is a place for learning necessary roles and skills and knowledge, and a place for enlivening and embodying the creative imagination. ✦

(1968)

# IV-6 *The Invitation to Die*

It seems that we have made giant strides in our understanding of man—his experience and his behavior—by comparing him with something else. Our models of man have been drawn from nature. Thus, we have looked at man as being like a rat, monkey, pigeon, or guinea-pig; we have assumed that factors that affect the condition of these animals likewise affect man, the observer of those animals. It is as if the sciences of human beings have espoused the motto, *"Nihil animalis a me alienum puto."*

And we have compared man to man-made mechanisms and systems: to communication networks, servo-systems, computers, hydraulic systems, robots, and the like, with considerable payoff in understanding the being of man. It is as if we have sought to grasp man by understanding something he has made: *"Nihil machinae a me alienum puto."*

These approaches are embodied in the great efforts to comprehend man: Darwinism, Marxism, psychoanalysis, behaviorism, and physiology.

But there is another approach which I think has become timely, one that science prided itself in surpassing, but which I think can illumine man and the world more than it did hitherto: the approach of animism, or animalism, with the tendency to attribute human motives to the nonhuman beings in the world—a more sophisticated anthropomorphism. From this vantage point, the beings in the world are likened to me as free, conscious agents, with intentionality, and with a career that commences out of nothingness and returns to nothingness. The

Latin motto would be something like, *"Nihil mihi a mundi alienum puto"*—"Nothing of my experience can be irrelevant to understanding the world."

The current term for the renascent anthropomorphism, for the use of my experience, as I reflect upon it as a model for the comprehension of the world—and especially the comprehension of the other man in sickness and health, in self-fulfillment and self-destruction—is existential phenomenology. The effort to develop this as a disciplined way of inquiry, a science of persons, is a task of the emerging humanistic psychology.

I address the theme of suicide from the point of view of existential phenomenology.

From this standpoint, man is seen as this particular person, an embodied consciousness, free in a situation of time, place, society, and culture, living a body of specifiable (by others) structure and capabilities, and living in relation to particular other persons. His experience affects and is affected by the disclosed experience of others.

As a person, man is a center for orientation of the entire universe, a perspective through which being is refracted and experienced in a unique way. And man is an origin for action, action which impacts and changes the world (for him and for others), and it changes his own embodied being as well. [1]

A person, so conceived, is not a determined creature, although he encounters determiners as he pursues the fulfillment of his projects in time. Each project, momentary or enduring, to which he has committed himself discloses the world to him in a different way. Thus, a man's biology, anatomy, and physiology may be experienced by him as an obstacle to the fulfillment of some projects, as a facilitator of others. An obese body may handicap the running of a race, but may facilitate the project of pinning an adversary in a wrestling match.

The consciousness which a person is, or embodies, can be likened to an apparatus which receives the disclosures of being, albeit in a highly selective way. We are attentive to some disclosures of being, and inattentive to others, depending upon the projects which animate and direct our lives. And this consciousness of being occurs in numerous modes, sometimes serially, more often fused into an integrated fabric with perceptual, conceptual, imaginative, recollective, affective, and fantasy strands. My experience of you can be analyzed into perceptual, imaginative, conceptual, recollective, and fantasy components. Our experience of anything lends itself to investigation and reporting to another person through the act of reflection, a skill that can be learned.

So much for a sketchy overview of man, seen from the vantage point of existential phenomenology.[2]

To live as a person can be likened to amoeboid locomotion, but locomotion through time, rather than space. Man invents his future being—he imagines himself at some point in the future, whether fifteen seconds or five years ahead; this is one way to describe a project—as an imaginative experience of an as yet unlived way to be in the world. Active life then consists in transmuting the image into a reality that can be perceived by the self, and by others. In this way, life resembles the activity of the artist who transmutes an imaginative experience of his canvas or lump of clay into something that can be perceived. Activity extended in time is necessary for the transmutation. Man pulls himself into the future that he (or someone else) invents for him; he is not pushed by instincts or habit, nor pulled by environmental stimuli. However, a man can repress his experience of freedom or never be awakened to it, and experience himself as driven or controlled by habit, impulse, personal threats, suggestions or invitations from others.

If human life is the *experience* of life, then we can propose that he who experiences more, with greater intensity, lives more. If life occurs in time, then he who has more time has more life.

A person lives as long as he experiences his life as having meaning and value, and as long as he has something to live *for*—meaningful projects that will animate him and invite him into the future or entice him to pull himself into the future. He will continue to live as long as he has hope of fulfilling meanings and values. As soon as meaning, value, and hope vanish from a person's experience, he begins to stop living; that is, he begins to die.

I am going to propose that people destroy themselves in response to an invitation originating from others that he stop living. And that people live in response to the experience of chronic invitations to continue living in some way or in any possible way. Life and death can be seen fruitfully as responses to an invitation or the experience of an invitation. The invitation is extended by others, that is, it originates in someone's consciousness, sometimes as a conscious wish that the person stop existing, in that way, or at all, sometimes as an unconscious wish; sometimes not so openly, but rather as an indifference to the continued existence of the person in question. In whatever mode the wish for death, or the indifference to continued existence, appears, it is communicated to the one whom we might call the suicide. He experiences himself as being invited to stop living, and he obliges. (Actually, he may only be invited to stop that way of living.) He may accept the invitation by shooting himself, taking sleeping pills, jumping off a bridge, or jumping into the path of a car; or he may commit suicide more slowly by stopping his projects, disintegrating himself such that he is ostensibly killed by germs and viruses that have killed him because his immunity mechanisms have been called out of action; or he commits suicide by suspending or diminishing his vigilance toward all the things that are always present to kill a person, but which ordinarily he averts or neutralizes when he experiences his existence as having value, when he has things to do, and projects to fulfill.

I am going to postulate that there are in our bodies some self-destruct mechanisms that are always present.[3] And in the environment there are agencies that can release these self-destruct mechanisms. Physicians have catalogued all the germs, bacteria, and viruses that can become self-destruct agencies. I am proposing that we have enough inside us to kill an army, but that usually these are held in abeyance as long as the person experiences his life as meaningful and hopeful and valuable. Anything that diminishes a person's experience of hope, meaning, and value to his continued existence has simply released the activity of the self-destruct mechanisms faster than they would have been released by ordinary wear and tear.

I postulate that official views of life expectancy to which a person has been trained provide one source of accelerated self-destruction. Thus, many cultures have no role for more than a few people past a certain age; nor have they the food or shelter for more than a limited number of members of their tribe and group. And so when a person has reached the age at which he is expected to die, if he has been effectively socialized into the world-view of that culture, he obliges by dying. He is assisted in this project by the expectations of others that he will not be around for long. In fact, he may have become a dead being in the consciousness of others before he has died. (The parallel with voodoo death is obvious.) If there is any empirical validity to this analysis—and average death ages in various societies lend at least some credence to it—then it becomes meaningful to redefine "natural death from old age" as at once murder and suicide—an invitation to die, extended by others, that has been accepted by the victim.

People who have not been fully socialized and mystified may escape the death sentence by not taking seriously traditional or authoritative views as to the proper time to die; or they make take them seriously, but defy the invitations that they experience.[4]

Our society trains people to expect to live to riper ages than it did one hundred years ago. But we kill our citizens in another way—by encouraging them to believe that there is only one identity, one role, one way for them to be, one value for them to fulfill. When this ground for their existence is outgrown or lost, a person may begin to die or he may kill himself more quickly. I have in mind here those instances of people who kill themselves after the loss of money, work, a limb, their beauty, their sexuality, a loved one, or status, and those persons who, on reflection, discover that they no longer are the person they believed themselves to be. And so, by killing themselves, they are saying, in effect, that they believe they have only one incarnation that is possible for them, one way to live and be. When the ground or value of their existence is eliminated, so is their existence. I suspect that our socialization practices encourage people to believe that they can only *be* in one way such that they cannot imagine or invent new purposes, new identities, new lives when an old one has run its course. In fact, I believe that most of what we call mental and physical illness is evidence that the way in which the person had been living up to the point of his collapse has truly been outgrown and it is time for him to stop that way of life to invent a new way which is more compatible with health. But members of our healing and helping professions construe the signals that a way of life has been outlived as an illness to be cured, rather than a call to stop, reflect, meditate, dream, and invent a new self. The helping professions do not so much help a person to live as they help him to perpetuate a life that has been outgrown. I suspect that our ossified theories of disease and health have the sociological function of perpetuating the social, economic and political status quo. People stay vital, growing, fit, and zestful as a function of the way they live their lives. They live their lives for meaningful projects. When projects are outworn, it is time to re-project, not anesthetize the experience of despair, or disinfect the gut; because if the "sick" person resumes the life that was sickening him, it will soon kill him. Can it be that physicians, psychiatrists, psychologists, social workers, and clergymen help society retain its stability, its present class structure and distribution of wealth and freedom by encouraging people not to reinvent themselves when it is time to? Is it suicidal for a person to consult an established practitioner?[5]

When a person feels he cannot live any more in the way that he has been, when he feels trapped in frozen interpersonal relationships in a social system that he feels offers him no way out, he may fall physically ill, become schizophrenic or psychotically depressed, or commit murder or suicide. (In fact, to murder someone else is one way to get others, or the state, to kill you.) But the experience of entrapment is just that—an experience. Human consciousness being what it is, it can be mystified and trained in ways that fixate habits of construing; and it can be liberated such that a person, feeling trapped by one way of construing his situation, can untrap himself by an imaginative and creative reconstruing of the situation. We can ask, how do we typically train people in the activity of construing and in the activity of imagining? My view is that, typically, we train people to an impoverished imagination, to a banal image of their possibilities, and to conventional ways to attach meaning. We train people to repress their experience of freedom and to replace it with the conviction that in certain situations they "have no choice." Our way of socializing is effective at producing a social system that has an immense productive output and much material wealth, but at the cost of alienating most of us from the experience of our own possibilities—including the possibility of reinventing ourselves and reconstruing our situations of felt entrapment. Any social practices, such as stupefying television or mystifying mass media, that gain control over people's consciousness contribute to sickness, madness, and self-destruction just as they contribute to maintenance of the status quo. Any teacher who liberates, expands, or activates a person's consciousness creates a condition for richer life of longer duration.

The invitation to die, if given openly—"Why don't you drop dead"—can be vigorously declined. An invitation to die given in bad faith, as a fantasy wish that is communicated subvocally or that is conveyed as indifference, is more subtle and thus more difficult for a person to counter. I suspect that, just as Laing and Esterson were able to document the way family members of schizophrenic girls communicated their wish that the victim annihilate her own perspective and replace it with one that was alien, then denied it all,[6] so we might find, for people who kill themselves or who die before they "should," evidence of the wish that they die existing at some level of consciousness in the people around them. Or else we would find that the more speedily dying person experiences himself as not existing for others.

The implications that I see in this analysis are to the effect that it is possible to study a social system or an interpersonal nexus in order to see in what ways the invitations to die are communicated, to discover where they originate, and to explore ways to counter them. And it is possible to study socialization practices, medical and healing ideologies and practices, to ascertain in what ways they fail to activate a person's experience of his freedom, his creative imagination, and his freedom to reinvent himself, when one way of being has palpably become unlivable any longer. Surely there are other alternatives to entrapment than physical illness, psychosis, or suicide. I think we need, in our society, to take the precept, "Ye must be born again" out of Sunday School and put it into our public schools. I think we need to liberalize and pluralize our social structure, so that people can be taught a theory of personal growth that encourages them to let an incarnation die, without killing their embodied selves so that they can invent new ones, and find places and company to live them, until they die of being worn out. Meditation and retreat centers, rather than hospitals, where the invitation to live is seriously extended; and where guides are available to help a person kill off the identity he has outgrown (not his body) so he can invent a new one—these may be an answer to the problem of self-destruction. And if we make our society even more pluralistic, people can take a perspective that is unlivable in one scene to another where it is welcomed; or be encouraged to return to their old scenes, but in a reincarnated way. We need to learn how to invite people to explore and try more of their possibilities than modal upbringing seems to foster so that the invitation to live and grow is as fascinating as is the invitation to die.[7]

One mark of a good theory, as of an enlightened and growing perspective, is its power to reconcile contradiction.[8] A good theory of suicide should make both living-behavior and dying-behavior intelligible. I think that Bakan's recent book[9] contains the ingredients of such a theory, one which students of suicide might well examine carefully. Earlier (1959, 1960, 1961) I offered some rather crude speculations that I regard as less documented versions of Bakan's later and more sophisticated concepts. I spoke of "inspiritation," "spirit-titre," and "dispiritation," all terms that refer to the extent to which a person is integrated. When a person is inspirited, according to these views, his body is maximally organized or integrated such that behavior is frictionless (muscles and endocrine and neural systems are synergic), and subjectively, the person is characterized by good morale, enthusiasm, a sense of meaning, direction, and purpose in his existence. Events, relationships, and situations can dispirit a person, such that the entire system that a man is becomes less resistant to infectious diseases and entropic forces. Thus, according to this view, for one person to disconfirm another, to reduce his hope, or to diminish the value he invests in his aims and purposes is to accelerate his rate of dying. To inspirit a person is to augment and confirm his values and purposes, to increase his experience of meaning in his existence, and to render him more resistant both to physical and mental diseases.[10]

Bakan has introduced the concept of "deferential" dying—wherein an organism does to itself what it anticipates and believes the environment is going to do to it—and the concept of "telic decentralization." The latter term refers, in humans, to a relinquishing of the purposes that give direction and meaning to a person's life (at the phenomenological level) and isomorphically permit the organization of subordinate processes to operate unchecked by the higher *telos*—a factor in cancer and other physical diseases. Bakan adduces a great deal of empirical evidence to buttress his thesis, and to me it makes a great deal of sense. Moreover, both his theory and mine have many practical implications. If a person carries within him the means whereby his body can destroy itself and if the environment carries myriad means for destroying a person, the problem to be explained is not suicide or death, but rather, living in the face of so many physical pathogens and so many experiences of invitation to abandon life.

One person can invite another to change his being in many ways. I can invite you to change the meanings you attach to things and events to reconstrue your world.[11] I can invite you to change from the inauthentic way to the authentic way.[12] It follows that I can invite you to try living again when you have experienced yourself as invited to die, when your purposes have worn out, when it seems that there is no place for you and your way of being a person in a given time and place, and when you feel you have already been abandoned by others. I can invite you to reinvent yourself, your purposes, and you might become reinspirited, characterized by renewed telic centralization.

Disintegration, telic decentralization, is posited by Bakan as both a condition of self-destruction and a condition for growth, for further differentiation of an organism or a person. I believe that growth is characterized as a kind of dying (the end of the tether, the end of projects, giving up, becoming psychotic to some degree) followed by a rebirth—of new challenges and fascinations and invitations. These formulations adumbrate nicely with Bakan's. The suicide, especially the younger suicide, may be seen as one who has reached the end of his tether, of his projects, and he will, unless effectively invited to live, erroneously believe that he cannot live further, and so he kills himself. Let us, then, as therapists and healers, inquire into the phenomenon of invitation, since it appears to affect physiology, experience, and behavior. ✦

## References

[1] *See R.D. Laing,* The Politics of Experience *(New York: Pantheon, 1967) for a more detailed formulation of a person from the viewpoint of existential phenomenology.*

[2] *Further development of these ideas is given in S.M. Jourard,* Disclosing Man to Himself *(Princeton: Van Nostrand, 1968).*

[3] *Bakan has proposed a mechanism which he calls "telic decentralization," which goes a long way toward making this phenomenon intelligible. See D. Bakan,* Disease, Pain and Sacrifice: Toward a Psychology of Suffering *(Chicago: University of Chicago Press, 1968).*

[4] *It occurs to me that one approach to the problem of aging people who do not wish to die of boredom, nor yet add to the problem of overpopulation, is to create an agency, like an employment agency, specifically for people in their sixties and older, with international connections. Men and women who have been obliged to retire, and who might then age and die rapidly, could be given the opportunity to "export" themselves to other places, other countries even, where their knowledge and competence would be welcomed, rather than be assessed as obsolete. We already export obsolete munitions, automobiles, buses, and machinery to developing countries.*

[5] *See T. Szasz,* The Myth of Mental Illness *(New York: Hoeber, 1961).*

[6] *Cf. R.D. Laing,* Self and Others *(London: Tavistock, 1961) and R.D. Laing and A. Esterson,* Sanity, Madness and the Family *(London: Tavistock, 1964).*

[7] *A psychotherapeutic implication that I see here is the following: If research can show that some regimen, some profession, some role carries with it a high probability of developing serious illness, and a low mean age for dying, then an unenlightened person living in that way is speeding up his dying. A therapist's job would be to let him know these facts, so that if he continues living in that way, it is tantamount to suicide. Of course the patient could choose that path if he wished. An intense but brief life is, for many persons, preferable to a long, safe, and boring existence.*

[8] *Cf. Franklin J. Shaw,* Reconciliation, at Theory of Man Transcending, *edited by S.M. Jourard and D.C. Overlade (Princeton: Van Nostrand, 1966).*

[9] *Bakan, op.cit.*

[10] *S.M. Jourard,* The Transparent Self *(Princeton: Van Nostrand, 1964).*

[11] *Cf. G.A. Kelly,* The Psychology of Personal Constructs *(New York: Norton, 1955).*

[12] *Cf. Jourard,* Disclosing Man to Himself.

# *IV-7* Privacy: The Psychological Need

Only the exterior of a man's being is visible to others. His experience—his "being-for-himself"—remains perpetually private. None save the experiencing person can ever know his thoughts, feelings, wishes and imaginings in direct perspective. Others can know *about* a man's experience only if that man wishes to make it known, through full self-disclosure. Without such free disclosure, a man's experience can only remain, the subject of inference and conjecture. In this sense, we are condemned to privacy, just as we are condemned to freedom.

Our behaviour is visible. It affects other people. It enriches the experience of others, and it can impinge upon their freedom. The responsible leaders of any society have a vested interest in controlling the behaviour of the society's members, for without this control the society would be chaotic. The entire process of socialisation—from infancy, through the school and college years, up into adulthood—aims at training people to confine their actions to prescribed roles. If family, age, sex and occupational roles are properly enacted, people can anticipate how others will behave toward them; and the roles will define how a man feels he must behave toward others.

Society enforces conformity with the assortment of roles in various ways. Overt agents of "social control" are empowered to meet violations with sanctions, graded in severity. The lawbreaker may be fined or imprisoned. Parents chastise or withdraw tokens of affection from children who are "not nice." Friends and associates ostracise the bore, or the ill-mannered person. People come to fear these sanctions, the more so because they "internalise" them in the form of conscience. And the fear of retribution is thus reinforced by the possibility of guilt for violating what has become one's personal code.

A more insidious move directed against people whose action appears unacceptable or unintelligible is the "mental-illness" sanction. If someone cannot or will not behave in pre-scribed ways, he may be regarded not as evil or sinful, but mentally ill. As soon as that happens, his behaviour is viewed as the excrescence of a disease process. He no longer exists as a responsible, free citizen. He is seen as the container of "psycho-dynamics" that produce bizarre or unacceptable con-duct. He becomes a "mental patient" if he comes to the atten-tion of psychiatrists.

## "Mental Illness"

Once a man has been so stigmatised, his career changes radically. He may be sent to a hospital, there to be "treated" with tranquilising pills, electroshock, leucotomy or psycho-therapy. Or, if he lives in a enlightened community, he may be-come an outpatient, and report weekly for conversations with a therapist, alone, or in groups. If he changes in certain ways deemed "normal" by the appropriate authority, he may be rated as "cured".

Medical professionals and laymen are both coming to realise that the psychiatric and psychotherapeutic treatment of people designated "mentally ill" is another form of social con-trol. Psychiatrists like Thomas Szasz and R.D. Laing, and soci-ologists like Thomas Scheff, document how off-beat experience and action, and inescapable crises of existence, are denigrated and invalidated by calling them mental illness. Psychiatry once seemed to be a discipline that might be able to rescue man-kind from needless suffering. But it appears to have fallen into the role of a further agency to make people conform to the social status quo. At its worst, it can destroy private life.

If a man violates other people's notions of appropriate and sane action he risks sanctions that can be extreme. But if he conforms slavishly to the conventional definitions of roles, he increases the odds that he will sicken, in the physical sense. And he will very likely find his existence becoming cramped, boring and even a kind of trap with no exit save physical break-down, suicide, "acting out" his difficulties in extra-legal ways by committing "crimes," or "going mad" (whatever he construes madness to be). The illness rates of any civilised society represent a kind of index as to the unfitness of that society for men to live, breathe and grow in.

That recurrent or chronic illness of all kinds is the regular outcome of excessive conformity is a truth increasingly recognised by growing numbers of sentient physicians. They are coming better to understand the process by which illness comes about. People *behave* themselves into a stress illness like heart disease, arthritis or peptic ulcers. These diseases are the outcomes of a way of being—with other people in one's life: a mendacious, role-playing public charade that conceals the true impact that one's regimen is having upon one's total being. Even infectious diseases are known to be contacted when one's "resistance" has been diminished, not just by inadequate rest and diet, but by demoralising, hopeless status quos.

**Political Medicine**

Indeed, if people get sick because of the way they behave, then treatment that solely tranquilises, relieves pain, cuts out bad tissue, or disinfects the gut or wound, represents a kind of political act. These treatments restore a mystified person to the very way of life that generated his breakdown. Much of contemporary medicine can be likened to combat surgery. On the battlefield, the surgeon's task is to keep as many soldiers in action as he can. In modern society, the front line is suburban boredom or dehumanised working conditions. The doctor may, if he is too busy or not very enlightened, function as a kind of medical commissar, keeping people "at it," the while serving as middleman for the pharmaceutical houses.

In a sense, role-conformity entails a kind of "private life." The sufferer from excessive conformity must conceal from others, and ultimately from himself, those modes of experience and action that would transgress definitions of what is sane, proper and respectable. If the sufferer has repressed his own experience, it can be said that he is keeping his true life private, even from himself.

If a man finds his roles in life stifling or meaningless and discloses his discontent or confusion in speech and action, he meets severe sanctions. If he conceals his distress and impersonates a contented, conforming citizen, he may break down physically or run the risk of being invalidated as a psychotic. Is there no third option?

Inviolable places to be private—i.e., free and self-disclosing—represent a way out of the dilemma above. The experience of psychotherapists and students of personality growth attest that those people maintain themselves in physical health and in psychological and spiritual fitness who preserve some arena where they can be off-stage. Their "private place" may be the forests, a cottage, a pad or a monastic cell. Or it may be an ambience like a pub, a club or a mistress's bedroom. There, the person can do or be as he likes or feels, and if he is with others, he feels confirmed for being the growing, changing person he is. He does not (in Sartre's phrase) feel the intrusive and controlling pressure of others' looks. He can shut off the television, close his newspapers, unplug the radio and be free from the plethora of efforts to control and constrain his action and experience into serving the Establishment at his expense.

As society becomes increasingly urbanised; and as techniques for the control of experience and action become increasingly refined and effective (as in the subtleties of advertising, propaganda and subliminal persuasion); and as techniques for eavesdropping on people at a distance, unknown to the person involved, become ever more diabolical—so it becomes more difficult and more important to discover private places. A nation of men who are always conscious of being looked at, and half-conscious of being manipulated and controlled through assorted mass media is a nation in danger. A society that would endure, and more, that its citizens would find worth living in, must provide the possibility of private places, and ensure their privacy.

## Solitude Abhorred

But private places are seen as dangerous by proponents of the status quo. The leader of any organisation or nation must have some feedback to guide his governing and controlling actions. A boss may spy on his employees, a husband upon his wife, or a government secret agent upon some suspected subversive agent. If the atmosphere within a society is one of distrust and suspicion, privacy becomes a hostile, possibly subversive act. Primitive societies recognise this; and in some the native who does anything outside the view of his fellows is regarded as some kind of witch. He is punished appropriately. Some aspects of our more urban upbringing train people so that they regard solitude as loneliness, and the man who seeks his own company as an oddity.

Secret societies of all kinds are always viewed with suspicion by people who are not members. Revolutions come into being from plans hatched in the hidden conclaves of a secret society. But the doctor-patient relationship in psychotherapy can be a kind of secret society. If the healer sees himself as a kind of teacher or guru rather than as a further agent of socialisation, he may aim at helping the sufferer gain a perspective on society and his position in it, and show him how to transcend the "social determiners" of his existence. On this view, psychotherapists are perhaps agents of social subversion—just as, on the opposing view, they can be para-medical commissars.

Privacy, the privilege of choosing by whom one will be seen, is a necessity for growth, meditation and the initiation of change in one's existence. It is precious and hard to come by. I believe that, without the possibility of privacy, a society suffers collectively—from high rates for illness of all kinds—and people suffer individually. I believe that a real contribution to public health and well-being would be made if every community provided, not just a hospital for the repair of the damage resulting from insensate conformity, but retreats to which bored, trapped and dispirited people could go to renew themselves. If existing mental hospitals could be replaced by attractive, modern equivalents of temples of self-renewal, without social stigma, it would be a radical advance toward a civilised, pluralistic society, allowing people to go their own way. In these temples, there might be a new kind of professional healer—a kind of enlightened guru who can guide people who have been *over-socialised* into new ways of being, into using their own resources fully, without threatening the worthwhile basis of society.

Until such time as society becomes more civilised and secure, and pressure to conformity in all arenas of existence have been mitigated, the quest for privacy must be the responsibility of the individual.

I have studied the act and consequences of self-disclosure for a number of years. I think chronic self-concealment is a factor in malaise and disease of all kinds. But indiscriminate self-disclosure is a risky business so long as society remains "one dimensional," with a single set of standards and aims. There are occasions when disclosure of one's experience to others could be suicidal. But private places, to which one can repair in solitude or with trusted friends, are appropriate places for a person to be and to disclose himself, without pretence or guile. The man who can find neither the place, nor the friend or loved one with whom he can drop guard and pretences is a desperate man indeed.

All indications are that such men are very numerous in every city. They form the queues at every doctor's clinic, and consume the incredible output of our pharmaceutical manufacturers. Until a more pluralistic society has been achieved, it would seem that the layman must learn, or be taught, how to "play social games" with elegance and precision (when he is on stage), and be liberated within so that (when he is off stage) he can live a more satisfying, diverse, growth-yielding private life. This "liberation within" poses a challenge to education, medicine, psychology and psychiatry. And the quest for a more pluralistic society, which confirms variety in living, is the task of the enlightened politician and the voter. ✦

[1967]

# IV-8 The Fear that Cheats Us of Love

If we want to be loved, we must disclose ourselves. If we want to love someone, he must permit us to know him. This would seem to be obvious. Yet most of us spend a great part of our lives thinking up ways to avoid becoming known.

Indeed, much of human life is best described as impersonation. We are role players, every one of us. We say that we feel things we do not feel. We say that we did things we did not do. We say that we believe things we do not believe. We pretend that we are loving when we are full of hostility. We pretend that we are calm and indifferent when we actually are trembling with anxiety and fear.

We not only conceal ourselves; we also usually assume that the other person is in hiding. We are wary of him because we take it for granted that he too will frequently misrepresent his real feelings, his intentions or his past, since we so often are guilty of doing those very things ourselves.

As a therapist and research psychologist I often meet people who believe that their troubles are caused by things outside themselves—by another person, bad luck or some obscure malaise—when in fact they are in trouble because they are trying to be loved and seeking human response without letting others know them. For example, a husband and wife may come to me with a problem they think is purely sexual in origin but instead it turns out to be a frustration that has arisen because these two people can't communicate with each other.

Of course we cannot tell even the people we know and love everything we think or feel. But our mistakes are nearly always in the other direction. Even in families—good families—people wear masks a great deal of the time. Children don't know their parents; parents don't know their children. Husbands and wives are often strangers to each other.

One has only to think of the astronomical rate of divorce and the contemporary conflict between parents and children, one has only to hear the anxiety and pain expressed in the therapist's office when these closest of all relationships are touched upon, to know that it is possible to be involved in a family for years, playing one's role nicely and never getting to know the other members of the family—who also are playing roles.

A few years ago a colleague and I devised a questionnaire with which we sought to find out what people were willing to disclose to others. We discovered that even with those they cared about most, people shared little of their true feelings or their most profound longings and beliefs; revealed little of what they really thought on such touchy subjects as sex, self-image, religion.

Why is this so? For a great variety of reasons, some obvious, some not; some sensible, some profoundly harmful. But the most important reason springs from the very nature of the human enterprise itself. Paradoxically, we fail to disclose ourselves to other people because we want so much to be loved.

Because we feel that way, we present ourselves as someone we think can be loved and accepted, and we conceal whatever would mar that image. If we need to believe that we are without hostile impulses, that we are morally superior to other people, we won't give anything away that spoils that image.

Another reason we hide is to protect ourselves from change. Change is frightening to most people. Here is a young bride, for example, who returns from her honeymoon still lost in the romantic haze of being in love, blissfully happy and convinced that this is the way it is always going to be. But what happens?

One day her husband comes home, troubled over some problem at work, and broods in silence or snaps at her irritably. She in turn finds that getting meals and cleaning house—even when they're done for the chosen beloved—are not all that satisfying. Her feelings are changing. But instead of facing the fact that nothing in life stands still, she tries to pretend, to herself and to her husband, that she feels exactly as she did before.

The truth is that we want to think of ourselves as *constant.* Once we have formed our image of who and what we are, we proceed to behave as if that were all we ever could be. We "freeze," as though we had taken a pledge to ourselves that even if we did change, we'd try not to notice it.

And we don't want the other person to change either. Once he is labeled husband or child or father or unselfish friend, we have no wish to disturb that image. If something is happening inside him that may make him behave differently toward us, we don't want to hear about it.

Still another reason we don't disclose ourselves is that we were never taught how. On the contrary, unless we were very lucky as children, we were taught more about how to conceal ourselves from other people than about how to disclose ourselves. And we are still playing roles that we adopted almost before we can remember.

As small children we are and we act our real selves. We say what we think; we scream for what we want; we tell what we did. Then quite early we learn to disguise certain facts about ourselves because of the painful consequences to which they lead.

In fact, our own self-deceptions, painfully acquired, are among the strongest factors in our inability to reveal ourselves.

Personal ambition and economic pressures also give us powerful reasons for concealing what we really are. We grow up in a world where it is important to get ahead, and you can't do that without competing with other people. To put it bluntly, we want the job the other person wants, so of course we aren't going to be talking to him very candidly. Nor are we going to be honest with our professional superiors if being so reflects to our discredit. Our society itself exerts pressures on a person to suppress all but those characteristics that are considered acceptable.

All of us hide behind the iron curtain of our public selves. And with our "intimates" we again fail to disclose ourselves because we are so vulnerable to those we love. Under special pressures we might tell the stranger on the train about our longings and lusts and frailties, but how can we talk about them to those we love, who might be hurt by such revelations?

And of course it is true that we should not gratuitously hurt those we love. In the intimacy of daily life we *must* at times hide our feelings. But it is fatally easy to assume from this that we must never tell the truth when it will hurt. Every therapist, for example, is familiar with the man who, because his marriage is profoundly dissatisfying to him, is carrying on an affair. His involvement with another woman may break up his marriage; yet he says that he cannot talk about his basic dissatisfaction with his wife "because it will hurt her"!

Finally, we are uncertain about our roles as men and women, and this uncertainty confuses us about how to communicate with those we love. What is it to be a good husband, a good wife, a good father, a good mother? What is it to be a man, a woman?

If people find it too difficult to impersonate the ideal version of "masculine" and "feminine" current in their time, they will hide their deviant attitudes. I've noticed recently, for example, that women who come for therapy tend to withhold whatever is spontaneous and authentic about themselves if those characteristics do not fit the social role they've been led to believe is appropriate. They try not to sound aggressive, strong, ambitious. They're afraid that even the therapist will reject them.

Men, on the other hand, hide what prevents them from seeming strong and masculine. Our researches showed that in general men tend to disclose considerably less than women do—and are told less. Often fathers seem to be the last to know anything subjective about their children; they talk a lot less about themselves to their sons and daughters than mothers do. All this may be changing for the young; but males 30 and over have been brought up in a world in which they have been taught to hide their feelings of weakness, their fears and their hurts, in order to appear tough, achieving, unsentimental.

If we have such good reasons not to disclose ourselves, why should we? Admittedly there are times when telling everything is unwise and hurtful. Neither can we always avoid playing roles. Often they are inescapable; they must be played or else the social system will not work. We *are* teachers and businessman, housewives and mothers; and as responsible people we often must discipline ourselves to these roles.

Moreover, each person is entitled to be a "self" and entitled to keep that self private when he feels that he is not yet ready to disclose it. Healthy personalities aren't always fully visible. Chronic self-revelation may be idolatrous or even destructive in certain circumstances.

What matters is that we should be able to be private when we wish, when that's meaningful, and to be quite open and transparent when that's appropriate. That is all we should be trying for; but that is a great deal. We are warm, live, human, growing creatures; and when we suppress our identities completely, serious consequences follow.

For there is a limit to intuitive understanding. If we must spend much time together, if our lives are bound together, if we must collaborate for common ends, we are in trouble if we cannot communicate.

Thus a wife who finds her husband silent and preoccupied may believe that there is another woman in his life; a husband who finds his wife unresponsive in bed may blame himself for a problem that is really hers. When our loved ones do disclose themselves, we find all our preconceptions altered, one after another, by the facts as they come forth, since our previous ideas were based on insufficient evidence.

Another reason disclosure is so important is that without it we really cannot know ourselves. Or to put it another way, we learn to deceive ourselves while we are trying to deceive others. For example, if I never express my sorrow, my love, my joy, I'll smother those feelings in myself until I almost forget that they were once part of me.

What is the truth about ourselves? Often we ourselves don't know. But if I feel so safe in your presence that I am willing to try to disclose myself to you, I'll find out about myself just by talking about how I feel and what I need and whether my needs are defensible.

When we cannot communicate we not only fail to have access to our inner selves but we also are under psychic and bodily stress. It's hard work trying not to be known and it brings a lot of patients to doctors and therapists.

Perhaps the most important reason for self-disclosure is that without it we cannot truly love. How can I love a person I don't know? How can the other person love me if he doesn't know me?

Indeed, we often marry strangers. In our society people commonly marry in a romantic haze. They marry an image, not a person—an image spun out of their own needs and fantasies. Often a courtship, instead of being a period of mutual exposure of the self and study of the other, is a period of mutual deception, a period in which the couple construct false public selves. It is not rare for a person to fall in love with, court and marry someone and then, much later, come face to face with that person's real self and wonder. How did I ever get joined with him?

"He changed," a woman complains. Perhaps—but perhaps he never really was the person she thought she loved.

Obviously, it is hard to pick the right husband or wife if our concept of the other person is not accurate. And having picked someone we don't know or understand, how can we behave in loving ways that make him happy? If I care, I care about what he needs, what he is, what he wants, how I am failing him. But I cannot do this unless I know what he needs and what he wants and I cannot know this unless he tells me.

And then how can I feel my love to be real if this person, allegedly so beloved, is not to be trusted with my innermost thoughts and feelings? In my heart I know that if I love someone, I display my love by letting him know me. Loving requires trust and openness one to the other, a metaphoric nakedness. We must drop our defenses.

The inability to communicate is especially dangerous to a close and meaningful sexual relationship. Given a reasonable lack of prudery, a lusty sex life grows best out of a relationship between two persons who can disclose themselves to each other in all areas of their lives without fear of being hurt.

The wife who takes little interest in sex may really be complaining that this man is a stranger who comes to her without disclosure of himself, a stranger with whom she feels no bond. Sex deteriorates when a couple cannot establish a close, mutually revealing, *nonsexual* relationship; the very defenses one uses to keep from being known and possibly hurt by the spouse one cannot understand are the same defenses that impede spontaneity in sex.

Parents and children too need to know each other. Most mothers love their children, but the children may be languishing emotionally because the mother does not or will not learn what each child needs from her to grow, to become a loving person.

Self-disclosure is as important a part of growing as it is of love, and growth is a part of change. The real self is continually evolving. One's needs, wishes, feelings, values, goals and behavior all change with age and experience.

I think of this illustration, with which the therapist is most familiar: Here is a woman who married at a stage of her life in which she was passive, dependent and easily won by a dominant man whose sense of his own strong identity was reinforced by her helplessness. In time she discovers that she has become more self-reliant; she is less easy to please; she is more able to assert difference.

Now she doesn't know what to do. If she is herself, if she expresses herself, she may make her spouse feel very insecure; so she usually goes on trying to pretend that she is what she was before.

The same thing can happen to the man who falls in love with a dominant woman because he needs to be taken care of. Eventually he may outgrow this need, and then, unless she can change too, they are at an impasse.

But can they change? Of course they can. Often a person imagines that his partner is as immobile as a rock and will always be that way. Having decided this, a husband or wife then digs in for a lifetime of dissatisfaction—or institutes divorce proceedings. But many a spouse, following a bitter divorce, has been dumfounded to discover that the discarded partner *has* changed. The stodgy, unromantic ex-husband has become more attentive to his appearance, more considerate of women, more romantic and impractical; the fretful, nagging wife blooms with good will.

This is certainly evidence that both can change, but it is evidence also that they did not feel free to change while they lived together.

Freedom and the right to grow are a difficult and painful gift for a couple to give each other, but there is no alternative. People outgrow the roles in which they have been cast by their partners, and when they have grown and changed, each must be able to let that fact be known so that the partner he or she loves can take it into account.

This is indeed a frightening prescription, but it's a consoling one too. For if changing and growing are dangerous in marriage, it is equally true that many marriages fail because of a lack of such growing, and many a foundering marriage is saved by an acknowledged change in one or both partners. A great many divorces might be avoided if both partners were willing to disclose to each other what they were thinking and then together "reinvent" their marriage.

I have been making the point that without the ability to disclose ourselves to each other, we are in serious trouble. But what can we do about it?

First of all, we can ask ourselves how many things we feel free to talk about. Can we let it be known that we are full of paradox and contradiction, that we change from day to day, that we are often self-deceived and unable to understand ourselves? Can we say, "I was the one who was wrong" and mean it?

In marriage can we talk freely to our husband or wife about what's bothering us? Can we discuss our sexual longings, needs and disappointments? Can we really *hear* what the other person is saying about these things? As mothers can we really hear our children when they are complaining about us or expressing a need we didn't think they should have? In our perplexing world can we hear and understand people of other generations, backgrounds, races? And make ourselves clear to them?

What we need is to be able to realize what troubles us and what it is in ourselves and in the other person that prevents us from understanding and loving. If we are authentically communicating, we will drop pretense, defenses, duplicity and bad faith. We will stop using our behavior as a gambit designed to disarm the other fellow.

Husbands and wives need tough, and candid talk aimed at dispelling misunderstandings. They need to understand how they differ, what they respect and love in each other, what they hold in common—yes, and what enrages them in each other. If we speak honestly, we must be able to say, "What you are doing right now makes me angry."

Complaints are to an interpersonal relationship what pain is to the body—a sign that something is wrong, that something must be done. I often advise quietly martyred patients to learn the art of complaining. For example, a working wife may simmer day after day because when she comes home from work she has to do all the household chores without help from her husband. In time she may stop loving him out of sheer anger and frustration. How much better if she had expressed herself clearly and strongly in the very beginning!

To be sure, it may happen that a person complains on the basis of irrational and unrealistic needs and demands. But it is good to get even these complaints out into the open where husband or wife can rebut or where, at the very least, there will be an impasse and both will see that something must be done.

What is it we must be able to trust the other person to do? To be patient and gentle while we are exploding in wrath? Of course not. What we need is to know that he will neither belittle, betray nor unjustly punish us; that he will respond to us honestly, see us as real and in turn respond to us really and honestly. If we would be trusted, we must be trustworthy; and we demonstrate that first by being honest ourselves and then by being honest in our responses.

It became apparent early in my researches that disclosure begets disclosure and secrecy begets secrecy.

Self-disclosure comes too from a grace that I can only call *flexibility*. We need to abandon our fears that the other person will grow away from us or leave us and replace these fears with a genuine concern for *his* growth and happiness. Husbands and wives often feel they love each other when they mean they want to possess each other. This is not love. People who love each other will be genuinely concerned about each other's welfare. They will actively want the other to grow, even if it shakes their own security.

In fact, a good relationship of any kind is one that can be re-invented if necessary, one that carries within it always the seeds of new growth.

Indeed, I often counsel people whose marriage is at the breaking point but who still find it meaningful to live together to try to invent a new marriage with each other. If necessary, they might try living apart for a while, visiting each other on weekends. They might try lending their children to foster parents or living with another family or going on separate vacations. What is hoped for is that each will find himself married to a new partner he can live with—the old spouse grown in some new dimension.

In any case, courageous self-disclosure is especially needed today in our swiftly moving world, where, in fact, few relationships *can* stand still. More than ever we need to be able to invite disclosure from our changing, wandering children. And more than ever men and women—in marriage and out—need to feel free to talk to each other.

If a man and woman can share new insights, if they can explore them together, if she can tell him that she still feels like a woman and that she still sees him as a man, if he can tell her that he really wants her to be free but he just doesn't want to feel deserted, then they can make it together.

But a word of warning is in order. We can get so uptight about needing to be candid with each other that we probe for disclosure whether it's forthcoming or not. It won't work. Parents should not try to bring an end to the silence a child evidently wants; wives should not go about saying to an abstracted and worrying husband, "What are you thinking about?" Instead, we *invite*. We invite by our own disclosure; we invite by behaving toward others in ways that will satisfy their basic needs.

We have learned the art of communication when we realize that it is not all a matter of words. Obviously we use our bodies when we want to communicate sexually with each other. But touch is a superb means of communication at other times too. Less "civilized" people have long understood this. The most primitive mode of establishing contact with another person is to touch him-to hold his hand, or to hug him.

The trouble is that in America we have many taboos about touching each other. We seem to live as though we had an invisible fence around us. In research I have recently undertaken, I have found that many people literally are almost never touched except in sexual encounter. In the preliminary stages of these studies I watched pairs of people in conversation in coffee shops in San Juan, London, Paris and in my own college town in Gainesville, Florida. I counted the times that one person touched another during a one-hour sitting. The scores were: San Juan, 180; Paris, 110; London, 0; Gainesville, 2.

Yet nonverbal understanding is at least as important as verbal. It can be a way of releasing our real selves when our limited words won't do it.

I remember a case in which a man in his late 20s, very obsessed with his own manliness, consulted me for help when he found he couldn't finish a thesis on which he was working. We proceeded through the beginning stages of therapy swiftly enough and then we reached an impasse of intellectualized chitchat.

During one session when the chitchat died out there was a period of silence, and the patient sat there with a look of desperation on his face. I felt an impulse to take his hand and hold it. In a split second I pondered as to whether I should do such a thing. I did it. I took his hand and gave it a firm squeeze. He grimaced, and with much effort not to do so, he burst into racking sobs. The dialogue proceeded from there.

Human beings appear to have a built-in need for self-disclosure. We want to know the other person is *there*; we want to know what we are thinking by *saying* it and hearing it resonate in the other's response; we want to share.

Presumably we'll never be able to do this fully. There will always be the loneliness of never wholly reaching those we love. Loneliness is not a curable disease for human beings. But we can ameliorate it, and it may indeed be growing less instead of greater. Certainly the young are much more candid about sexual matters, morality, radical politics, the way they think of each other, than people used to be; and they don't have their elders' inability to communicate across national boundaries, sex boundaries, race and class boundaries. Families too may become different, less well defined, less traditional, more open to the world.

In any case we need people, in families and out, who will talk freely enough to help one another explore for new understanding, new ways of living, new ways to love and grow. Self-disclosure is a way of sharing, a way of learning from each other. ✦

[1971]

# *IV-9* Some Notes on the Experience of Commitment

## I

A commitment is my pledge to use my time and resources, to actualize someone's vision of a good or better world. I can only *do* what I deem worth doing, and so at any moment, I am doing those things, to produce that future which I regard as most important, valuable and good. Each act of mine, thus, is the embodiment of a commitment. But importance is not a property of a task or of a future. Importance is an experiential act, a *praxis.* It is something I accord to and withdraw from acts, things, and the future. When I committed myself to write this paper, I was sharing someone's view that a journal containing others' articles on commitment, together with my contribution, was worthwhile. If I did not attribute value to the issue of *Humanitas* which existed in the editors' imagination, I would not now be typing out these reflections.

## II

Commitment entails attribution of importance by someone to a future someone envisions. Each act embodies a commitment to actual-ize this future. When commitment is thus understood, some light can be shed on interpersonal influence, or manipulation. Each commitment of mine is a declaration to myself and to others (if I tell them truly what I deem important) of what will reward my efforts. When I reveal my commitments, other people are then in a position to help or hinder me in my efforts to actualize the valued future. Moreover, when others know what I deem important, they can influence my action so it serves *their* futures. If you have some of the means by which I can fulfill my commitment, you can bribe me, or you can threaten my chances to produce this future. Among human beings, the tokens of "reinforcement," which make up Skinnerian behavior-modification procedures, work as reinforcing only if they are accorded value and importance by the person being influenced. It is difficult to influence a person when you do not know his commitments.

## III

I can see commitment as a response to the experience of a calling or a call. If commitment is a response to an invitation or a call to regard something as important enough to drop other activities, then we can see how leaders, teachers and prophets function. Each man embodies his commitments, and lives them out through his action. Action affects the world, making it fit for some beings to live in, unfit for others. Each new commitment calls for a change, a re-ordering of a person's hierarchy of values. And each new commitment calls for a change in action. Every man carries with him a vision of utopia, and his action is undertaken to bring this utopia into being. A great leader, like Moses, Christ, Churchill, Gandhi, or DeGaulle, is able to present a vision of utopia, of a promised land, and to invite people to the necessary effort to find, to defend, or to create this promised land. The great leader calls upon people to abandon their separate and private projects, and pool and coordinate their efforts to actualize a utopia for all. A great teacher is a great orator, whether his idiom is the spoken word, or exemplary action. When a teacher shows off, when he displays enthusiasm for what he does, when it appears to the learner that life is richer when one has the knowledge or skill, then the learner commits himself to the project of achieving mastery.

It is important to me to know some dimensions of a person's utopia, because I want to know whether I can live in it if it ever comes into being. The Promised Land was good for those Hebrews who lived in the Way; but it was hardly utopia for the

Canaanites. Utopia for the Nazis and for much of the Arab world is hardly a future for which many Jews would gladly commit themselves. Each commitment is an aspect of the person's utopia. The teacher, the leader, the prophet invite and call others to commit themselves to a utopia. It is important, then, to know whose utopia you are committing yourself to actualize through your action.

## IV

Commitment makes action possible. Man finds himself in the position of the shark, which has no air-bladder, and must keep swimming throughout his life, else he will sink to the bottom of the sea. Unless man acts, at least western man, he feels himself at the mercy of a malevolent fate; and he may feel that he does not exist. For many men of the west, the motto is *ago, ergo sum.* If there is nothing that I can do, because I feel impotent and helpless, and if there is nothing that seems important enough to do, I may feel I do not exist. Therefore, a man may cling to his commitments, those he made yesterday or in childhood, as if his life depended upon him honoring them. And, of course, his life does depend upon them. Yet, the very act of honoring these commitments may require action which is quite inimical to the life, growth and well-being of the actor. Here we find the dilemma of neurotics, and also the dilemma of the generations during a time of rapid social and cultural change. How to tolerate the dread and experience of wordlessness that is occasioned by suspension of commitments, in order to make newer, more viable commitments?

It appears to be devilishly difficult to abandon a commitment once one has invested time and action to honor it. Couples who commit themselves to one another in marriage find it difficult to un-commit when death or divorce call for a separation. To commit oneself wholly to a new spouse or friend seems impossible if there had been authentic commitment to the other. The work of mourning appears to be necessary as a kind of ritual to bury the amputated part of oneself that the abandoned commitment represents. *Partir, c'est mourir un peu.* To give up one's commitment to his work, to his spouse and children, is indeed a kind of death. And new commitments, when they happen, are a kind of rebirth.

## V

Because some commitments are difficult to abandon, and yet life is unlivable for the person so committed, some light is shed upon functions of psychedelic drugs, and the various "transpersonal" means for producing altered states of consciousness. Man's usual way of being in the world is a committed way, and the life that is lived in pursuit of those aims may be painful, unlivable. Persons, especially young people who "trip" often with psychedelic drugs before they have gotten fully committed to some task, some role, some way of life, may find their powers of attributing importance to long range projects grossly impaired. Overly committed persons may find that psychedelic drugs, or any of the meditative disciplines, make it possible for them to become less "attached" to their projects of this world. The young person who weakens his attachment to projects in this world finds himself in the position of the much older man who, in preparation for death, gradually lets go his commitments which, paradoxically enough, have kept him alive. An overly committed person finds that he is paying too high a price to pursue his goals, and he may need help to reduce his commitment in order to commit himself to some other future.

## VI

A knotty question is this: How can we account for people committing themselves to goals which are not related to gratification of one's own basic needs. It is not difficult to understand why people commit themselves to tasks which result in food and shelter, love, or fame. It is more difficult to understand why someone commits himself to help others, or to do difficult things in the world because life is more interesting and meaningful for so doing. When commitment is experienced as a call from God, from family or community, a call which asserts that something is unquestionably worth doing, there is no problem. But when such commitments wear out, as they do, we then face the problem of attribution of importance. When God is experienced as dead, when a person leaves his family and community, then the commitments which he honored in response to those "calls" may be dropped. A person may then simply, and unreflectingly take on the values and commitments of the place in which he now finds himself. But if he cannot share those values, and if God is dead to him, then he is in the position of being required to play God himself—if God is the supreme attributor of importance. If a man experiences himself as empty, as valueless, then he will also regard his attributions of value as rather weak, or non-compelling. Perhaps we all need to be confirmed in our attributions of value, as Buber tells us, in order that we can make the commitments which make human life possible. ✦

[1972]

# *V* Appendices

# $V$-$1$    Bibliography from Disclosing Man to Himself

1. Bakan, D. A reconsideration of the problem of introspection. *Psychol. Bull.*, 1954, 51, 105-118.

2. Bakan, D. *Duality in human existence.* Chicago: World Book Pub. Co., 1966.

3. Barron, F. Freedom as feeling. *J. Humanistic Psychol.*, 1961, 1, 91-100.

4. Bartlett, F. C. *Remembering.* Cambridge: Cambridge Univ. Press, 1932.

5. Berdyaev, N. *The meaning of the creative act.* New York: Collier, 1962.

6. Bettelheim, B. *The informed heart.* Glencoe: The Free Press, 1960.

7. Blum, A., *et al. Utopiates. The uses and users of LSD-25.* New York: Atherton, 1965.

8. Braatoy, T. *Fundamentals of psychoanalytic technique.* New York: Wiley, 1958.

9. Buber, M. *I and thou.* New York: Scribners, 1958.

10. Buber, M. *Between man and man.* Boston: Beacon Press, 1955.

11. Bugental, J. F. T. *The search for authenticity: An existential-analytic approach to psychotherapy.* New York: Holt Rinehart & Winston, 1966.

12. Cohen, E. *Human behavior in the concentration camp.* New York: Grosset and Dunlap, 1960.

13. Deikman, A. J. Experimental mediation. *J. Nerv. ment. Dis.*, 1963, *136*, 329-343.

14. Edwards, A. L. *The social desirability variable in personality assessment and research.* New York: Dryden, 1957.

15. Ellis, A. *Reason and emotion in psychotherapy.* New York: Lyle Stuart, 1962.

16. Festinger, L. *A theory of cognitive dissonance*. Evanston: Row, 1957.

17. Fiedler, F. A comparison of therapeutic relationships in psychoanalytic, nondirective and Adlerian therapy. *J. Consult. Psychol.*, 1950, 14, 436-445.

18. Fisher, S., and Cleveland, S. P. *Body-image and personality*. Princeton: Van Nostrand, 1958.

19. Frank, J. D. *Persuasion and healing*. Baltimore: Johns Hopkins Press, 1961.

20. Frank, L. K. Tactile communication. *Etc. Rev. gen. Semant.*, 1958, 16, 31-79.

21. Frankl, V. E. *From death camp to existentialism*. Boston: Beacon Press, 1959. Also published in paperback under the title, *Man's search for meaning*. New York: Washington Square Press, 1963.

22. Frankl, V. E. Dynamics, existence and values. *J. Existent. Psychiat.*, 1961, 2, 5-16.

23. Fromm, E. *The forgotten language*. New York: Rinehart, 1951.

24. Gendlin, E. T. *Experiencing and the creation of meaning*. Glencoe: The Free Press, 1962.

25. Gendlin, E. T. A theory of personality change. In Worchel, P., and Byrne, D., *Personality change*. New York: Wiley, 1964.

26. Goffman, E. *The presentation of self in everyday life*. New York: Doubleday, 1959.

27. Goffman, E. *Asylums, Essays on the social situation of mental patients and other inmates*. New York: Doubleday, 1961.

28. Harlow, H. The nature of love. *Amer. Psychol.*, 1958, 13, 673-685.

29. Heidegger, M. *Being and time*. London: SCM Press, 1962.

30. Heider, F. *The psychology of interpersonal relations*. New York: Wiley, 1958.

31. Hoffer, E. *The true believer*. New York: Harper, 1951.

32. Hora, T. The process of existential psychotherapy. *Psychiat. Quart.*, 1960, 34, 495-504.

33. Hora, T. Transcendence and healing. *J. Existent. Psychiat.*, 1961, 1, 501-511.

34. Husserl, E. *Ideas: General introduction to pure phenomenology*. London: Allen & Unwin, 1931.

35. Huxley, A. *The doors of perception, and heaven and hell*. New York: Harper, 1954.

36. James, W. *The varieties of religious experience.* New York: Modern Library, 1944.

37. Jourard, S. M. Self-disclosure and other-cathexis. *J. Abnorm. soc. Psychol.*, 1959, 59, 428-431.

38. Jourard, S. M. Age and self-disclosure. *Merrill-Palmer Quart. Beh. Dev.*, 1961, 7, 191-197.

39. Jourard, S.M. *Personal adjustment.* An approach through the study of healthy personality. New York: MacMillan, 1963 (2nd ed.) (a).

40. Jourard, S. M. *Some observations by a psychologist of the Peace Corps' "outward bound" training program at Camp Crozier, Puerto Rico.* Washington, D. C.: Peace Corps, 1963(b).

41. Jourard, S. M. *The transparent self.* Princeton: Van Nostrand, 1964.

42. Jourard, S. M., and Landsman, M. J. Cognition, cathexis, and the 'dyadic effect' in men's self-disclosing behavior. *Merrill-Palmer Quart. Behav. Dev.*, 1960, 6, 178-186.

43. Jourard, S. M., and Remy, R. M. Perceived parental attitudes, the self, and security. *J. Consult, Psychol.* 1955, 19, 364-366.

44. Jourard, S. M., and Secord, P. F. Body-cathexis and personality. *Brit. J. Psychol.*, 1956, 46, 130-138.

45. Jung, C. G. *Two essays on analytical psychology.* New York: Meridian Books, 1956.

46. Jung, C. G. Symbol formation In *Coll. Works*, Vol. 8, pp. 45-61.

47. Kazantzakis, N. *The Odyssey, a modern sequel.* New York: Simon and Schuster, 1958.

48. Kelly, G. *The psychology of personal constructs.* New York: Norton, 1955.

49. Kesey, K. *One flew over the cuckoo's nest.* New York: Signet, 1963.

50. Kessen, W., and Mandler, G. Anxiety, pain, and the inhibition of distress. *Psychol. Rev.*, 1961, 68, 396-404.

51. Kretschmer, W. Die meditativen Verfahren in der Psychotherapie. *Zeit. f. Psychother. u. Med. Psychol*, 1951, 1, No. 3.

52. Laing, R. D. *Transcendental experience in relation to religion and psychosis.* In *The politics of experience and the bird of paradise.* London: Penguin, 1967.

53. Laing, R. D. *The self and others.* London: Tavistock Institute Press, 1962.

54. Laing, R. D. *The 'divided' self.* London: Tavistock, 1960.

55. Laing, R. D., and Cooper, D. *Reason and violence.* London: Tavistock, 1964.

56. Laing, R. D., and Esterson, A. *Sanity, madness and the family.* London: Tavistock, 1964.

57. Laing, R. D., Phillipson, H., and Lee, R. *Interpersonal perception.* A theory and a method of research. London: Tavistock, 1966.

58. Leary, T., Alpert, R., and Metzner. *The psychedelic experience.*

59. Luijpen, W. A. *Existential phenomenology.* Pittsburgh: Duquesne Univ. Press, 1963.

60. Lyons, J. *Psychology and the measure of man.* New York: Free Press, 1965.

61. Maher, B. A. *Progress in experimental psychology.* New York: Academic Press, 1964.

62. Maslow, A. H. *Toward a psychology of being.* Princeton: Van Nostrand, 1962.

63. Maupin, E., Individual differences in response to a Zen meditation exercise. *J. Consult. Psychol.,* 1965.

64. May, R. Intentionality, the heart of human will. *J. Humanistic Psychol.,* 1965, 5, 202-209.

65. Merleau-Ponty, M. *The phenomenology of perception.* London: Routledge and Kegan Paul, 1962.

66. Miller, H. *The air-conditioned nightmare.* New York: New Directions, 1945.

67. Mowrer, O. H. *The crisis in psychiatry and religion.* Princeton: Van Nostrand, 1961.

68. Mowrer, O. H. *The new group therapy.* Princeton: Van Nostrand, 1964.

69. Murphy, G. *Personality, a biosocial approach to origins and structure.* New York: Harper, 1947.

70. Murphy, G. *Human potentialities.* New York: Basic Books, 1958.

71. Orne, M. T. The social psychology of the psychological experiment: with particular reference to demand characteristics and their implications. *Amer. Psychol.,* 1962, 17, 776-783.

72. Polanyi, M. *Personal knowledge. Towards a post-critical philosophy.* New York: Harper and Row, 1964.

73. Powell, Jr., W. J. A comparison of the reinforcing effects of three types of experimenter response on two classes of verbal

behavior in an experimental interview. Unpub. Ph. D. dissertation, Univ. of Florida, 1963.

74. Privette, Gayle. Some factors in transcendent behavior. *Teachers College Record*, 1965, 66.

75. Rank, O. *Will therapy*. New York: Knopf, 1947.

76. Rapaport, D., Gill, M., and Schafer, R. *Diagnostic psychological testing:* the theory, statistical evaluation, and diagnostic application of a battery of tests. Chicago: Year Book Publishers, 1946.

77. Reich, W. *Character analysis*. New York: Orgone Institute Press, 1949.

78. Reich, W. *The murder of Christ*. New York: Orgone Institute Press, 1953.

79. Reich, W. *Listen, little man*. New York: Orgone Institute Press, 1948.

80. Reifel, Lee. Unpublished research, University of Florida, 1965.

81. Reitan, H. and Lackey, L. Unpublished research, University of Florida, 1966.

82. Ribble, Margaret, *The rights of infants*. New York: Columbia Univ. Press, 1943.

83. Rivenbark III, W. R. Unpublished research, University of Florida, 1963, 1964.

84. Rogers, C. *Counseling and psychotherapy*. Boston: Houghton Mifflin, 1942.

85. Rosenthal, R. The effect of the experimenter on the results of psychological research. In B. A. Maher (Ed.), *Progress in experimental personality research*. New York: Academic Press, 1964, 79-114. Also *Experimenter effects in behavioral research*. New York: Appleton-Century-Crofts, 1967.

86. Sartre, J. P. *Being and nothingness*. An essay on phenomenological ontology. London: Methuen, 1956.

87. Sartre J. P. *La critique de la raison dialectique*. Paris: Librairie Gallimard, 1960.

88. Sartre, J. P. *The psychology of imagination*. New York: Citadel Press, 1961.

89. Sartre, J. P. *The problem of method*. London: Methuen, 1963.

90. Schachtel, E. G. *Metamorphosis*. New York: Basic Books, 1961.

91. Scheff, T. *Being mentally ill*. Chicago: Aldine, 1966.

92. Secord, P. F., and Jourard, S. M. The appraisal of body-cathexis: Body-cathexis and the self. *J. Consult. Psychol.*, 1953, 17, 343-347.

93. Secord, P. F., and Backman, C. *Social psychology*. New York: McGraw-Hill, 1965.

94. Shaw, F. J. *Reconciliation:* A theory of man transcending. Jourard, S. M. and Overlade, D. C. (eds.) Princeton: Van Nostrand, 1966.

95. Sivadon, P., and Gantheret, F. *Reeducation corporelle des fonctions mentales*. Paris: Editions Sociales Francaises, 1966 (in press).

96. Spitz, R. *"Hospitalism," in Psychoanalyt. Stud. Child. I.* New York: International Univ. Press, 1945.

97. Stratil, M. Unpublished research, 1966.

98. Sulzer, J. Chiropractic as psychotherapy. *Psychotherapy: theory, research and practice.* 1964, 2.

99. Szasz, T. *Pain and pleasure. A study of bodily feelings.* New York: Basic Books, 1957.

100. Szasz, T. *The myth of mental illness.* New York: Harper, 1961.

101. Tawney, R. H. *Religion and the rise of capitalism.*

102. Time-Life. *The drug takers.* New York: Time, Inc., 1965.

103. Trocchi, A. A revolutionary proposal. In *City Lights Journal, No.2.* San Francisco: City Lights, 1964, 14-36.

104. Van Kaam, A. *Existential foundations of psychology.* Pittsburgh: Duquesne Univ. Press, 1966.

105. Watts, A. W. *The way of Zen.* New York: Mentor, 1959.

106. Watts, A. W. *Nature, man, and woman.* New York: Mentor, 1960.

107. Watts, A. W. *The joyous cosmology.* New York: Vintage, 1965.

108. Webb, W. B. The choice of the problem. *Amer. Psychol.*, 1961, 16, 223-227.

109. Weber, M. *The Protestant ethic.* New York: Scribner, 1948.

110. Werner, H. *The comparative psychology of mental development.* Chicago: Follett, 1948.

111. Whitaker, C., and Malone, J. P. *The roots of psychotherapy.* New York: Blakiston, 1953.

112. Wilson, C. *The outsider.* London: Gollancz, 1956. (Paperback edition: London, Pan Books, 1963.)

# *V-2* Bibliography from The Transparent Self

1. Alexander, F. *Psychosomatic Medicine*. New York: Norton, 1950.

2. Allport, G., *Becoming*. New Haven: Yale Univ. Press, 1955.

3. Anonymous, "A New Theory of Schizophrenia," *J. abn soc. Psychol.*, 1958, 57, 226-236.

4. Bakan, D., *Pain, Disease, And Sacrifice. Toward A Psychology Of Suffering*. Chicago: Univ. of Chicago Press, 1968.

5. Barr, S., *Purely Academic*. New York: Simon & Schuster, 1958.

6. Berne, E., *Games People Play*. New York: Grove, 1964.

7. Block, J., "The Assessment of Communication. Role Variations As a Function of Interactional Context," *J. Pers.*, 1951, 21, 272-286.

8. Block, J., and Bennett, Lillian, "The Assessment of Communication. Perception and Transmission As a Function of the Social Situation." *Hum. Relat.*, 1955, S. 317-325.

9. Buber, M., "Elements of the Interhuman," William Alanson White Memorial Lectures. *Psychiatry*, 1957, 20, 95-129.

10. Buber, M., *I and Thou*, New York: Scribners, 1958.

11. Buber, M., *The Knowledge of Man*. New York: Harper & Row, 1965.

12. Bugental, J. F. T., *The Search For Authenticity. An Existential Analytic Approach To Psychotherapy*. New York: Holt, Rinehart & Wooston, 1965.

13. Cameron, N. and Magaret, Ann, *Behavior Pathology*. Boston: Houghton Mifflin, 1951.

14. Cannon, W. B., (Voodoo death—chapter on suicide).

15. Canter, A., "The Efficacy of a Short Form of the MMPI to Evaluate Depression and Morale Loss," *J. consult. Psychol.*. 1960, 24, 14-17.

16. Christenson, W. N., Kane, F. D., Wolff, H. G., and Hinkle, L. E. Jr., "Studies in Human Ecology: Perceptions of Life Experiences As a Determinant of the Occurrence of Illness." *Clin. Res.*, 1958, 6, 238.

17. Combs, A., and Snygg, D. *Individual Behavior.* (2nd. ed.), New York: Harper, 1959.

18. Cooke, T. F., "Interpersonal Correlates of Religious Behavior," unpublished Ph. D. Dissertation, Univ. of Florida, 1962.

19. Davis, F. H., and Malmo, R. B., "Electromyographic Recording During Interview," *Amer. J. Psychiat.*, 1951, 107, 908-916.

20. Dittes, J. E., "Extinction During Psychotherapy of GSR Accompanying 'Embarrassing' Statements," *J. abn. soc. Psychol.*, 1957, 54, 187-191.

21. Dunn, H. L., "High-level Wellness for Man and Society," *Amer. J. Pub. Health*, 1959 (b), 49, 786-792.

22. Durkheim, E., *Suicide.*, Glencoe: Free Press, 1951.

23. Engel, G. L., "Studies of Ulcerative Colitis, V. Psychological Aspects and Their Implications for Treatment." *Amer. J. Digest. Dis.*, 1958, 3, 315-337.

24. Eysenck, H.J., "The Effects of Psychotherapy: an Evaluation," *J. consult. Psychol.*, 1952, 16, 319-324.

25. Fiedler, F. E., "A Comparison of Therapeutic Relationships in Psychoanalytic Non-directive, and Adlerian Therapy," *J. consult. Psychol.*, 1950, 14, 436-445.

26. Fiedler, F. E., "A Note on Leadership Theory: The Effect of Social Barriers between Leaders and Followers," *Sociometry*, 1957, 20, 87-94.

27. Foote, N. N., and Cottrell, L. S., *Identity and Interpersonal Competence.* Chicago: Univ. of Chicago Press, 1955.

28. Frank, J. D., *Persuasion and Healing.* Baltimore: Johns Hopkins Univ. Press, 1961.

29. Frankl, V. E., *The Doctor and the Soul, An Introduction to logotherapy.* New York: Knopf, 1955.

30. Frankl, V. E., *From Death Camp to Existentialism.* Boston: Beacon Press, 1959.

31. Freud, S., *The Interpretation of Dreams.* New York: Basic Books, 1955.

32. Fromm, E., *The Art of Loving.* New York: Harper, 1956.

33. Fromm, E., *Man for Himself*. New York: Rinehart, 1947.

34. Fromm, E., *The Sane Society*. New York: Rinehart, 1955.

35. Gergen, K., "Social Reinforcement of Self-presentation Behavior," unpublished Ph.D. Dissertation, Duke Univ., 1962.

36. Goldstein, K., *Human Nature in the Light of Psychopathology*. Cambridge: Harvard Univ. Press, 1947.

37. Goodman, G. E., "Emotional Self-disclosure in Psychotherapy," unpublished Ph.D. Dissertation, Univ of Chicago, 1962.

38. Greenspoon, J., "The Reinforcing Effect of Two Spoken Sounds on the Frequency of Two Responses," *Amer. J. Psychol.*, 1955, 68, 409-416.

39. Heider, F., *The Psychology of Interpersonal Relations*. New York: Wiley, 1958.

40. Henry, W. E., and Cumming, Elaine, "Personality Development in Adulthood and Old Age," *J. proj. Tech.*, 1959, 23, 383-390.

41. Hinkle, L. E., and Wolff, H. G., "Ecologic Investigations of the Relationship between Illness, Life Experiences and the Social Environment," *Ann. Int. Med.*,1958, 49, 1373-1388.

42. Hinkle, L. E., "On the Assessment of the Ability of the Individual to Adapt to His Social Environment and the Relation of This to Health and High-level Wellness," unpublished report presented to subcommittee for the Quantification of Wellness, National Office of Vital Statistics, Washington, D. C., 1959.

43. Hora, T., "The Process of Existential Psychotherapy," *Psychiat. Quart*, 1960, 34, 495-504.

44. Horney, K., *Neurosis and Human Growth*. New York: Norton, 1950.

45. Horney, K., *The Neurotic Personality of Our Time*. New York: Norton, 1936.

46. Husserl, E., *Ideas: General Introduction to Pure Phenomenology*. London: Allen and Unwin, 1931.

47. Huxley, A., *Brave New World*. Garden City, New York: Sun Dial Press, 1932.

48. Jahoda, Marie, *Current Concepts of Positive Mental Health*. New York: Basic Books, 1958.

49. Jourard, S. M., "Age and Self-disclosure," *Merrill-Palmer Quart. Beh. Dev.* 1961, 7, 191-197.

50. Jourard, S. M., *Disclosing Man to Himself*. Princeton: Van Nostrand, 1968..

51. Jourard, S. M., "The Effects of Experimenters' Self-disclosure on Subjects' Behavior," in Spielberger, C. (ed.), *Current Topics in Clinical and Community Psychology*. New York: Academic Press, 1969. 109-150.

52. Jourard, S. M., "Ego Strength and the Recall of Tasks," *J. abnorm. soc. Psychol.* 1954, 49, 51-58.

53. Jourard, S. M., "Identification, Parent-cathexis, and Self-esteem," *J. consult. Psychol.*, 1957, 21, 375.

54. Jourard, S. M., "Moral Indignation: A Correlate of Denied Dislike of Parents' Traits," *J. consult. Psychol.*, 1954, 18, 59-60.

55. Jourard, S. M., *Personal Adjustment. An Approach through the Study of Healthy Personality*. New York: Macmillan, 1958 (2nd ed., 1963).

56. Jourard, S. M., "Religious Denomination and Self-disclosure," *Psychol. Rep.*, 1961, 8 446.

57. Jourard, S. M., *Self-disclosure: An Experimental Analysis of the Transparent Self*. New York: Wiley, 1971.

58. Jourard, S. M., " Self-disclosure and Grades in Nursing College," *J. appl. Psychol.*, 1961, 45.

59. Jourard, S. M., "Self-disclosure and Other Cathexis," 244-47. *J. abn. soc. Psychol.*, 1959, 59, 428-431.

60. Jourard, S. M., "Self-disclosure Patterns in British and American College Females," *J. soc. Psychol.*, 1961, 54, 315-320.

61. Jourard, S. M., "Self-disclosure in the United States and Puerto Rico," unpublished data, 1963.

62. Jourard, S. M., and Landsman, M. J., "Cognition, Cathexis, and the 'Dyadic Effect' in Men's Self-disclosing Behavior," *Merrill-Palmer Quart. Behav. Dev.*, 1960, 6, 178-186.

63. Jourard, S. M., and Lasakow, P., "Some Factors in Self-disclosure," *J. abn. soc. Psychol.*, 1958, 56, 91-98.

64. Jourard, S. M., and Richman, P., "Disclosure Output and Input in College Students," *Merrill-Palmer Quart. Beh. Dev.*, 1963, 9, 141-148.

65. Jourard, S. M., and Secord, P. F., "Body-cathexis and Personality," *Brit. J. Psychol.*, 1955, 46, 130-138.

66. Jung, C. G., *Modern Man in Search of a Soul*. New York: Harcourt Brace (Harvest Books), 1933.

67. Kesey, K., *One Flew over the Cuckoo's Nest*. New York: Signet, 1963.

68. Krasner, L., "Studies of the Conditioning of Verbal Behavior," *Psychol. Bull.*, 1958, 55, 148-170.

69. Leary, R., *Interpersonal Diagnosis of Personality.* New York: Ronald, 1957.

70. Laing, R. D. *The Divided Self.* Pelican Books. 195 .

71. Laing, R. D. *The Politics of Experience and The Bird of Paradise.* London: Penguin. 1967.

72. Laing, R. D., *The Self and Others.* Chicago: Quadrangle, 1962.

73. Laing, R. D., and Esterson, A., *Sanity, Madness and the Family.* London: Tavistock, 1964.

74. Lewin, K., *A Dynamic Theory of Personality.* New York: McGraw-Hill, 1935.

75. Lewin, K., "Some Social-psychological Differences between the United States and Germany," in Lewin, G. (ed.), *Resolving Social Conflicts: Selected Papers on Group Dynamics*, 1935-1946. New York: Harper, 1948.

76. Lindquist, E. F., *Design and Analysis of Experiments in Psychology and Education.* Boston: Houghton Mifflin, 1953.

77. Luijpen, W., *Existential Phenomenology.* Pittsburgh: Duquesne University Press, 1963.

78. Marcuse, H., *One-dimensional Man.* London: Routledge & Kegan Paul, 1964.

79. Maslow, A. H., *Motivation and Personality.* New York: Harper, 1954.

80. Maslow, A. H., *Toward a Psychology of Being.* Princeton: Van Nostrand, 1961.

81. McLuhan, M., *Understanding Media, Extensions of Man.* New York: McGraw-Hill, 1964.

82. Mechanic, D., and Volkert, E. H., "Stress, illness behavior and the sick role," *Amer. Social Rev.*, 1961, 26, 51-58.

83. Melikian, L., "Self-disclosure among University Students in the Middle East," *J. soc. Psychol.*, 1962, 57, 259-263.

84. Miller, J. G., "Toward a General Theory for the Behavioral Sciences," *Amer. Psychol.*, 1955, 10, 513-531.

85. Moloney, J. C., *The Magic Cloak. A Contribution to the Psychology of Authoritarianism.* Wakefield, Mass.: Montrose Press, 1949.

86. Mowrer, O. H., *The Crisis in Psychiatry and Religion.* Princeton: Van Nostrand, 1961.

87. Murphy, G., *Personality, a Biosocial Approach to Origins and Structure.* New York: Harper, 1947.

88. Orwell, G., *1984.*

89. Parsons, T., "Illness and the Role of the Physician: A Sociological Perspective," *Amer. J. Orthopsychiat.,* 1951, 21, 452-460.

90. Parsons, T., and Bales, R. F., *Family, Socialization, and Interaction Process.* Glenco: Free Press, 1955.

91. Perls, F., *Gestalt Therapy Verbatim.* Lafayette, Calif.: Real People Press, 1969.

92. Popper, K. R., *The Open Society and Its Enemies.* Princeton: Princeton Univ. Press, 1950.

93. Potter, S., *One-Upmanship; being some account of the activities and teaching of the Lifemanship Correspondence College of Oneupness and Gameslifemastery.*       New York: Holt, 1952

94. Powell, W. J., "Personal Adjustment and Academic Achievement of College Students," unpublished M.A. Thesis, Univ. of Florida, 1962.

95. Reich, W., *Character Analysis.* New York: Orgone Press, 1948.

96. Reik, T., *Listening with the Third Ear.* New York: Harcourt, Brace, 1949.

97. Rickers-Ovsiankina, Maria, "Social Accessibility in Three Age Groups," *Psychol. Reports,* 1956 2, 283-294.

98. Rickers-Ovsiankina, Maria, and Kusmin, A. A., "Individual Differences in Social Accessibility," *Pyschol. Rep.,* 1958, 4, 391-406.

99. Riesman, D., *The Lonely Crowd.* New Haven: Yale Univ. Press, 1950.

100. Roethlisberger, F. J., and Dickson, W. J., *Management and the Worker.* Cambridge: Harvard Univ. Press, 1939.

101. Rogers, C. R., "The Characteristic of a Helping Relationship," *Pers. Guid. J.,* 1958, 37, 6-16.

102. Rogers, C. R., "The Concept of the Fully Functioning Person," in Rogers, C. R., *On Becoming a Person.* Boston: Houghton Mifflin, 1961.

103. Rogers, C. R., *Freedom to Learn.* Columbus, Ohio: Merrill, 1969.

104. Rogers, C. R., "A Theory of Psychotherapy with Schizophrencies and a Proposal for Its Empirical Investigation," in Dawson, J. G., Stone, H. K., and Dellis, N. P., *Psychotherapy with Schizophrenics.* Baton Rouge: Univ. of Louisiana Press, 1961.105.

105. Rogers, C. R., and Dymond, R. F., *Psychotherapy and Personality Change.* Chicago: Univ. of Chicago Press, 1954.

106. Rosenthal, D., and Frank, J. D., "Psychotherapy and the Placebo Effect," *Psychol. Bull.*, 1956, 53, 294-302.

107. Ruesch, J., *Disturbed Communication.* New York: Norton, 1957.

108. Sartre, J. P., *Being and Nothingness.* London: Methune, 1956.

109. Sartre, J. P., *No Exit.*

110. Schmale, A. H., "Relation of Separation and Depression to Disease," *Psychosom. Med.*, 1958, 20, 259-277.

111. Shutz, W., *Joy.* New York: Grove, 1967.

112. Selye, H., *The Physiology and Pathology of Exposure to Stress.* Montreal: Acta, 1950.

113. Shapiro, A. K., "A Contribution to a History of the Placebo Effect," *Behav. Sci.*, 1960, 5, 109-135.

114. Shaw, F. J., *Reconciliation, a Theory of Man Transcending* (S. M. Jourard, and D. C. Overlade, eds.). Princeton: Van Nostrand, 1966.

115. Skinner, B, F., *Science and Human Behavior.* New York: Macmillan, 1953.

116. Skinner, B. F., "Teaching Machines," *Science*, 1958, 128, 969-977.

117. Skinner, B. F., *Walden Two.* New York: Macmillan, 1948.

118. Smith, Dorothy M., "A Nurse and a Patient," *Nursing Outlook*, February 1960.

119. Smith, S., "Self-disclosure Behavior Associated with Two MMPI Code Types," unpublished M. A. Thesis, University of Alabama, 1958.

120. Sorokin, P., "The Mysterious Energy of Love," *Main Currents*, September, 1958. Foundation for Integrated Education, Inc., New York.

121. Spielberger, C. (ed.), *Current Topics in Clinical and Community Psychology.* New York: Academic Press, 1969.

122. Stahmer, H., *Speak, That I May See Thee.* New York: Macmillan, 1969.

123. Standal, S. W., and Corsini, R. J. (eds.), *Critical Incidents in Psychotherapy.* Englewood Cliffs, N. J.: Prentice-Hall, 1959.

124. Stupp, H., and Luborsky, L., *Research in Psychotherapy* (Volume 2). Washington: American Psychological Association, 1962.

125. Szasz, T., *The Myth of Mental Illness.* New York: Hoeber, 1961.

126. Tillich, P., *The Courage to Be.* New Haven: Yale Univ. Press, 1952.

127. Truax, C. B. and Carkhuff, R. R., *Toward Effective Counseling and Psychotherapy: Training and Practice.* Chicago: Aldine, 1967.

128. Van Kamm, A., "Phenomenal Analysis: Exemplified by a Study of the Experience of 'Really Feeling Understood,'" *J. individ. Psychol.,* 1959, 15, 66-72.

129. Webb, E. J., Campbell, D. T., Schwartz, R. D., and Sechrest, L., *Unobtrusive Measures. Nonreactive Research in the Social Sciences.* Chicago: Rand-McNally, 1966.

130. Whitehorn, J. C., "The Goals of Psychotherapy," in Rubinstein, E. A., and Parloff, M. B. (eds.), *Research in Psychotherapy.* Washington, D. C.: American Psychological Association, 1959.

131. Wolff, H. G., *Stress and Disease.* Springfield: C. C. Thomas, 1953.

132. Zief, R. M., "Values and Self-disclosure," unpublished Honors Thesis, Harvard Univ., 1962.

# *V-3* Sidney M. Jourard Bibliography

## BOOKS

*Personal Adjustment*, MacMillan, 1958.

*Personal Adjustment,* (second edition), MacMillan, 1963.

*Healthy Personality,* (third edition), MacMillan, 1974.

*Healthy Personality,* (fourth edition Jourard and Landsman), MacMillan, 1980.

*Self-Disclosure: An Experimental Analysis of the Transparent Self,* Wiley-Interscience, 1971.

*The Transparent Self,* Van Nostrand Insight, 1964.

*The Transparent Self,* (second edition), Van Nostrand Rheinhold, 1971.

*La Transparence de Soi,* Saint-Ives (Saint-Foy Quebec), 1974.

*Japanese Edition of The Transparent Self* (title in Japanese characters), Arranged with Litton Educational Publishing through Chares E. Tuttle, Tokyo.

*Disclosing Man to Himself,* Van Nostrand, 1968 (out of print).

*Zelfkennis als Kracht* (Dutch *Disclosing Man to Himself)*, Lemniscaat-Rotterdam.

*Healthy Personality* (Japanese Edition in Japanese text), MacMillan published in Japan by Sangyo Nohritsu Tanki Daigaku through Charles Tuttle Co. Tokyo, 1974.

*La Personalidad Saludable* (*Healthy Personality* in Spanish), Sidney Jourard/Ted Landsman, Editorial Trillas, Printed in Mexico, Authorized by MacMillan Publishing Co., 1987.

*Reconciliation A Theory of Man Transcending,* Jourard and Overlade, edited work of Franklin J. Shaw, Van Nostrand Insight Book, 1966.

# ARTICLES

Jourard, S.M. "The Appraisal of Body Cathexis: Body Cathexis and the Self" (with Secord). *Journal of Consulting Psychology.* October, 1953, Vol. 17, No. 5.

Jourard, S.M. "Ego Strength and the Recall of Tasks." *Journal of Abnormal and Social Psychology*, January, 1954, Vol. 49.

Jourard, S.M. "Identification, Parent Cathexis and Self-Esteem." *Journal of Consulting Psychology.* 1957, Vol. 21, No. 5.

Jourard, S.M. *Personal Adjustment: An Approach Through the Study of Healthy Personality.* New York: Macmillan, 1958.

Jourard, S.M. "Counseling and Psychotherapy, Personality Theory and Counseling Practice." First Annual Conference on Personality Theory. University of Florida, January 5–7, 1961.

Jourard, S.M. "Sex in Marriage," *Journal of Humanistic Psychology*, Fall, 1961, Vol. 1, No. 2.

Jourard, S.M. "Some Lethal Aspects of the Male Role." *J. Existent.* Winter, 1962.

Jourard, S.M. *"The Role of Spirit And 'Inspiriting' In Human Wellness, J. Existent.* Winter, 1963.

Jourard, S.M. "The Awareness of Potentiality Syndrome." *Journal of Humanistic Psychology.* Fall, 1966, Vol. 6, No. 2.

Jourard, S.M. "An Exploratory Study of Body Accessibility." *British Journal of Social and Clinical Psychology*, 1966, Issue 5.

Jourard, S.M. "Some Psychological Aspects of Privacy." *Law and Contemporary Problems.* Duke University, Spring, 1966, Vol. 31, No. 2.

Jourard, S.M. and Overlade, Dan C. (eds.) *Reconciliation: A Theory of Man Transcending.* New York: D. Van Nostrand, 1966. (Out of print.)

Jourard, S.M. "Automation, Stupefaction and Education." *Humanizing Education: The Person in Process.* ASCD Proceedings, Washington, D.C., 1967.

Jourard, S.M. "Experimenter-Subject Dialogue: A Paradigm for A Humanistic Science of Psychology." In J. Bugental (Ed.) *Challenges of Humanistic Psychology.* McGraw Hill, 1967.

Jourard, S.M. "The Human Challenge of Automation. *Humanitas.* Spring, 1967.

Jourard, S.M. "Privacy, the Psychological Need." *New Society.* May, 1967.

Jourard, S.M. (Ed.) *To Be or Not To Be/Existential-Psychological Perspectives on the Self.* University of Florida Monographs, Social Sciences #34. Gainesville, Florida: University of Florida Press, 1967.

Jourard, S.M. "To Be or Not To Be Transparent" and "The Experience of Freedom." Esalen Institute, Big Sur: Esalen Publishing, 1967.

Jourard, S.M. *Disclosing Man to Himself.* Princeton: D. Van Nostrand, 1968.

Jourard, S.M. "Education for a New Society, Emerging Universities and National Concerns." Conference Proceedings, Ball State University, Feb., 1968.

Jourard, S.M. and Leo A. Kormann. "Getting to know the experimenter and its effect on psychological test performance." *Journal of Humanistic Psychology.*. 1968, 8(2), 155–159.

Jourard, S.M. and Jane E. Rubin. "Self-Disclosure and Touching: A Study of Two Modes of Interpersonal Encounter And Their Inter-Relation. *Journal of Humanistic Psychology.* 1968, 8(1), 39–48.

Jourard, S.M. Material in *Ways of Growth* by Herbert Otto and John Mann. New York: Grossman, 1968.

Jourard, S.M. "The Beginnings of Self-Disclosure." *Voices: The Art & Science of Psychotherapy.* 1970, Spring, Vol. 6(1), 42–51.

Jourard, S.M. and Robert Friedman. "Experimenter-Subject'Distance' and Self-Disclosure." *Journal of Personality & Social Psychology.* 15(3), 278–282.

Jourard, S.M. and Peggy E. Jaffe. "Influence of an Interviewer's Disclosure on the Self-Disclosing Behavior of Interviewees." *Journal of Counseling Psychology.* 1970, 17(3), 252–257.

Jourard, S.M. "Reinventing Marriage: The Perspective of a Psychologist" in *The Family In Search of a Future. Alternate Models for Moderns.* Herbert Otto, Ed. Appleton Century Crofts, 1970.

Jourard, S.M. and Jaquelyn L. Resnick. "Some Effects of Self-Disclosure Among College Women." *Journal of Humanistic Psychology.* 1970, Spring, Vol. 10(1), 84–93.

Jourard, S.M. "Suicide: An Invitation to Die." *American Journal of Nursing.* 1970, Feb., Vol. 70(2), 269, 273–275.

Jourard, S.M., Bloch, Ellin L., Goodstein, Leonard D., Jaffe, Peggy E. "Comment on 'Influence of an Interviewer's Disclosure on the Self-Disclosing Behavior of Interviewees.'" *Journal of Counseling Psychology,* 1971, Nov., Vol. 18(6), 595–600.

Whitman, Ardis. "The Fear that Cheats Us of Love" (on Jourard's work), *Redbook*, October, 1971.

Jourard, S.M. "On Kemp's Article, 'Existential Counseling.'" *Counseling Psychologist.* 1971, Vol, 2(3), 41.

Jourard, S.M. "Prophets as Psychotherapists and Psychotherapists as Prophets;" *Voices*, Fall, 1971.

Jourard, S.M. "Psychology, Control or Liberation." *Journal of Interpersonal Development.* 1971–72, Vol. 2, pp. 65–72.

Jourard, S.M. *"Self Disclosure: An Experimental Analysis of the Transparent Self,"* New York: Wiley Interscience, 1971.

Jourard, S.M. *The Transparent Self,* Revised edition. New York: Van Nostrand Reinhold, 1971.

Whitman, Ardis. "The Invitation to Live" (on Jourard's work). *Reader's Digest*, April, 1972.

Jourard, S.M. "Some Dimensions of the Loving Experience." *In Love Today, A New Exploration.* Herbert Otto, Ed. New York: Association Press, 1972.

Jourard, S.M. "Some Notes on the Experience of Commitment." *Humanitas*, 1972.

Jourard, S.M. "Some Reflections on a Quiet Revolution." *Professional Psychology.* 1972, Fall, Vol. 3(4) 380–381.

Jourard, S.M. "An Odyssey Within." *Personal Growth*, June, 1973, No. 18.

Jourard, S.M. *Healthy Personality.* New York: Macmillan Publishing Co., 1974. 4th edition currently revised by Ted Landsman.

Jourard, S.M. "Some Lethal Aspects of the Male Role." In *Men and Masculinity*. Prentice-Hall, 1974.

Jourard, S.M. and J.J. Barrell. "Being Honest with Persons we Like." *Journal of Individual Psychology*, 1976, Vol. 32, No. 2, pp. 185–193.

Jourard, S.M. "Some Ways of Unembodiment and Re-Embodiment." *Somatics.* 1976 Aut. Vol. 1(1) 3–7.

Jourard, S.M. "Education as Dialogue." *Journal of Humanistic Psychology*, Winter, 1978, Vol, 18, #1.

Jourard, S.M. "Marriage is for Life." *Journal of Marriage and Family Counseling.* July, 1975.

## UNDATED AND OTHER ITEMS

Jourard, S.M. "Fascination: A Phenomenological Perspective on Independent Learning." *The Theory and Nature of Independent Learning.* International Textbook Company. 1967 Gerald T. Gleason ed.

Jourard, S.M. "Human Revolution: Confronting the Realities of 'Them' and 'Us.'" *To Nurture Humanness: Commitment for the 70s.* ASCD, 1201 16th St., N.W. Washington, D.C. 20036

Jourard, S.M. "Growing Awareness and the Awareness of Growth." *Ways of Growth: Approaches to Expanding Awareness.*

*"Self Disclosure: An Experimental Analysis of the Transparent Self."* AAP "Voices" (no reference)

*"Ehe Furs Leben-Ehe Zum Leben"* (Marriage Is For Life) translated into German for "Familiendynamik," April 1992 Stuttgart, Germany.

*"A Future For Psychotherapy* AAP, "Voices" Vol. II, 1975 issue 39

*"Astrological Sun Signs of Self-Disclosure"* AHP Journal Winter, 1978

*"A Way To Encounter"* "Confrontation: Encounters with Self and Interpersonal Awareness" edited by, Leonard Blank, Gloria Gottsegan, Monroe G. Gottsegan, 1971 Macmillan

*"Reinventing Marriage: The Perspective of a Psychologist"* "The Family In Search of A Future" edited by Herbert A. Otto 1970 Meredith Corporation (Appleton, Century, Crofts)

*"Controversial Issues In Human Relations Training Groups"* Edited by Kenneth T. Morris Ph.D., Kenneth M. Cinnamon Ph.D., Charles C. Thomas, Publisher, 1976 (this book was dedicated in memory of Sidney Jourard)

*"An Odyssey Within"* "Personal Growth" 1973, Explorations Institute, Berkeley, CA Jim Elliot publisher/editor

*"Humanism and Behavior"* "Dialogue and Growth," A. Wandersman, P. Popp, D. Ricks, Pergamon Press 1976

*"The Invitation to Die"* "On the Nature of Suicide," Edward Schneidman Editor, Jossey-Bass, 1966

*"Toward A Psychology of Transcendent Behavior"* "Explorations In Human Potentialities" Herbert Otto, Editor, Charles C. Thomas, Publisher 1966

*"Changing Personal Worlds: A Humanistic Approach to Psychotherapy"* "Humanistic Psychology" edited by David Welch, George A. Tate, Fred Richards, Prometheus Books, 1978 (paper presented at Cornell University on Human Behavior)

*"A Humanistic Revolution In Psychology"* The Social Psychology of Psychological Research, edited by Arthur G. Miller, 1972

# JOURARD COLLECTION

(This material is available at West Georgia State College, Carrollton, GA. The boxes indicate storage areas in the archives there.)

Jourard, Sidney M. "A study of Self-Disclosure." *Sci. Amer.*, May, 1958, 198, 77–82.

Jourard, Sidney M. "A Way To Encounter." University of Florida. 1970. Box 11.

Jourard, Sidney M. "Age and Self-Disclosure." 1960. Box 12.

Jourard, Sidney M. "An Exploratory Study of Body-Accessibility." *British J. of Social and Clinical Psychology* (1966), 5, 221–231.

Jourard, Sidney M. *An Introduction to the Theory and Measurement of Ego Strength.*

Jourard, Sidney M. Article: "And Always Let Your Conscience Be Your Guide." December 1956. Box 16.

Jourard, Sidney M. "Assessing Personality Health": Proposed Interview Outlines, 1956. (Folder 1) Box 15.

Jourard, Sidney M. "Assessing Personality Health": Proposed Interview Outlines, 1956. (Folder 2) Box 15.

Jourard, Sidney M. "Assessing Personality Health": Proposed Interview Outlines, 1956. (Folder 3) Box 15.

Jourard, Sidney M. "Authenticity in Therapy": Discussion With J.F.T. Bugental, 1963. Box 11.

Jourard, Sidney M. "Being, Becoming, and Choosing Oneself." Talk to AAUW, January 19, 1961. Box 12.

Jourard, Sidney M. "Being With Others Versus Manipulating Others." April 6, 1961. Box 11.

Jourard, Sidney M. "Body-Cathexis." Article J. Consult. 1953. Box 16.

Jourard, Sidney M. "Body-Cathexis." Oral Version For APA. Box 16.

Jourard, Sidney M. "Body-Image and Cultural Norms," APA meeting-September, 1959. Box 12.

Jourard, Sidney M. "Body Size and Body Cathexis For Females." Box 16.

Jourard, Sidney M. "Body Size and Body Cathexis." 1953. Box 16.

Jourard, Sidney M. Camp Study: Presented To Southern Soc. April, 1952. Box 16.

Jourard, Sidney M. Carbons For Manuscript. Box 16.

Jourard, Sidney M. Center of Man Lectures (1969) Box 11.

Jourard, Sidney M. Clinic Patients-Real-Self Communication. 1957. Box 14.

Jourard, Sidney M. *Comments on the "Bedside Manner" in Nursing,* January 12, 1959.

Jourard, Sidney M. "Committee For the Quantification of Wellness: Notes on the Nature of Man." February, 1959. Box 13.

Jourard, Sidney M. "Concepts of Mom and Perception of Women" (With Secord) 1955. Box 16.

Jourard, Sidney M. "Development of a Procedure For Quantifying Psychiatric Evaluation." Box 16.

Jourard, Sidney M. Dialogue With Joe Adams. March, 1969. Box 11.

Jourard, Sidney M. Disclosure: Nursing Personnel. "Self-Disclosure Between Statuses" (Role Categories) 1962. Box 11.

Jourard, Sidney M. Encounter Groups. Papers on encounter by several different persons. Box 10.

Jourard, Sidney M. Esalen-type Centers and Institutes. Information on Various ones. (Folder 1) Box 10.

Jourard, Sidney M. Esalen-type Centers and Institutes. (Folder 2) Box 10.

Jourard, Sidney M. "Factor Analysis of a Measure of Self-Disclosure." 1963. Box 11.

Jourard, Sidney M. "Factor Analysis of a Measure of Self-Disclosure." Unp. manu., UF.

Jourard, Sidney M. and Patricia Richman. "Factors in the Self-Disclosure inputs of College students." *Merrill-Palmer Quart.,* 1963, 9, 141–148.

Jourard, Sidney M. and Landsman, Murray J. "Feelings Versus Intellect As Factors in Men's Interpersonal Behavior." Box 13.

Jourard, Sidney M. and Landsman, Murray. *Feelings Versus Intellect as Factors in Men's Interpersonal Behavior,* April 24, 1959.

Jourard, Sidney M. Fellowship: Public Health. Mental Health Consultant, 1950. Box 16.

Jourard, Sidney M. Frank Shaw Correspondence. Box 13.

Jourard, Sidney M. Group Transparency. 1969. Box 11.

Jourard, Sidney M. Guide to Healthy Personality (Carlson) Box 10.

Jourard, Sidney M. Healthy Personality: Popular Article. (Summer, 1959) Box 12.

Jourard, Sidney M. *Healthy Personality*. Popular Book. Ms. Box 12.

Jourard, Sidney M. "Healthy Personality." Popular Version Drafts. 1956. Box 15.

Jourard, Sidney M. *Healthy Personality and Pastoral Counseling*, Proceedings, Workshop in Pastoral Counseling, University of Florida, August 24–28, 1959.

Jourard, Sidney M. Healthy Personality and Self-Disclosure. *Mental Hygiene* (1959) 43, 499–507.

Jourard, Sidney M. Hi Level Wellness Committee. (Folder 1) Box 13.

Jourard, Sidney M. Hi Level Wellness Committee. (Folder 2) Box 13.

Jourard, Sidney M. "Hostility, Self-Disclosure and Health." Don Hartsough. February, 1959. Box 13.

Jourard, Sidney M. Individual Variance Project. Box 16.

Jourard, Sidney M. Individual Variance Score. J. Clin. Psy. 1957. Box 14.

Jourard, Sidney M. Infirmary Study: 1961: Interviews, Self-Disclosure. Box 12.

Jourard, Sidney M. Interpersonal Communication Project, 1956. Box 15.

Jourard, Sidney M. Interviews W. Med. Patients. 1962. Box 11.

Jourard, Sidney M. Inward Look, Spirit, and Healthy Personality. Presented at the 1960 meetings of the Southeastern Psychological Association, Atlanta, Georgia.

Jourard, Sidney M. "Is The Family Disintegrating?" Box 12.

Jourard, Sidney M. *Knowing Patients and Effective Nursing*, February 2, 1959.

Jourard, Sidney M. Lethal Aspects of the Male Role. (The Incomplete Man) Prepared for presentation at the 1960 meeting of the SEPA, Atlanta, GA, in a symposium entitled "The Complete Man."

Jourard, Sidney M. "Letting Others Know You." May 13, 1958. (Popular Article) Box 14.

Jourard, Sidney M. Like and Knowing As Factors in Self-Disclosure Among Males. Box 10.

Jourard, Sidney M. "Love of Parents and Moral Indignation." Emory University. Annoyances Study. Box 10.

Jourard, Sidney M. Fred Richards' "Man As Artist." December, 1970. Box 11.

Jourard, Sidney M. Minnesota League For Nursing Workshop. November 9-10, 1961. Box 11.

Jourard, Sidney M. *Motivation, Manipulation and Morality*, University of Florida, March 25, 1959.

Jourard, Sidney M. APGA Talk: "Non-Intellective Factors in Academic Success" January 13, 1960. Box 12.

Jourard, Sidney M. *Notes on the Integration of Mental Health and Psychiatric Concepts in the Curriculum and Practice of Health Professions*, February 2, 1959.

Jourard, Sidney M. *Notes on the "Quantification of Wellness."* October 16, 1958.

Jourard, Sidney M. Notes on Quantification of Wellness. Prepared for meeting of the Subcommittee on the Quantification of Wellness. Washington, D.C. November 18, 1958. Box 13.

Jourard, Sidney M. "Notes on Resistance, Technique, and Spontaneity in the Psychotherapist." (for J. Exist. Psychiat.) 1961. Box 11.

Jourard, Sidney M. *Notes Toward A Formulation of the Theory of Ego Strength.*

Jourard, Sidney M. and Powell, William J. "Objective Evidence of Immaturity in College Underachievers." APA Paper on Self-Disclosure and Security in Achievers. Box 11.

Jourard, Sidney M. and Powell, William J. "Objective Evidence of Immaturity in College Underachievers. Paper read at APA, 1962.

Jourard, Sidney M. On Reinforcement of Real-Self-Being in Psychotherapy. SEPA Symposium, 1959: Behav. Approaches to Therapy. Box 13.

Jourard, Sidney M. "Of What Stuff Are Dreams Made?" Popular Article. February 15, 1962. Box 11.

Jourard, Sidney M. Operant Conditioning of Self-Disclosure. An Experimental Analysis of Self-Disclosure. A Request for Research Support Submitted by H.S. PennyPacker and S.M. Jourard. Box 10.

Jourard, Sidney M. Out of Touch: the Body Taboo. *New Society*, November, 1967.

Jourard, Sidney M. Parent Identification and Parent Cathexis. (Original Paper) Box 16.

Jourard, Sidney M. Parent-Identification and the Self. Box 16.

Jourard, Sidney M. Parental Cathexis and Security. 1954. Box 16.

Jourard, Sidney M. Pfeiffer, Carl Pre L.S.D. Tests (Drug Test Given To Peter Rosenbaum.) Box 16.

Jourard, Sidney M. Policemen and College Students Paper (Self-Disclosure.) 1957. Box 14.

Jourard, Sidney M. Symposium, SEPA, 1960. Positive Mental Health. Box 12.

Jourard, Sidney M. Project Replication. Unp. manu., 1968.

Jourard, Sidney M. Quote from Morris L. West's *The Ambassador.* Box 10.

Jourard, Sidney M. "Real-Self Responding versus Deliberate Reinforcement (Manipulation) in Counseling and Psychotherapy." April 25, 1959. Box 13.

Jourard, Sidney M. "Religion and Self-Disclosure." Box 11.

Jourard, Sidney M. "Repeated Rorschach" Study. Box 13.

Jourard, Sidney M. Research in Self-Disclosure Chapter. Self-Disclosure Monograph. Box 11.

Jourard, Sidney M. "Review of Self-Disclosure Findings." December 11, 1958. Box 13.

Jourard, Sidney M. "Re-Write for Needs Chapter." Box 15.

Jourard, Sidney M. Rorschach Productivity and Self-Disclosure. *Precept Mot. Skills*, 1961, 13, 232.

Jourard, Sidney M. "Self-Disclosure: A Factor in Personality Health, Illness, Therapy and Research." 1957. Box 14.

Jourard, Sidney M. "Self-Disclosure and Interpersonal Competence." Faculty ratings of students on interpers. comp. Box 12.

Jourard, Sidney M. "Self-Disclosure and Marriage." 1957. Box 14.

Jourard, Sidney M. "Self-Disclosure and MMPI" (Code-Type 1957) (Stewart Smith's Thesis) Box 12.

Jourard, Sidney M. "Self-Disclosure and the MMPI." Unp. manu., UF.

Jourard, Sidney M. "Self-Disclosure and the Mystery of the Other Man." April 3, 1959.

Jourard, Sidney M. "Self-Disclosure and Other-Cathexis." Box 13.

Jourard, Sidney M. "Self-Disclosure and Other Cathexis." *J. abnor. soc. Psychol.*, 1959, 59, 428–431.

Jourard, Sidney M. *Self-Disclosure and Other-Cathexis.* A reprint from the Journal of Abnormal and Social Psychology, Vol 59, No. 3, November, 1959.

Jourard, Sidney M. Self-Disclosure, Other Concepts, and Interpersonal Behavior. Paper read at APA, 1958.

Jourard, Sidney M. Self-Disclosure and Personality Health (Talk For APGA Meeting, November 20, 1958.) Box 13.

Jourard, Sidney M. "Self-Disclosure and Rorschach Productivity." 1959. Box 13.

Jourard, Sidney M. and Jane Rubin. "Self-Disclosure and Touching." Unp. manu., UF, 1968.

Jourard, Sidney M. and Jane Rubin. "Self-Disclosure and Touching: A Study of Two Modes of Intimacy." University of Florida. Box 10.

Jourard, Sidney M. "Self-Disclosure Article: First Version; Raw Data 1957. Box 14.

Jourard, Sidney M. "Self-Disclosure: English Subjects From University of Nottingham." Box 14.

Jourard, Sidney M. "Self-Disclosure Experiments." Box 10.

Jourard, Sidney M. "Self-Disclosure." Fam. Couns. Box 14.

Jourard, Sidney M. "Self-Disclosure." Final Version. 07/26/57. J.A.S.P. Box 14.

Jourard, Sidney M. "Self-Disclosure, Grades, and Interpersonal Competence." Box 12.

Jourard, Sidney M. "Self-Disclosure: Guidance Workshop (Summer, 1959) Box 12.

Jourard, Sidney M. "Self-Disclosure: Nurses." Box 14.

Jourard, Sidney M. "Self-Disclosure, Other-Cathexis, Personality-Ratings, and Guessability." Box 14.

Jourard, Sidney M. & Pat Richman. Intake-Output Study. "Self-Disclosure Output and Intake Among College Students." University of Florida. 1962. Box 11.

Jourard, Sidney M. "Self-Disclosure Patterns in British and American College Females. *J. Soc. Psychol.,* 1961, 54, 315–320.

Jourard, Sidney M. "Self-Disclosure Patterns of Nursing-College 'Drop-Outs.'" University of Florida. Box 10.

Jourard, Sidney M. SEPA, 1970: Self-Disclosure Research. Box 11.

Jourard, Sidney M. "Self-Disclosure Research: papers, Data to Date." Unpublished and published researches in S-D by me, students, and others. Box 10.

Jourard, Sidney M. "Self-Disclosure Slides" (Colored) Box 10.

Jourard, Sidney M. "Self-Disclosure: The Scientist's Portal to Man's Soul." Talk to University of Florida Seminar. 04/11/58. Box 14.

Jourard, Sidney M. Sermon Given at Beth Israel Synagogue. Gainesville, Florida. October 6, 1961. Box 11.

Jourard, Sidney M. *"Servo" Theory and Evaluating Nursing Students,* May 21, 1959.

Jourard, Sidney M. "Sex and Race As Factors In Self-Disclosure." 1958. Box 14.

Jourard, Sidney M. "Sex Problems and Counseling College Students." (APGA Talk, 1961) Box 12.

Jourard, Sidney M. Similarity-To-Parents Project. 1956. Box 16.

Jourard, Sidney M. and P. Lasakow. "Some Factors in Self-Disclosure." *J. Abnor. Soc. Psychol.,* 1958, 56.

Jourard, Sidney M. and Patricia Richman. "Some Factors in the Self-Disclosure Inputs of College Students." & "Disclosure Output Versus Disclosure Intake Among College Students." Box 11.

Jourard, Sidney M. "Some Implications of Self-Disclosure Research For Counseling and Psychotherapy." Paper Read at Conf., UF 1960.

Jourard, Sidney M. "Some Lethal Aspects of the Male Role." (For J. Exist. Psychiat.) Submitted May, 1961. Box 11.

Jourard, Sidney M. "Some Remarks on the Impact of Existentialist Thought on American Psychology." Presented July 19, 1961 at the University of Florida. Box 11.

Jourard, Sidney M. *Subcommittee for the Quantification of Wellness.* March 18, 1959.

Jourard, Sidney M. "Suicide: The Invitation to Die." University of Florida. Presented March 10, 1968 at the Institute on Suicidology in Chicago, Illinois, Box 11.

Jourard, Sidney M. "Ten Minute Interviews: Self-Disclosure." Box 14.

Jourard, Sidney M. Symposium 1960 S.E.P.A.: "The Complete Man." Box 12.

Jourard, Sidney M. *The Development of a Procedure for Quantifying Psychiatric Evaluation.* December 1956.

Jourard, Sidney M. and Jacquelyn Resnick. The Effect of High Revealing Subjects on the Self-Disclosure of Low Revealing Subjects. Unp. manu., JF, 1969.

Jourard, Sidney M. and Peggy E. Jaffe. "The Influence of Interviewer's Disclosure on the Self-Disclosing Behavior of Interviewees." Unp. man., UF.

Jourard, Sidney M. "The Phenomenon of Resistance in the "psychotherapist." (For SEPA, 1961) Box 12.

Jourard, Sidney M. "The Phenomenon of Resistance in the Psychotherapist." Adapted from a paper presented at the meeting of the Southeastern Psychological Association. Gatlinburg, Tennessee. April 14, 1961.

Jourard, Sidney M. "The Phenomenon of Resistance in the Psychotherapist." *Counseling Center Discussion Paper.* Vol. 7, No. 13, December 1961.

Jourard, Sidney M. NIH Grant Request: The Reinforcing Value of Self-Disclosure. 1963. Box 11.

Jourard, Sidney M. The Relative Disclosability of Personal Subject-Matter. University of Florida. Box 10.

Jourard, Sidney M. "The Study of Self-Disclosure: An Empirical and Conceptual Odyssey." (Biblio, Van Nostrand Ms) 1962. Box 11.

Jourard, Sidney M. and Lasakow, Paul. *The Study of Self-Disclosure Behavior, Influence of Target-Persons, Aspects of Self, and Group-Differences on Self-Disclosure.*

Jourard, Sidney M. Thesis Proposals. Box 11.

Jourard, Sidney M. "To Whom Can You Give Personalized Care?" (Talk, Student Nurses Convention, 1960.) Box 12.

Jourard, Sidney M. *Transparent Self.* 1963. Box 11.

Jourard, Sidney M. "What is the Purpose of a University? How is this Reflected at the University of Florida?" (For Comment: A Student Publication) 4/19/62. Box 11.